SPIRITUAL LIVES

General Editor
Timothy Larsen

SPIRITUAL LIVES

General Editor

Timothy Larsen

The *Spiritual Lives* series features biographies of prominent men and women whose eminence is not primarily based on a specifically religious contribution. Each volume provides a general account of the figure's life and thought, while giving special attention to his or her religious contexts, convictions, doubts, objections, ideas, and actions. Many leading politicians, writers, musicians, philosophers, and scientists have engaged deeply with religion in significant and resonant ways that have often been overlooked or underexplored. Some of the volumes will even focus on men and women who were lifelong unbelievers, attending to how they navigated and resisted religious questions, assumptions, and settings. The books in this series will therefore recast important figures in fresh and thought-provoking ways.

Andrew Jackson

Old Hickory in Christian America

JONATHAN M. ATKINS

OXFORD
UNIVERSITY PRESS

Great Clarendon Street, Oxford, OX2 6DP,
United Kingdom

Oxford University Press is a department of the University of Oxford.
It furthers the University's objective of excellence in research, scholarship,
and education by publishing worldwide. Oxford is a registered trade mark of
Oxford University Press in the UK and in certain other countries

© Jonathan M. Atkins 2025

The moral rights of the author have been asserted

All rights reserved. No part of this publication may be reproduced, stored in a retrieval system, transmitted, used for text and data mining, or used for training artificial intelligence, in any form or by any means, for commercial purposes, without the prior permission in writing of Oxford University Press, or as expressly permitted by law, by licence or under terms agreed with the appropriate reprographics rights organization. Enquiries concerning reproduction outside the scope of the above should be sent to the Rights Department, Oxford University Press, at the address above.

You must not circulate this work in any other form
and you must impose this same condition on any acquirer

Published in the United States of America by Oxford University Press
198 Madison Avenue, New York, NY 10016, United States of America

British Library Cataloguing in Publication Data

Data available

Library of Congress Control Number: 2024946422

ISBN 9780198852353

DOI: 10.1093/9780191886812.001.0001

Printed and bound by
CPI Group (UK) Ltd, Croydon, CR0 4YY

The manufacturer's authorised representative in the EU for product
safety is Oxford University Press España S.A. of el Parque
Empresarial San Fernando de Henares, Avenida de Castilla,
2 – 28830 Madrid (www.oup.es/en).

For J. Mills Thornton III

Contents

Preface ix

1. "I was brought up a rigid Presbeterian . . ." 1
2. "I think I would have made a pretty good saddler" 13
3. "May the great 'I am' bless and protect you" 27
4. "my reputation is dearer to me than life" 41
5. "the remarkable interposition of Heaven" 57
6. "God alone is the searcher & judge of hearts" 77
7. "providence will spare me untill my enemies are prostrate" 97
8. "I find myself a solitary mourner . . ." 115
9. "We want them . . . free from colision with the whites" 133
10. "My negroes shall be treated humanely" 153
11. "Providence . . . has chosen you as the guardians
    of freedom" 173
12. "I await with resignation the call of my god" 193

Selected Bibliography 209
Index 217

Preface

As the writer of Ecclesiastes might have put it: of making many books about Andrew Jackson there is no end. Scores of authors have produced biographies of the American military hero and president. Countless other studies examine various aspects of his life and career. The intense interest in Jackson is understandable. During his lifetime, his image so dominated the second quarter of the nineteenth century that American historians long referred to his era as the "Age of Jackson." For the next century, Americans usually ranked the Hero of New Orleans among their greatest presidents, proclaiming him the champion of the "common man" against powerful economic and political interests. Later generations rejected Jackson's patriotic persona, depicting him instead as a lawless, reckless, and disturbed individual, driven by either unbridled passions or a pathological desire for self-vindication. Modern Americans usually damn him as the embodiment of western civilization's evils, making him the scapegoat for the national sins of racism, slavery, and ruthless conquest.

The shifting interpretations justify yet another Jackson biography. This work presents an account of Jackson's life through an aspect that may shock readers today: his belief in Christianity. Arda Walker first summarized Jackson's beliefs in an article published in 1945, but most historians still either ignore or dismiss his religious affirmations. Some have recognized their influence, including his first serious biographer, James Parton; Jon Meacham, the author of the most acclaimed recent account; and Robert V. Remini, whose three-volume work remains the most comprehensive study of Jackson's life.[1] A few recent scholars have looked closely at his religious beliefs and their impact, most notably Gary Scott Smith, Daniel Gullotta, and Miles Smith IV.[2] In a broader study, Sam Haselby has argued that Jackson contributed significantly to the development of an American "religious nationalism," presumably the foundation for the Christian nationalism that in recent years has appeared as a potent and populist political force.[3]

With respect for these works, and conscious of Jackson's possible influence on what scholars usually refer to as a "civil religion," I hope

x   *Preface*

in this biography to take a different approach. Here, my intention is to integrate Jackson's faith into a narrative that traces its influence on the course of his life and career. As the following pages demonstrate, the importance of Christianity ebbed and flowed through the various stages of Jackson's life. He became more devout as he aged, but he always considered himself a Christian. Despite contemporary and modern contentions, he never experienced a dramatic moment of conversion, a fact that put him at odds with prominent religious leaders of his day. Throughout his life, he blended Christian tenets with the ethic of honor that pervaded antebellum Southern culture, and—like many believers—he sometimes twisted Christian principles to justify his actions. Nevertheless, Jackson's faith provided him with a moral compass that explained to him his experiences and his world. Recognizing his adherence to Christianity thus offers modern readers deeper insight into his character and a window into the role of religion in early American culture.

While I designed this work to contribute to historians' understanding of Jackson and his age, I also intend for it to serve general readers as an introduction to a controversial figure—an account that counters popular assumptions that simplistically portray him as an ignorant, overbearing, obnoxious, hot-tempered, temperamental, hate-driven, violent, and murderous powder keg. To be sure, Jackson could lose his temper and act ruthlessly, but like all humans, he was a complex, complicated, and often contradictory individual. Living in an era more accustomed to violence than our own—and having witnessed atrocities and cruelties unimaginable to most modern Americans—he showed little reluctance toward taking matters into his own hands, even when the outcome might lead to his own or to another's death. But he was also intelligent, with a relatively good education for his time despite his lack of formal schooling. He formed himself into a respected gentleman well regarded by contemporaries for his courtly manners, his hospitality, and especially his courteous treatment of women. He displayed natural gifts both as a military commander and as a politician, and while vilification of his foes filled his private correspondence, only occasionally did he vent these rants in public. And though he sometimes feigned uncontrollable outbursts to intimidate those around him, he usually kept his anger in check, suppressing his emotions when an explosion might work against him.

Preface xi

Readers will see that I have relied heavily on Jackson's writings, letting him tell his own story as much as possible. While not the ignorant fool often presumed, he did spell inconsistently, and his grammar and language usage at times could be confusing. Rather than correct his wording or perpetually insert "[*sic*]" to indicate mistakes, I have followed the practice of *The Papers of Andrew Jackson* to retain "fidelity to the original text," presenting Jackson's writings as he wrote them while adding "[*sic*]" or other bracketed modifications only in quotations where his wording might seem incomprehensible.[4] Likewise, while I have prepared the work for modern readers, wherever suitable, I prefer to use the language of Jackson's era. To my knowledge, for instance, Jackson never called the president's home the "White House," so I have avoided use of this term. Similarly, I refer to what we know today as the "State of the Union" address as the president's "Annual Message," which would be delivered to Congress in print rather than as an oration. I should note, too, that the basics about the course of Jackson's life are generally well established, so for factual information I most often rely on Parton's and Remini's biographies, along with Mark Cheathem's shorter but more-recent *Andrew Jackson, Southerner*, which makes important points about subjects that seemed less relevant to Parton's or Remini's generations.[5] Rather than repeatedly refer to these sources, the notes cite them only when providing direct quotations or unique or particularly pertinent facts or interpretations.

Finally, readers can rest assured that I have no intention in this work either to defend or to celebrate Jackson. Respecting his religious beliefs and noting his complex character should not exonerate him. His flaws were many, and while he profoundly affected American development, we still have trouble coming to terms with his legacy. Nevertheless, I hold to the perhaps outdated belief that a historian's first responsibility is not to praise or condemn but to understand and explain. Through this approach, I hope to offer both academics and students a better sense of just who this significant but provocative figure actually was.

Thanks to modern technology, preparing this book required no extensive travel and only a little digging to find a few obscure documents. Still, no historical work is an individual effort, and I need to thank several individuals and institutions for their help along the way. My gratitude first goes to Timothy Larsen, editor of the *Spiritual Lives* series,

xii   *Preface*

for suggesting I take on Jackson after concluding that the subject I initially proposed—James K. Polk—lacked the significance necessary for the series. Jackson indeed proved the better choice, and I've sincerely appreciated Tim's encouragement, guidance, and patience. My deepest thanks also go to Daniel Feller, who recently retired as editor of the Jackson papers. Dan not only took time to read the whole book, but his deep knowledge of Jackson's world saved me from numerous egregious errors while encouraging me to think through my conclusions more carefully. A sabbatical at Berry College allowed me to make significant progress in spring 2023, and the assistance of several student workers helped complete the mundane but necessary tasks. The staff at Berry's Memorial Library and at the Tennessee State Library and Archives likewise graciously assisted me in obtaining important sources. At Berry, I've been blessed to work for more than twenty years with Larry Marvin, Christy Snider, and Matt Stanard, accomplished scholars and good friends who read either all or part of the manuscript and offered support and insightful comments. I'm grateful, too, to Mark Cheathem, Barry Hankins, Daniel Gullotta, and the three readers for Oxford University Press, each of whom presented challenging thoughts that I think improved the finished product. Tom Perridge and Aimee Wright at Oxford meanwhile made the production process a joy to work through.

At home, Christie, as always, provided her love and companionship as I carried the work through its completion, and as we together cared for our son with autism while helping our daughter get her start on her own as a young adult. The dedication expresses my gratitude to a mentor who has had perhaps the most profound influence on my career.

Notes

1. Arda Walker, "The Religious Views of Andrew Jackson," *East Tennessee Historical Society's Publications* 17 (1945): 61–70; James Parton, *Life of Andrew Jackson*, 3 vols. (Boston and New York: Houghton, Mifflin & Company, 1859–60); Jon Meacham, *American Lion: Andrew Jackson in the White House* (New York: Random House, 2008); Robert V. Remini, *Andrew Jackson: The Course of American Empire, 1767–1821* (New York: Harper & Row, 1977; rpt. Baltimore: Johns Hopkins University Press, 1998); Remini, *Andrew Jackson: The Course of American Freedom, 1822–1832* (New York: Harper

Preface xiii

& Row, 1981; rpt. Baltimore: Johns Hopkins University Press, 1998); Remini, *Andrew Jackson: The Course of American Democracy, 1833–1845* (New York: Harper & Row, 1984; rpt. Baltimore: Johns Hopkins University Press, 1998). Throughout, Remini's volumes are cited using abbreviated versions of their subtitles.

2. Gary Scott Smith, "Andrew Jackson: Providentialist President," in *Religion in the Oval Office: The Religious Lives of American Presidents* (New York: Oxford University Press, 2015), 123–58; Daniel Nicholas Gullotta, "To Make a Christian of Andrew Jackson," Ph.D. dissertation, Stanford University, 2023; Miles Smith IV, "What Andrew Jackson Could Teach Donald Trump about Religion," *The Gospel Coalition*, July 21, 2017, https://www.thegospelcoalition.org/blogs/evangelical-history/what-andrew-jackson-could-teach-donald-trump-about-religion/.

3. Sam Haselby, *The Origins of American Religious Nationalism* (New York: Oxford University Press, 2015).

4. "Editorial Method," Sam B. Smith, Harriet Chappell Owsley, Harold D. Moser, Daniel Feller et al., eds., *The Papers of Andrew Jackson*, 12 vols. to date (Knoxville: University of Tennessee Press, 1980–present), 1:xxxi. This work is cited hereafter as *PAJ* with volume and page numbers.

5. Mark R. Cheathem, *Andrew Jackson, Southerner* (Baton Rouge: Louisiana State University Press, 2013).

1
"I was brought up a rigid Presbeterian . . ."

Andrew Jackson never knew his father. In 1765, the elder Andrew Jackson, along with his wife Elizabeth and their two young sons, had come to Great Britain's North American colonies with thousands of other northern Irish migrants of Scottish descent. Most Scots-Irish immigrants entered the colonies through Philadelphia and moved inland to the frontier, with many taking the "Great Wagon Road" along the eastern ridge of the Appalachians to the Southern backcountry. Family legend contended that the Jacksons came instead through Charleston and walked the 170 miles to the Waxhaws region along the indistinct line separating North from South Carolina. However they arrived, the elder Jackson claimed a tract of about two hundred acres along Twelve Mile Creek in North Carolina, where he built a log cabin for his family and set out to carve a farm out of the wilderness. The challenge proved too much for him. Weakened from overwork and exhaustion, he died in early 1767, shortly before the birth of his third son and namesake on March 15.[1]

Distraught over her husband's death, Elizabeth Jackson turned to her kin for comfort and support. All five of her sisters and their families had also migrated to the Waxhaws. One sister, Jane Crawford, probably crossed the Atlantic with the Jacksons, along with her husband James and their eight children. Jane's brother-in-law, Robert Crawford, first came to the Waxhaws a few years before, and as an early arrival, he had acquired some of the area's best lands, including the farm for James's family. The Jacksons, like most other latecomers, could afford only the less-expensive lands in nearby North Carolina.

Andrew Jackson. Jonathan M. Atkins, Oxford University Press. © Jonathan M. Atkins 2025.
DOI: 10.1093/9780191886812.003.0001

2   *Andrew Jackson: Old Hickory in Christian America*

Still, they remained in close touch with their relations, and the clan immediately responded to Elizabeth's tragic and unexpected loss.[2]

Elizabeth's in-laws brought her husband's body back to the Waxhaws for proper burial as family members took in the widow and her young sons. Some later claimed that Elizabeth stayed with her sister Margaret and her husband George McCamie in North Carolina until after Andrew's birth. Andrew Jackson himself insisted that he was born in his uncle James Crawford's home, only a mile away from the McCamies but in the South Carolina portion of the Waxhaws. Regardless of the exact location of his birth, Andrew became part of James's household. Jane Crawford always suffered from poor health, so Elizabeth assumed the role of caretaker and housekeeper for her sister. Eventually, her oldest son, Hugh, would be sent to live with the childless McCamies, but Andrew and his brother Robert remained for the next several years with their mother at the Crawfords.[3]

The Waxhaws community in which Andrew Jackson spent his earliest years consisted overwhelmingly of migrants whose ancestors, like the Jacksons, had moved from Scotland to Ireland throughout the seventeenth century. King James I had encouraged Ireland's colonization with hopes of displacing the native Celtic population with loyal Scots, and by the mid-1600s Scots had established several plantations in northeastern Ireland's Ulster province. In County Antrim, near the town of Carrickfergus, Jackson's forebears and their neighbors supported themselves through farming, supplemented by weaving linen and wool cloth.[4] Some families, like the Crawfords, prospered in their new land. Most migrants, though, continued to face the high rents, poor harvests, and uncertainties in the wool industry that had plagued them in Scotland. These pressures—along with the resentment of the native Irish population, religious discrimination, and condescension or indifference from often-absent English landlords—compelled thousands of Scots in Ireland to relocate once again in the eighteenth century, this time to British North America.[5]

Scots-Irish settlers first came to the Waxhaws in the early 1750s. By the time of Andrew Jackson's birth, the scattered cluster of farms and houses had become one of the most heavily populated communities on South Carolina's frontier. Stretching back about ten miles from the confluence of the Catawba River and Waxhaws Creek, the region took its name from a Native American people that the rival Catawba

"I was brought up a rigid Presbeterian . . ." 3

nation had destroyed a generation earlier. The conquerors declined to occupy their victims' lands, so migrants coming down from the Great Wagon Road met little resistance as they moved in to set up their farms.[6] Here, the migrants found the soil ideal for growing wheat, which allowed them to replicate fairly closely the community of small farmers and weavers they had known in Ulster. Twenty years after the first European settlers arrived, William Moutrie, a commissioner on the team surveying the line dividing North from South Carolina, noted in his journal that the Waxhaws contained "pretty good lands" with "a great many large wheat fields, very few negroes among them; all their work is done by plowing and English husbandry."[7]

Andrew Jackson thus spent his earliest years in a relatively stable environment. By the time of his birth, the Waxhaws had grown into an ethnically homogenous community of about one thousand inhabitants. While not wealthy, he grew up around modest comfort, for James Crawford apparently had enough to support his in-laws as well as his own wife and offspring. Like other Waxhaw farmers, the Crawfords moved away from subsistence farming to sell their crops to South Carolina's rice plantations along the coast. Camden, forty-five miles southeast, emerged as the backcountry's market center, and Jackson's uncle Robert Crawford became the Waxhaws' unofficial agent for Camden's principal merchant, Joseph Kershaw, a connection that established Robert as one of the Waxhaws' most prominent men.[8] Meanwhile, the Waxhaws of Jackson's youth generally remained free of major conflict. Tensions occasionally flared between the original settlers at the center of the Waxhaws and the less-fortunate, later-arriving inhabitants on the community's outskirts. The Catawbas, the nearest Native Americans, mostly stayed away from the settlement, while the larger and more dangerous Cherokee nation had ended their raids on the frontier in the early 1760s. Waxhaw residents likewise stayed out of the "Regulator" uprisings, when settlers protested the colonial government's custom of ignoring the backcountry. African American slaves meanwhile made up only about 10 percent of the population, a proportion too small to threaten a serious rebellion.[9]

The Presbyterian church lay at the center of the Waxhaws community. "I was brought up a rigid Presbeterian," Jackson recalled years later, and the church offered him and his kin much more than either an opportunity to worship or an explanation of the cosmos.

4   *Andrew Jackson: Old Hickory in Christian America*

In Ulster, Presbyterianism had become a crucial component of the identity of the Scottish migrants and their descendants, for their faith distinguished them from the Catholic Irish natives and the English landed elites of the established Church of Ireland. In America, the Presbyterian church provided a bond that tied Scots-Irish settlers together. It also served as the basis for social organization and authority. In Ulster, officials in the established church doubted Presbyterians' loyalty to the crown and aggressively pressured them to conform; in South Carolina, the Anglican church also had government support, but the founders offered toleration from the colony's earliest days. For most of the eighteenth century, the low-country planters who dominated the colonial assembly paid little attention to the backcountry settlements. Presbyterian ministers and elders thus emerged as the Waxhaws' political as well as social leaders, and before South Carolina set up a local court in Camden in 1771, the church became the principal forum for resolving disputes among the community's inhabitants.[10]

The Waxhaws emerged as one of the church's strongholds in the Southern backcountry. Within a few years after their arrival, the first settlers built a meeting house, and in 1759, thirty-year-old William Richardson came to serve as its minister. Richardson had been ordained by the church's Synod in Philadelphia, and prior to coming to South Carolina, he had worked with Samuel Davies, the leader of Virginia's Scots-Irish Presbyterians. Once in the Waxhaws, he married Agnes Craighead, the daughter of a nearby local minister. Charles Woodmason, an Anglican cleric sent in the 1760s to strengthen South Carolina's established church on the frontier, knew and respected Richardson, despite their denominational differences. He described Richardson as "A good sort of man," "sensible, Moral, Religious and Moderate," and he acknowledged that Richardson led a devoted flock. Woodmason may have exaggerated when he claimed that "Seldom less than 9, 10, 1200 People assemble of a Sunday" at the Waxhaws church, but his observation testifies to the inhabitants' commitment to the Presbyterian version of the faith.[11]

Although he liked Richardson, Woodmason had little respect for most Waxhaw Presbyterians, describing them as "a Sett of the most Lowest vilest Crew breathing."[12] Richardson's congregants adhered to the "Old Side" sect of the faith, which rejected the revivals of the "Great Awakening" that had raged through colonies farther

"I was brought up a rigid Presbeterian . . ." 5

north before the Waxhaws' settlement. The revivals of "New Side" Presbyterians called for evidence of personal conversion among believers, which led proponents to accept a less-rigid commitment to orthodoxy while encouraging challenges to leaders who appeared "unconverted." "Old Side" ministers and elders distrusted the revivals and stressed instead the importance of church authority and discipline.[13] Joined with memories of conflict with Catholic "papists" in Ireland, and of discrimination from the established church's "Black Robes," Old-Side beliefs contributed to Waxhaw Presbyterians' intense resistance to outsiders. Though a tolerated sect and largely isolated from colonial officials, backcountry Presbyterians became intensely insular, clannish, exclusionary, self-righteous, and distrustful of all other denominations.[14]

Waxhaws Old-Siders particularly despised Baptists, a sect new to the South that gained a widespread following after a series of revivals beginning in the 1750s. Not only did Baptists win converts from the Scots-Irish flock, their emotion-driven worship and dramatic accounts of conversion experiences embodied the extremism and disorder to which New Side Presbyterians appeared headed.[15] Fearful of persecution, Presbyterians and Baptists put aside their differences to resist representatives of the established Anglican church. Woodmason claimed that the people of the Waxhaws treated him like "an Wolf strayed into Christs fold to devour the Lamb of Grace," and he recounted several instances of Presbyterians shunning him, interrupting his services, and denying him food or shelter once they discovered his status as an Anglican minister. Even his friend Richardson had to keep his distance. On one visit to the region in 1768, Woodmason called at Richardson's residence after a wealthy Presbyterian refused to let him eat, rest, or warm himself in his tavern, but Richardson "denyed being at Home—Not being willing to give offence to his flock in entertaining a person who was drawing off the People from them."[16]

Richardson's association with Samuel Davies—one of the Awakening's leading revivalists—made him at least sympathetic to New Side views, and at times he had tried to counter his congregation's sectarianism. A year before snubbing Woodmason, he had invited the Anglican missionary to preach at the Waxhaw meeting house. A rainstorm prevented Woodmason from coming on the appointed day, and the church's elders' "not being agreeable" vetoed rescheduling the

6   *Andrew Jackson: Old Hickory in Christian America*

visit. Richardson also met resistance when he attempted to replace the traditional Scottish psalter with the newer hymns of the English noncomformist Isaac Watts.[17] Tense relations with his congregants may have contributed to Richardson's early death, apparently from suicide, in 1771. Woodmason lamented Richardson as "a victim to Moderation" and noted that the Waxhaw Presbyterians afterward "fell into Confusion and Parties," leaving the church without a permanent minister until 1779. Nevertheless, local elders, temporary appointments, and occasional visiting itinerants continued to lead the services and kept the church at the center of the settlement well after Richardson's demise.[18]

Andrew Jackson's mother appears to have been one of the Waxhaw church's most devoted members. The community remembered Elizabeth Jackson as a pious woman, a good friend of Agnes Richardson, and deeply committed to her faith. She and her husband had attended the church's services while they lived in North Carolina, despite their farm's distance from the meeting house. Now, as a widow living with her in-laws, she instilled Presbyterian doctrine in her sons from their earliest days. William Richardson likely baptized Andrew shortly after his birth, and the minister often visited the Crawford home to lead prayers and review the children's instruction in the Westminster Catechism, a series of questions and answers that summarized the church's core beliefs. Elizabeth likewise regularly took her sons to the church's Sunday meetings and reinforced the church's lessons at home, likely with the support of uncle James, who, as one of the Waxhaws' leading men, probably served as a church elder. Years later, Jackson well remembered how his mother loved Isaac Watts's hymns and often sang them to her children.[19]

Andrew, of course, started attending services too young to pay attention to sermons, but as he grew, he would have picked up Bible stories and basic Christian principles from church, his family, and the cultural presumptions of the people around him. The Westminster Catechism he recited with his brothers and cousins relied heavily on the thought of French theologian John Calvin, whose teachings provided Ulster Presbyterianism's guiding principles. From the Catechism, Jackson learned that an all-powerful, all-knowing God had created the world for His pleasure. He created man to oversee his creation, but when Adam failed to keep God's Covenant of Works, misery and punishment for sin fell on all creation. Nevertheless, God had elected some fallen humans to salvation through a Covenant of Grace founded

"I was brought up a rigid Presbeterian . . ."   7

on the death and resurrection of Jesus, who suffered the punishment that the elect deserved. Still, God demanded from all humanity strict obedience to His word as outlined in the Ten Commandments and in the Lord's Prayer. As good Calvinists, Presbyterians assumed that they stood among God's elect and that God's will lay behind all natural occurrences and human events. He blessed His people when pleased and disciplined them when they strayed, and though enemies may torment them, His chosen ones knew He would provide protection and vindication for the faithful.[20]

Andrew's early schooling undoubtedly reinforced these teachings. Ulster Presbyterians wanted the elect to be able to read the Scriptures for themselves, so at some point his mother or uncle would have given him his earliest instruction. Then, when he was six or seven, he and his brothers started attending a common school in a cabin just across the North Carolina line. There, Jackson practiced reading and writing while learning the basic rules of arithmetic. Meanwhile, he grew into an energetic boy who loved to have fun. Thin for his age, he played, raced, fought, and wrestled. Other Waxhaw boys remembered him as intensely competitive. One classmate recalled usually beating the younger and lighter Andrew when wrestling, "but he wouldn't stay throwed," always bouncing up to continue the fight. Jackson also witnessed the cockfights and thoroughbred races that were popular past times on the frontier, and in his early years, he developed the love for horses that would continue throughout his life. By his teen years, Jackson had so impressed his elders with his natural ability to train and handle the animals that he gained their respect for his judgment on a racehorse's worth.[21]

Jackson also impressed his neighbors as a bright and intelligent boy. At an early age, he displayed a good command of words. He could speak fluently and effectively, and his quick mind appeared to give him a promising future. At some point, his mother concluded that he should train to become a minister. Surely the thought of her youngest becoming a man of God thrilled Elizabeth's pious soul, but practical considerations influenced her as well. After her husband's death, her brother-in-law James secured the title to the North Carolina lands, which he put in the name of her three sons.[22] Elizabeth knew, though, that dividing the 200 acres between two, let alone three, of her children would leave them with farms too small to support families of their own. Probably, she expected either Hugh or Robert to work and

8   *Andrew Jackson: Old Hickory in Christian America*

eventually take over the land; the other son could be apprenticed to learn a trade, while Andrew could pursue the professional career for which he showed an aptitude. The ministry stood as a prestigious position among Scots-Irish Presbyterians; few trained ministers came to the region, and more churches would likely be constructed as the backcountry settlements matured. Andrew's education and ordination could thus secure for him employment and status as a community leader in one of the colonies' churches. Perhaps Elizabeth even dreamed of him one day filling the vacant pulpit in the Waxhaws.

So, in 1776, at age nine, Andrew and his cousin Will Crawford moved in with their uncle Robert so they could attend a school taught by William Humphreys at the Waxhaws meeting house. There, they spent three years learning the basics of Latin, Greek, and other subjects necessary to prepare them for professional careers. Jackson also recalled spending a term at an academy in Charlotte, North Carolina, probably after Humphreys closed his school in 1779. Little evidence remains to show how seriously Jackson took his studies. Clearly, he did not become a scholar. Later in life, he occasionally used Latin phrases, but he neither became fluent in a foreign language—living or dead— nor demonstrated a deep love for the classics. At the same time, his schooling expanded his awareness and helped him develop skills that would later help him gain respect and social prestige. Despite political opponents' later criticism of his supposed ignorance and lack of education, his correspondence and public statements revealed a familiarity with classical stories and the works of writers like Plutarch, Shakespeare, and Alexander Pope. According to his private secretary while president, Oliver Goldsmith's *Vicar of Wakefield* was Jackson's favorite book, "after the Bible, of course," and as an adult he collected an impressive library of historical, biographical, and theological works. While ownership of books is no guarantee of having read them, he apparently read more than his detractors acknowledged. Meanwhile, his early education helped him develop a clear, strong, and direct writing style. Though later he relied on his staff or associates to draft and refine his official papers, Thomas Hart Benton recalled in his memoirs that the thoughts in Jackson's papers "were his own, vigorously expressed," with his writing coming out as "a vigorous flowing current."[23]

As a boy, though, Jackson seldom displayed the piety expected for a minister in training. Those who knew him in his youth described

"I was brought up a rigid Presbeterian . . ." 9

him as confrontational and headstrong. A slave woman who nursed him through an illness later recalled that he was "the most mischievous of all the youngsters thereabouts; always up to some prank and getting into trouble." Others in the Waxhaws found him "self-willed, somewhat overbearing, easily offended, *very* irascible, and, upon the whole, 'difficult to get along with.'" He especially became known for his swearing. His thin skin, short temper, and eagerness to fight also made a lasting impression. Once, some boys overloaded a gun so its unexpectedly strong kick would knock him down when he fired it; their trick worked, but Jackson immediately got up and swore, "By G-d, if any one of you laughs, I'll kill him!" One boy who knew him claimed that, "of all the boys he had ever known, Andrew Jackson was the only bully who was not also a coward."[24]

Jackson's youthful behavior showed him to be a strong-willed boy who likely needed male guidance. Possibly, he resented the loss of his father and his mother's dependence on the Crawfords. He became very close to his mother, and while no evidence suggests that either James or Robert Crawford mistreated their nephew, neither ever became a father figure for him. His uncles had their own offspring to care for, so both left the Jackson boys to Elizabeth, who likely indulged them when they needed discipline.

At the same time, Jackson learned much of his aggressive behaviors from the men of the Waxhaws. For many, if not most in the community, Presbyterianism had become, in one historian's words, "more a lingering memory than an active faith," but even the faithful held fast to their understanding of *honor*, a set of values that traced its roots back to the earliest civilizations. Honor stressed a man's need to maintain the respect of his peers by demonstrating his courage and his commitment to his comrades. An honorable man would show his loyalty to his friends and never hesitate to fight alongside them. Participating in vices bonded him in fraternity with his fellows while also showing his worth: he could hold his liquor, compete in any contest, and gamble to prove his willingness to take risks, no matter the potential costs. Likewise, an honorable man took care of those dependent on him, and he stayed true to his word, regardless of the consequences. Most significantly, a man of honor avoided shame. Losing one's good name would be more devastating than sacrificing personal integrity, so a man of honor would fight to dispel accusations of cowardice, dishonesty,

10 *Andrew Jackson: Old Hickory in Christian America*

cheating, or disloyalty. On the frontier, preserving honor might require fighting in bare-fisted boxing or wrestling matches that could end with the victor gouging out the eye of his foe. Regardless of the risk, an honorable man would fight to the death before submitting to an insult to his name.[25]

Honor would become a central component of the Southern culture in which Jackson came to maturity and lived as an adult. Throughout his life, it would prove for him a more important set of guiding principles than would Christianity. Like for the adults he observed in the Waxhaws, though, he never saw a serious conflict between his faith and his honor, despite Christian teachings about loving one's enemies, self-denial, submissiveness, and avoiding the world's sinfulness. Tensions might emerge between the two ethics, but the men of Jackson's youth apparently acted honorably while considering themselves faithful Presbyterians. William Richardson and his successors probably limited the challenges to their flock to condemning internal disputes and chiding members for missing church services. Most likely, they discouraged immoral behavior and excesses like drunkenness, profligacy, and Jackson's favorite sin, swearing. But almost certainly, they held back from insisting that their male congregants choose between their faith and their honor. Years after leaving the Waxhaws, Jackson as an adult occasionally recalled advice and admonitions from his Christian mother, such as "never to sue a man or indict him for slander," but his responses to conflicts more often reflected the ethic of honor than they did the teachings of Jesus.[26]

The demands of honor did not completely overwhelm Jackson's religious instruction. As an adult, Jackson recognized the different claims of honor and religion, but his commitment to upholding his name never caused him to doubt that he was a Christian. A few years before his death, he stated that, from his young adulthood on, he read three chapters of the Bible each day, and throughout his life, his public and private comments showed that he well knew the Bible's stories and basic teachings.[27] To be sure, he would refuse to join a church until late in life, and he went through long periods of years when religion or spiritual matters appeared at best of little importance. Still, he never denied belief in the existence of God, and though he moved away from the narrow sectarianism and the Calvinist deity of his youth, he never challenged Christianity's orthodox teachings. The possibility remains

"I was brought up a rigid Presbeterian . . ." 11

that, had he been able to remain in the stable environment of the colonial Waxhaws, supported by his clan and with the church a central institution, he would have outgrown his youthful excesses, fulfilled his mother's wishes, and upheld his honor as a leading Presbyterian minister. That he did not perhaps can be attributed more to unforeseen circumstances than to his personality or his upbringing.

Notes

1. Hendrik Booraem, *Young Hickory: The Making of Andrew Jackson* (Dallas: Taylor Trade Publishing, 2001), 1–4, 215–216n.2; Patrick Griffin, *The People with No Name: Ireland's Ulster Scots, America's Scots-Irish, and the Creation of a British Atlantic World, 1689–1764* (Princeton, 2001).
2. Booraem, *Young Hickory*, 2–4, 8–9.
3. Booraem, *Young Hickory*, 10–12, 14–16; Peter N. Moore, *World of Toil and Strife: Community Transformation in Backcountry South Carolina, 1750–1805* (Columbia: University of South Carolina Press, 2007), 2.
4. Griffin, *People with No Name*, 9–11, 25–32; James G. Leyburn, *The Scotch-Irish: A Social History* (Chapel Hill: University of North Carolina Press, 1962), 87–98, 108–16.
5. Griffin, *People with No Name*, 14, 67–79, 159; Leyburn, *The Scotch-Irish*, 157–69; Benjamin Bankhurst, *Ulster Presbyterians and the Scots Irish Diaspora, 1750–1764* (New York: Palgrave Macmillan, 2013), 13–19.
6. Booraem, *Young Hickory*, 6; Leyburn, *The Scotch-Irish*, 210–23; Moore, *World of Toil and Strife*, 15–17.
7. Charles S. Davis, "The Journal of William Moultrie While a Commissioner on the North and South Carolina Boundary Survey, 1772," *Journal of Southern History* 8 (November 1942):552.
8. Booraem, *Young Hickory*, 14–16; Kenneth E. Lewis, *The Carolina Backcountry Venture: Tradition, Capital, and Circumstance in the Development of Camden and the Wateree Valley, 1740–1810* (Columbia: University of South Carolina Press, 2017), 123–28, 196; Moore, *World of Toil and Strife*, 20–25, 56–58; J. M. Opal, *Avenging the People: Andrew Jackson, the Rule of Law, and the American Nation* (New York: Oxford University Press, 2017), 23, 241n. 19.
9. Moore, *World of Toil and Strife*, 2, 25–31, 38–39; Rachel N. Klein, *Unification of a Slave State: The Rise of the Planter Class in the South Carolina Backcountry, 1760–1808* (Chapel Hill: University of North Carolina Press, 1990), 47–77; James H. Merrill, *The Indians' New World: Catawbas and Their Neighbors from European Contact through the Era of Removal* (Chapel Hill: University of North Carolina Press, 1989), 192–215; Richard Maxwell Brown, *The South Carolina Regulators* (Cambridge, MA: The Belknap Press of Harvard University Press, 1963).
10. Andrew Jackson to Ellen Hanson, March 25, 1835, John Spencer Bassett, ed., *Correspondence of Andrew Jackson*, 7 vols. (Washington: Carnegie Institution,

12 *Andrew Jackson: Old Hickory in Christian America*

1926–1935), 5:333, hereafter cited as *Correspondence* with volume and page numbers; Peter Brooke, *Ulster Presbyterianism: The Historical Perspective 1610–1970* (New York: St. Martin's Press, 1987), 14–92; Moore, *World of Toil and Strife*, 2–3, 44, 54–58; Griffin, *People with No Name*, 20–25, 100–101; Lewis, *Carolina Backcountry Venture*, 72–73, 115.

11. Richard J. Hooker, ed., *The Carolina Backcountry on the Eve of the Revolution: The Journal and Other Writings of Charles Woodmason, Anglican Itinerant* (Chapel Hill: University of North Carolina Press, 1953), 14, 132–33; Moore, *World of Toil and Strife*, 1.

12. Hooker, ed., *Carolina Backcountry on the Eve of the Revolution*, 14.

13. Griffin, *People with No Name*, 39, 100–101; Leyburn, *The Scotch-Irish*, 278–81; Leonard J. Trinterud, *The Forming of an American Tradition: A Re-examination of Colonial Presbyterianism* (Philadelphia: The Westminster Press, 1949), 53–165.

14. Moore, *World of Toil and Strife*, 9, 32–34, 42.

15. Donald G. Mathews, *Religion in the Old South* (Chicago: University of Chicago Press, 1977), 23–28; Thomas S. Kidd and Barry Hankins, *Baptists in America: A History* (New York: Oxford University Press, 2015), 26–29, 35–38; Griffin, *People with No Name*, 164–65.

16. Hooker, ed., *Carolina Backcountry on the Eve of the Revolution*, 34–35, 43; Moore, *World of Toil and Strife*, 34–36.

17. Hooker, ed., *Carolina Backcountry on the Eve of the Revolution*, 14, 93–94, 150–62.

18. Hooker, ed., *Carolina Backcountry on the Eve of the Revolution*, 134–35; Booraem, *Young Hickory*, 18–22.

19. Booraem, *Young Hickory*, 4–5, 9, 18–21; William B. Bynum, "'The Genuine Presbyterian Whine': Presbyterian Worship in the Eighteenth Century," *American Presbyterians* 74 (Fall 1996):157–70; Meacham, *American Lion*, 16–17.

20. "The Westminster Shorter Catechism," The Westminster Presbyterian, A Ministry of the Presbytery of the United States, in the Free Church of Scotland, http://www.westminsterconfession.org/confessional-standards/the-westminster-shorter-catechism.php; Leyburn, *The Scotch-Irish*, 58–59, 70, 74–76; Griffin, *People with No Name*, 47–49; Bankhurst, *Ulster Presbyterians and the Scots Irish Diaspora*, 1, 64–66; Andrew R. Holmes, *The Shaping of Ulster Presbyterian Belief and Practice, 1770–1840* (New York: Oxford University Press, 2006).

21. Booraem, *Young Hickory*, 22, 40–41; Parton, *Life of Andrew Jackson*, 1:59–61, 67; Leyburn, *The Scotch-Irish*, 57, 73–74; Cheathem, *Andrew Jackson, Southerner*, 9–10.

22. "Deed from Thomas and Sarah Ewing," *PAJ*, 1:3–4; Booraem, *Young Hickory* 21–22, 34; Leyburn, *The Scotch-Irish*, 74, 273–78.

23. Meacham, *American Lion*, 16, 18–19; Booraem, *Young Hickory*, 27–34; Parton, *Life of Andrew Jackson*, 1:61–63, 67–68, 3:604; Opal, *Avenging the People*, 2–3; Thomas Hart Benton, *Thirty Years View; or A History of the Working of the American Government for Thirty Years, from 1820 to 1850* (New York: D. Appleton and Company, 1883), 1:738.

24. Parton, *Life of Andrew Jackson*, 60, 64–65; Booraem, *Young Hickory*, 42.

25. Mathews, *Religion in the Old South*, 7; Elliott J. Gorn, "'Gouge and Bite, Pull Hair and Scratch': The Social Significance of Fighting in the Southern Backcountry," *American Historical Review* 90 (February 1985):18–43; Bertram Wyatt-Brown, *Southern Honor: Ethics and Behavior in the Old South* (New York: Oxford University Press, 1982), 3–114.

26. Andrew Jackson to Ezra Stiles Ely, September 3, 1829, *PAJ*, 7:404; Bertram Wyatt-Brown, "Andrew Jackson's Honor," *Journal of the Early Republic* 17 (Spring 1997):1–36; Remini, *Course of American Empire*, 11–12.

27. Parton, *Life of Andrew Jackson*, 3:633; Meacham, *American Lion*, 17–18.

2

"I think I would have made a pretty good saddler"

Revolution and war shattered the world of Jackson's youth. Around the same time he entered William Humphreys's school, the Second Continental Congress in Philadelphia declared the American colonies' independence from Great Britain. Heritage and experience predisposed the Scots-Irish in the Waxhaws to distrust the crown and the English-dominated British Parliament. Memories of English hostility while in Ireland, like in the stories that Elizabeth Jackson related to her boys, drove most in Jackson's community to endorse independence. In the Revolutionary War's early stages, they expressed their approval from a distance. British forces concentrated at first on suppressing the uprising in New England and the Middle Atlantic region, so the Southern states witnessed relatively little action. Robert Crawford and a handful of men from the Waxhaws volunteered for service, and at least two Waxhaws neighbors joined in a retaliatory force against Britain's allies, the Cherokees, after a Cherokee raid annihilated a small American settlement in late 1776. Otherwise, life carried on in the Carolina backcountry as if there were no war.[1]

Once the conflict came to the Waxhaws, war hit the Jackson family especially hard. Unable to quash the rebellion in the north, British leaders turned to recovering their more valuable, cash crop–producing colonies in the South. In December 1778, a British army occupied Savannah on the Atlantic coast in nearby Georgia. As backcountry men volunteered to help drive out the invading force, Hugh Jackson, Andrew's sixteen-year-old brother, convinced his mother to let him join a company led by William Richardson Davie, the nephew of the Waxhaws' late Presbyterian minister. Davie's men headed for the

Andrew Jackson. Jonathan M. Atkins, Oxford University Press. © Jonathan M. Atkins 2025.
DOI: 10.1093/9780191886812.003.0002

14   *Andrew Jackson: Old Hickory in Christian America*

coast and participated in an indecisive assault on British infantry at the Battle of Stono Ferry. On the way, Hugh became ill. He defied orders to stay back and fought in the battle, but shortly after returning home, he died, apparently of "exhaustion," in June 1779.[2]

The Jacksons and Crawfords were still mourning Hugh's death when they came face-to-face with the enemy. After a six-month siege, General Benjamin Lincoln surrendered the city of Charleston and his 5,500-man army to General Henry Clinton, commander of the British forces in America. Clinton dispatched Lieutenant Colonel Banastre Tarleton's cavalry to deal with the remaining resistance in South Carolina. Near the Waxhaws, Tarleton's riders slaughtered a regiment of 350 Virginians, taking fifty prisoners after killing one-third and wounding one-half of the men. Tarleton then brought his troops to the Waxhaws to search for stragglers and supplies. Andrew Jackson joined his relatives and neighbors to hide in the surrounding woods while watching Tarleton's soldiers search their homes. Later, the boy remembered Tarleton coming close enough that he "could have shot him." After the intruders left, Jackson saw the effects of war for the first time when he helped his mother care for the wounded, who were brought to the Presbyterian meeting house as a makeshift hospital. Many of the men had been bayoneted or hacked with sabers, and Jackson heard their cries of anguish as he watched some of them die.[3]

The war in the Waxhaws was far from over. Shortly after the battle, about 1,000 Britons under Colonel Francis Rawdon came to Camden to patrol the backcountry and offer amnesty to those who agreed to take an oath of loyalty to Britain. Those who swore to the oath were expected to take up arms for the king, while those who refused would be labeled outlaws. Jackson's uncles, Robert and James Crawford, joined other leading Waxhaw men in the Patriot resistance. Andrew's brother Robert, now fifteen, may have participated in the resistance as well. Thirteen-year-old Andrew remained too young to fight, but he nevertheless gained his first military experience. His uncle Robert's home became a command center for the insurgents, and young Andrew likely listened in as his uncles planned strategy with William Davie and General Thomas Sumter, the commander of South Carolina's Patriot force. Meanwhile, Jackson drilled with the soldiers and helped with necessary tasks like unloading supply wagons, conveying messages, and performing odd jobs. Davie even took young Jackson along when

"I think I would have made a pretty good saddler"   15

he led his company in a raid against a British garrison on August 1, 1780, at Hanging Rock on the road to Camden. Jackson may have witnessed the battle, though more likely he stayed behind the lines to watch the men's horses.[4]

Despite these efforts, the backcountry resistance failed to free South Carolina from British control. When General Horatio Gates brought 3,000 American soldiers to attack Colonel Rawdon at Camden, General Charles Cornwallis, now commanding Britain's army in Charleston, quickly moved his main force to the backcountry, and Gates's poorly planned assault ended in a major American defeat on August 16. Two days later, Tarleton led 160 men in a surprise attack that defeated and dissolved Thomas Sumter's much larger American force at the Battle of Fishing Creek. Waxhaw Presbyterians now had to flee as British troops marched into the region to forage wheat for their next campaign. Cornwallis himself came to oversee the operations and set up his headquarters at Robert Crawford's house, where only two years earlier Andrew Jackson had practiced his lessons in Latin.[5]

While Cornwallis's men occupied the Waxhaws, Jackson and his mother took refuge with Peggy and George McCamie at the house of Susan Smart, a distant McCamie relative who lived about five miles south of Charlotte in North Carolina. Recollections from his hosts suggest he had grown into an older version of the bright but head-strong boy his family, friends, and schoolmates had known in the Waxhaws. He helped his hosts with chores around the house and with the early fall harvest, though he still found time for games with other teens and younger children. Women in the Smart family remembered him as kind, courteous, and charming, while the boys found him quarrelsome, competitive, and uncooperative. At least one pious eleven-year-old boy took great offense at Jackson's still-prolific swearing. His playmates at the Smart's household only had to put up with him for about three weeks, for in late September, Cornwallis's army left the Waxhaws and headed for Charlotte, forcing Patriotic Presbyterians to move on. The Jacksons probably spent the next few months with some other McCamie relatives at Guilford, North Carolina, until the British army's movements again drove them on. With nowhere else to go, the refugees returned to the Waxhaws.[6]

When the Jacksons returned home in February 1781, no significant British presence remained in the area besides Rawdon's two regiments

16 *Andrew Jackson: Old Hickory in Christian America*

in Camden. Loyalists controlled the region during the Patriots' absence, though, and as their rivals returned, they formed militia bands that raided Patriot settlers to try to force them to fight for the king, to settle old scores with family foes, or to prevent victims from recovering property that Loyalists had seized. Patriot supporters responded in kind, forming their own irregular units to defend themselves and launch retaliatory strikes. The conflict quickly degenerated into a bloody, brutal, and vicious civil war. Now fourteen, Andrew had reached the age to fight. With his brother and cousins, he rode with Patriot bands on some of their excursions, witnessing and perhaps participating in some of the cruel atrocities both sides committed against each other. His first combat experience probably came when he helped defend the house of an American officer, but the small victory came at a tragic cost. The group held off a Tory assault long enough for the officer to escape, but in the skirmish, Andrew's uncle, James Crawford, suffered a wound that a few weeks later would take his life.[7]

Jackson's experience as a partisan likewise lasted only a few weeks. Word came that General Sumter needed men to assist Nathanael Greene's American army, which was on its way to South Carolina. Patriots called for volunteers to meet at the Waxhaws' Presbyterian church on April 10, but when Robert and Andrew Jackson came to offer their services, they saw that a British squadron had already attacked and driven away the volunteers. As the soldiers burned down the meeting house, the Jackson brothers escaped to their cousin Thomas Crawford's home, but a group of British regulars and Loyalists apprehended them the next morning. According to Andrew's later account, his defiance then nearly cost him his life. As Tories ransacked the house, a British officer ordered him to polish the soldier's boots. The boy refused, claiming to be a prisoner of war and demanding to be treated with respect. Furious at his insolence, the officer lashed his sword at Jackson, who deflected the blow with his left arm but nevertheless suffered severe gashes on his hand and head. While Thomas's wife Elizabeth bandaged his wounds, the officer issued the same command to Jackson's brother. Sixteen-year-old Robert also refused, provoking another assault with a similar result.[8]

Robert's wounds proved more serious, but the commander's determination to move on prevented Elizabeth Crawford from treating the injury. Ordered to lead his captors to the house of a local Patriot

"I think I would have made a pretty good saddler"   17

leader, Andrew's quick thinking took them by a long and exposed route so the intended victim could see the squadron coming and have time to escape. Frustrated, the Britons rounded up their captives and forced them to march the forty-five miles to Camden, where they were imprisoned with 250 other Patriots in the town's small jailhouse. There, Jackson languished for two horrible weeks. Any sense of war as an adventure must have disappeared as he coped with the realities of prison life. His captors took his coat and shoes and separated him from his brother and cousins, putting each in different, overcrowded cells where the boys stood or sat in idleness and filth, overwhelmed by the stench of the poorly ventilated rooms. Tory guards harassed them and provided only small rations of bad food. Forty years later, Jackson remembered with appreciation how one British officer paid for additional provisions after learning about the prisoners' bleak conditions. Jackson also recalled using a dull razor to pry a small hole in a wall so he could watch General Greene's ultimately futile assault against Colonel Rawdon's men.[9]

Elizabeth Jackson finally obtained her boys' release when she persuaded a Patriot militia captain to include her sons in a prisoner exchange. Shortly before their release, though, smallpox had broken out among the prisoners. As they left the jail, Robert had already developed a serious case, and Andrew displayed the disease's early symptoms. The younger boy walked back to the Waxhaws while Robert and their mother rode the horses she had secured. Nevertheless, the journey took its toll. Robert died two days after their return, while Andrew lay in bed with a high fever, delirious, and, Elizabeth feared, near death. For three weeks, Jackson remained seriously ill. By late May, he began to recover, and the disease appeared to leave no lasting effects. But as he regained his strength, he experienced his most crushing blow yet. Elizabeth learned that two Crawford nephews were imprisoned with several other Waxhaw Patriots on a ship in Charleston harbor. With two other local women, she made the nearly two-hundred-mile trip to provide their kinsmen with some food and supplies. The other women returned six weeks after they left, but Elizabeth was not among them. Instead, they gave the boy the tragic news: while visiting a distant relative who lived just outside Charleston, Elizabeth became ill and died, probably from typhus caught from the prisoners she had assisted.[10]

18   *Andrew Jackson: Old Hickory in Christian America*

In two fast years, Jackson lost those closest to him. His mother's death hit especially hard. She had been a constant presence and his chief source of encouragement since his birth. He apparently never questioned her decision to aid others while he was still recovering from his own illness. Later, he would make several unsuccessful efforts to try to locate her unmarked grave.[11] Still, she left him at a crucial age, as had his brothers and closest kin. Beyond taking his family, the war had destroyed the secure home of his youth. The conflict must have also exposed him, at fourteen, to more hardships and greater cruelty than most adults face in a lifetime. The pain of these years undoubtedly affected him deeply. He learned that the future remains uncertain, that enemies can afflict devastation, and that death could come at any moment. Throughout his life, friends and foes noted his hostility toward his enemies—especially former allies whom he thought had betrayed him—and his determination to fight against them with every ounce of his being. He fought with all he had because he had learned that defeat could cost him everything.

At some point through his ordeals, Jackson may have asked, Where was God? If he doubted God's existence, he left no evidence of skepticism. Instead, he apparently continued to accept Christianity's basic tenets. According to Thomas Hart Benton, the adult Jackson possessed "a deep-seated vein of piety," as he remained "a firm believer in the goodness of a superintending Providence, and in the eventual right judgment and justice of the people. I have seen him at the most desperate part of his fortunes," Benton recalled, "and never saw him waver in the belief that all would come right in the end."[12] Possibly, surviving his ordeals stoked in Jackson this optimistic outlook. But while a degree of faith may have persisted, the tragedies Jackson experienced as a boy also failed to spark in him a dramatic conversion or a deeper reliance on the Almighty. Perhaps he thought God would one day inflict His wrath against the enemies he blamed for his troubles, but he saw vengeance as his own responsibility, not the Lord's. Clearly, the sectarian simplicity of "rigid Presbeterianism" no longer sufficed. Nothing indicates that he saw his troubles as punishment for sins that demanded repentance through prayer and fasting. Any thoughts about his becoming a minister were meanwhile buried with his mother, while maintaining his honor—all he had left—now became his obsession. Keeping his good name would venerate his family's memory and help

"I think I would have made a pretty good saddler"   19

him rise in status to attain the wealth and prestige that could gain control of his circumstances. Control, rather than faith, became for him the means for restoring the security that his enemies had taken away.

Jackson soon realized, too, that he would have to attain stature and gain control of his world on his own. After his mother's death, he first remained with his uncle, Robert Crawford, who was busy rebuilding his fortune out of the ruins of the Waxhaw community. The surrender of Cornwallis's army at Yorktown in October 1781 marked the end of the military conflict, but Crawford set up on his farm a supply station for Nathanael Greene's army, which kept a watch on the British force that continued to occupy Charleston while diplomats in Paris negotiated a peace treaty. Jackson helped out at the depot where he could, but once he regained his strength, Robert sent him to live with the family of Joseph White so he could learn the trade of a saddlemaker. Robert may have been putting Jackson into a sort of exile: in a run-in with John Galbraith, whom Greene had sent to oversee the station, Jackson had threatened "most avowedly" to send Galbraith "to the other world." But after six months, Jackson had had enough of saddlemaking. According to a Crawford family legend, one day while he was chopping wood, he threw down his axe, "swore that he was never made to hew logs," and walked away from the Whites.[13]

As an old man, Jackson chuckled, "I think I would have made a pretty good saddler," but at fifteen, he had no interest in the life of a tradesman. Self-willed, spurred by memories of his mother's encouragement, the survivor of several life-threatening ordeals, and already better-educated than most Waxhaw lads, he assumed that Providence had destined him for a higher station. New friends likely encouraged him in this belief. Several of Charleston's elite planter families had taken refuge in the Waxhaws during the city's occupation. Young men from these families included Jackson in their activities and likely stoked his conviction that he was more than a common laborer. When the refugees returned to Charleston after the British evacuated the city in December 1782, Jackson decided to go with them. He had probably visited the city at least once before on a business trip with his uncle, but now he went on his own with what money he had available—perhaps some funds his mother had stashed away, possibly from renting the family's farm in North Carolina. While in Charleston he may have planned to look for his mother's grave; forty years later he proclaimed

20 *Andrew Jackson: Old Hickory in Christian America*

himself "truly happy" when he learned about the house where she had died, and he fruitlessly asked a friend to locate her grave so he "might collect her bones & inter them with that of my father & brothers." But as a fifteen-year-old on his own in 1783, his main purpose was to make the acquaintances he needed for his advancement so he could join his friends as a bona fide member of the city's elite.[14]

As a result, Jackson spent most of early 1783 engaging in Charleston's elite past times. Socializing with some of the city's better families, he worked to adopt the genteel, courtly manners that later characterized his relations with friends and with those he respected. In Charleston, too, he probably first learned about dueling, a custom that French and British military officers had brought to the colonies, and that socially ranking Americans had quickly adopted as a means to display one's honor. Here, Jackson also experienced the dissolute side of privilege, drinking to excess, gambling recklessly, and likely frequenting the city's brothels. Meanwhile, his hope to launch a career failed. Beyond a congenial disposition, the spirit of a worthy competitor, and service as a good drinking companion for their sons, he had little to offer South Carolina's coastal aristocracy. His wealthy friends lost interest in him as his money ran out, while he probably grew tired of them and their self-indulgent, aimless lifestyle. Over the next few years, he would engage in the occasional "downright drunken debauch," but unlike numerous politicians and prominent men in his era, excess and depravity would never characterize his adulthood. After three months in Charleston, he was ready to move on. Risking his horse on a dice throw in a last-ditch effort to secure funds, he won £200, paid off his hotel bill, and left the city with no lasting friendships or connections.[15]

Jackson first returned to the Waxhaws, though he intended to remain only briefly. At some point, he had decided to become a lawyer. Like the ministry, the law stood as a profession of distinction, and in the aftermath of the Revolution, the departure of Loyalists had produced a shortage of attorneys in the Southern backcountry. An ambitious young lawyer could thus find plenty of business, and through it, he could make the connections necessary for obtaining wealth, social prestige, and security. Jackson's early schooling gave him the foundation for legal training, and other young men he knew and respected, including William R. Davie and cousin Will Crawford, had already

"I think I would have made a pretty good saddler" 21

embarked on careers in law. Never short on confidence, Jackson likely recognized that he possessed the characteristics necessary for a successful attorney. He had a quick mind, an aggressive and competitive disposition, and a command of language that could make him an effective advocate before either a judge or a jury.[16]

To pursue a legal career, Jackson eventually would need to "read law" with a practicing attorney; that is, he had to study legal texts in a lawyer's office while assisting the attorney's practice. At sixteen, he remained too young for a lawyer to take him on, so he spent the next two years preparing himself for his chosen profession. For a while, he brushed up on his skills at a local academy with other young men whose education the Revolution had disrupted. Briefly, too, he taught school, which helped solidify his reputation as a young man of education and promise. At least once, he took some of Robert Crawford's slaves to Salisbury, North Carolina, for sale to pay off one of his uncle's debts. Eventually, he moved to Martinsville, also in North Carolina, where he probably worked in a store owned by Thomas Henderson and Thomas Searcy while learning some basic law with a local planter, Charles Bruce. These men ranked among the most prominent figures in western North Carolina—Henderson's brother-in-law, Alexander Martin, had served as North Carolina's governor—and his acquaintance with them no doubt both furthered his ambition and assured him that he fit in well with those in the highest social ranks.[17]

Finally, shortly before his eighteenth birthday, Jackson concluded that he was ready. At first he applied to study in Morganton with Waightstill Avery, western North Carolina's most accomplished attorney. Avery, though, already had several prospective attorneys reading law in his office, so he had no room to take on Jackson as an additional student. Frustrated, Jackson instead moved to Salisbury to study with Spruce Macay, his cousin Will Crawford's former teacher.[18]

Salisbury residents later remembered Jackson, not as a serious student but as "the most roaring, rollicking, game-cocking, horse-racing, card-playing, mischievous fellow that ever lived" in the town. He lodged in a tavern with Will Crawford and John McNairy, a young local lawyer, and together the three became known as the "Inseparables," whose antics seemed either to enliven the town or threaten its peace. McNairy and Crawford were older and already had their law licenses, but Jackson emerged as the leading prankster. The trio drank a lot,

22   *Andrew Jackson: Old Hickory in Christian America*

gambled frequently, and regularly challenged other young men in horse races, foot races, and cockfights. Moving outhouses and stealing signposts appear among their favorite, milder practical jokes. In their most notorious escapade, they ransacked a room and burned its furniture at the tavern where they stayed. Near the end of his study, too, Jackson was arrested for "trespassing," which likely involved a property dispute that he quickly settled out of court.[19]

Yet Jackson did not neglect his education, which proved less about learning the law than about polishing the manners of a budding Southern gentleman. Salisbury residents remembered his conscientiousness about his appearance. He usually dressed his tall, thin frame well, wearing his long, sandy-colored hair tied in the back in a queue. Though his bout with smallpox surprisingly left few marks on his face, he was not especially handsome, but what he lacked in looks he made up for through charm and graciousness. Early biographers claimed that he developed a "presence" in these years, an aura that reflected his natural abilities as a leader while inspiring admiration, deference, or insecurity in others. Perhaps out of respect for his mother's memory, he continued to treat women with politeness and respect—at least women of his own or higher social status, as local Salisbury legend maintained that he frequented the town's brothel and preferred biracial sexual partners. His horsemanship continued to win the admiration of gentlemen, who sometimes brought their stock to him for his appraisal. With both men and women, he gained a reputation as a good conversationalist. Possibly, too, he attended the services of the local Episcopal church, the denomination of the elite friends he had known in Martinsville.[20]

Meanwhile, Jackson worked on smoothing his rough edges and curbing the recklessness he had displayed as a boy. His anger always had a short fuse, and his experience through the Revolution probably made him quicker to react to a possible offense or potential threat. But uncontrolled rage, he knew, did not reflect the character of a gentleman. Most likely, he practiced controlling his temper. Benton— whose relationship with Jackson ranged from trusted aide to bitter enemy to close political ally—concluded that Jackson's "temper was placable as well as irascible, and his reconciliations were cordial and sincere." James Parton, Jackson's first serious biographer, concluded that later visitors to Jackson's home expected to find him a barbarous

"I think I would have made a pretty good saddler" 23

man about whose "fierce ways and words they had heard so much"; instead, he usually impressed his guests as "the gentlest and tenderest of men." There were, he concluded, two Jacksons, and "instantaneously he could change from one Jackson to the other."[21] These observations suggest that Jackson never let raging passions dominate him. More likely, he could put on whatever face necessary to manipulate those around him and gain control of his circumstances. He would still get angry, but only rarely—almost always when facing a challenge to his honor—did he display this rage in public. More often, he would use the threat of his wrath and apparent unbridled fury to intimidate an opponent or underling, all the while remaining in complete control of himself.

Jackson also reined in his potentially destructive excesses so he could model the behavior of the planter elite he wanted to join. While he continued to drink, only occasionally did he get drunk with his "Inseparable" friends. He still wanted to win at cards, races, and cockfights, but he restrained his competitive streak and apparently learned to accept his losses graciously. Likewise, he curtailed his combativeness. As a budding man of honor, he never backed down from an insult, but no one in Salisbury remembered him as a bully. Instead, the town's residents considered him "not licentious nor particularly quarrelsome" and recalled he fought only when provoked. Benton attributed Jackson's later confrontations to "a temper which refused compromise and bargaining, and went for a clean victory or a clean defeat, in every case." Nevertheless, he acknowledged that Jackson would yield "on minor points, to his friends," while the "unpleasant concomitants" accompanying a personal confrontation quickly "passed away with all their animosities."[22] Only a few years before, his adolescent threat to kill an American officer compelled his uncle to send him away. Now, as a young law student, he learned to channel his anger into more socially acceptable forms of resolving disputes and defending his reputation.

Honorable behavior and genteel airs, though, could not completely whitewash Jackson's reputation as the "head of all the rowdies hereabout," and his mischievous streak almost deprived him of the gains he had made. As part of a committee to organize a Christmas ball at a dancing school he attended, he sent invitations to Molly and Rachel Wood—a mother and daughter with scandalous reputations

24 *Andrew Jackson: Old Hickory in Christian America*

who likely were prostitutes. To the shock of Jackson and Salisbury's elite, the Woods showed up at the event. While women raced for the exits, men demanded the Woods leave, which they did after identifying Jackson as the source of their invitations. Jackson insisted that he invited them as a joke and never expected them to come. His defense apparently sufficed enough for the scandal to blow over, but it may have cost him his position in Spruce Macay's office. Shortly after the incident, he left Macay's office to read law with John Stokes, a Revolutionary War veteran whom Jackson's mother may have tended to as a nurse in the Waxhaws' meeting house. Stokes had never married, and Jackson now may have needed a mentor without a wife to object to such a disreputable student.[23]

Throughout his time in Salisbury, Jackson never completely neglected his legal studies, and after reading with Stokes for six months, he concluded he was ready. In September 1787, he presented himself before the Salisbury Superior Court. After he satisfactorily answered a series of questions from two of the Court's judges, he received his license to practice law. Still only twenty, Jackson did not immediately open his own office. A different prospect now appeared promising. In December, his friend John McNairy was appointed superior court judge for Davidson County, four hundred miles to the west in North Carolina's recently opened lands past the Appalachian Mountains. McNairy promised to make Jackson his court's prosecutor, so Jackson agreed to join him and explore what possibilities the region might offer. With winter coming, they decided to delay their journey until the following spring, when travel over the mountains would be safer. In the meantime, Jackson drifted through the counties surrounding Salisbury, taking on a few cases but mainly continuing to hone his social skills—and engaging in a few pranks—before staying at the McNairy home in Martinsville to prepare for their departure.[24]

Finally, in Spring 1788, Jackson and McNairy joined several companions and headed west. Jackson later described this venture as "experimental," because he left open the possibility of returning to North Carolina if Davidson County failed to meet his expectations. Instead, the region that became Middle Tennessee became his home. For the rest of his life, he had little contact either with his cohort from his days as a law student or with the Waxhaw friends and relatives of his youth. Nevertheless, Jackson's early years in the Carolinas shaped

"I think I would have made a pretty good saddler"   25

him into the adult that would become a national hero. Part of the Waxhaws' legacy included a belief in God, knowledge of the Bible, and an understanding of fundamental Christian teachings. Childhood tragedy, though, had overwhelmed the simple faith of his boyhood and stripped away restraints on his determination to succeed. As he headed west, he remained more concerned about upholding his honor and achieving prestige and prominence than about practicing his religion.

Notes

1. Booraem, *Young Hickory*, 45; Amos Kendall, *Life of Andrew Jackson, Private, Military, and Civil, with Illustrations* (New York: Harper & Brothers, 1843), 11–13; Moore, *World of Toil and Strife*, 61–63; Lewis, *Carolina Backcountry Venture*, 190; Klein, *Unification of a Slave State*, 91–95; Jerome J. Nadelhaft, *The Disorders of War: The Revolution in South Carolina* (Orono: University of Maine at Orono Press, 1981), 47–49.
2. John S. Pancake, *The Destructive War: The British Campaign in the Carolinas, 1780–1782* (Tuscaloosa: University of Alabama Press, 1985), 30–35; Nadelhaft, *Disorders of War*, 50; Moore, *World of Toil and Strife*, 66–67; Booraem, *Young Hickory*, 47–48.
3. Pancake, *Destructive War*, 56–72; Nadelhaft, *Disorders of War*, 50–52; Robert Middlekauf, *The Glorious Cause: The American Revolution, 1763–1789* (New York: Oxford University Press, 1982), 438–49; "Jackson's Description of His Experiences during and Immediately Following the Revolutionary War," *PAJ*, 1:5; Booraem, *Young Hickory*, 49–50; Parton, *Life of Andrew Jackson*, 1:70–78; Kendall, *Life of Andrew Jackson*, 16.
4. Moore, *World of Toil and Strife*, 60–64; Pancake, *Destructive War*, 88–95; Middlekauff, *Glorious Cause*, 451–53; Nadelhaft, *Disorders of War*, 55–58; Booraem, *Young Hickory*, 45–65; Parton, *Life of Andrew Jackson*, 1:71–72.
5. Pancake, *Destructive War*, 95–107; Middlekauf, *Glorious Cause*, 449–62; Booraem, *Young Hickory*, 65–66.
6. Parton, *Life of Andrew Jackson*, 1:72–75; Booraem, *Young Hickory*, 71–84; Kendall, *Life of Andrew Jackson*, 40.
7. Pancake, *Destructive War*, 83–89; Klein, *Unification of a Slave State*, 102–104; Moore, *World of Toil and Strife*, 65–75; Booraem, *Young Hickory*, 85–88, 90–94; Parton, *Life of Andrew Jackson*, 1:85–87; Kendall, *Life of Andrew Jackson*, 41–47.
8. Booraem, *Young Hickory*, 94–99; Kendall, *Life of Andrew Jackson*, 48–50.
9. Andrew Jackson to Samuel Houston, August 8, 1824, *PAJ*, 5:431; Booraem, *Young Hickory*, 99–105; Kendall, *Life of Andrew Jackson*, 50–56.
10. Booraem, *Young Hickory*, 106–109; Meachem, *American Lion*, 57–59.
11. Meacham, *American Lion*, 13; Parton, *Life of Andrew Jackson*, 1:95.
12. Benton, *Thirty Years View*, 1:737.
13. "Jackson's Description," *PAJ*, 1:7; Booraem, *Young Hickory*, 111, 113–14, 116.

26 *Andrew Jackson: Old Hickory in Christian America*

14. "Jackson's Description," *PAJ*, 1:7; Andrew Jackson to James H. Witherspoon, August 18, 1824, *PAJ*, 5:438; Booraem, *Young Hickory*, 116–17.
15. Parton, *Life of Andrew Jackson*, 1:93–98, 106; Booarem, *Young Hickory*, 118–29; Kendall, *Life of Andrew Jackson*, 68–69.
16. Booraem, *Young Hickory*, 130–33.
17. Booraem, *Young Hickory*, 133–51; Parton, *Life of Andrew Jackson*, 1:98–101; Cheathem, *Andrew Jackson, Southerner*, 15.
18. Remini, *Course of American Empire*, 29.
19. Booraem, *Young Hickory*, 152–64; Remini, *Course of American Empire*, 27–31.
20. Parton, *Life of Andrew Jackson*, 1:105–106, 110–11; Booraem, *Young Hickory*, 147–48, 254–55n.11.
21. Benton, *Thirty Years View*, 1:738; Parton, *Life of Andrew Jackson*, 1:340.
22. Parton, *Life of Andrew Jackson*, 1:106, 112–113; Booraem, *Young Hickory*, 150–51; Benton, *Thirty Years View*, 1:737–38.
23. Parton, *Life of Andrew Jackson*, 1:105, 107–108, 110; Booraem, *Young Hickory*, 165–66, 179–81.
24. "Law License in North Carolina," *PAJ*, 1:10; Booraem, *Young Hickory*, 189–94.

3

"May the great 'I am' bless and protect you"

Andrew Jackson, John McNairy, and their companions left Martinsville for Nashville in late March 1788, just a few weeks after Jackson's twenty-first birthday. Six months later, they reached their destination. The travelers had spent the summer in Jonesborough, North Carolina's first town across the Appalachians, waiting for more migrants to arrive so they could join them on the remaining 200-mile trek through a mountainous and densely forested wilderness populated with potentially hostile Native Americans. While biding his time, Jackson raced horses and took on a few legal cases. In Jonesborough, he made his first known slave purchase, an eighteen-year-old woman named Nancy, though he may have owned a personal servant before. Possibly, too, he fought his first duel. Waightstill Avery, the attorney who had declined to take him as a legal student, opposed Jackson in a trial and made some remarks that the younger attorney considered insulting. Jackson immediately issued a challenge, which Avery reluctantly accepted. Whether their dispute actually reached, the field of honor is unclear. Whatever happened, both men emerged from the encounter unharmed. Their quarrel ended amicably, and Jackson declared his honor satisfied.[1]

Finally, after waiting nearly five months, an official guard came to escort Judge McNairy and his associates on the remainder of their trip. The party left Jonesborough in early October and three weeks later arrived at a cluster of cabins along the Cumberland River that had recently taken the name Nashville. Though Jackson had ventured west only to explore Nashville's prospects, he soon realized that he had found his new home. He immediately took up residence with the

Andrew Jackson. Jonathan M. Atkins, Oxford University Press. © Jonathan M. Atkins 2025.
DOI: 10.1093/9780191886812.003.0003

28   *Andrew Jackson: Old Hickory in Christian America*

Donelsons, the first white family to settle in the region. John Donelson, the family patriarch, had been killed two years before Jackson's arrival, so his widow, Rachel Stockley Donelson, offered free room and board to young men like Jackson who could help protect her homestead. In widow Donelson, Jackson found the maternal presence he had missed since his mother had died. Here, too, he struck up a lifelong friendship with John Overton, who would become Jackson's partner in several business ventures as well as a trusted political advisor. Meanwhile, Jackson hitched his fortunes to Nashville's future. As promised, McNairy appointed him his court's attorney. Jackson personally handled about half the cases that came before the Court, and his effectiveness at securing convictions so impressed Nashville's leaders that in late 1789 the North Carolina Assembly promoted him to attorney general for the state's entire western district, making him the chief prosecutor for each of the region's three counties.[2]

Jackson's official positions carried no salary, so his income mostly came from his thriving private law practice. He took as many cases as he could, on any sort of dispute or crime, so he could collect as many fees as possible, but he specialized in debt collection. The Cumberland region's dispersed settlement made it easy for settlers to avoid paying for their land or supplies, and the region's only other lawyer refused to bring suits against debtors. Jackson, then, became the attorney for Nashville's landowners, merchants, and creditors. Within his first month in Nashville, Jackson issued more than seventy writs to delinquent debtors, and to his clients' delight, he followed up successful suits by collecting the money that courts had awarded. Meanwhile, as the town elite's favorite attorney, he made numerous connections that brought him the contacts and information he needed to invest in the town's burgeoning commercial life. In his first few years in Nashville, he made several trips to Natchez in Spanish Territory on the Mississippi River to purchase goods—probably including slaves—and take care of errands for the town's leading figures. While in Natchez, he even took an oath of allegiance to the King of Spain—a vow that he probably viewed as little more than a business expense—so he could trade with the town's merchants. Possibly, too, he marketed some wares at a small store he may have set up nearby on the Stones River.[3]

While launching his legal and business career, Jackson also met the person with whom he wanted to share his life. Rachel, the youngest

"May the great 'I am' bless and protect you"   29

daughter of John and Rachel Stockley Donelson, was three months younger than Jackson. Contemporaries remembered her as an attractive young lady with an outgoing and vivacious—some would say flirtatious—personality. Her reputation as the settlement's best horsewoman would have immediately attracted Jackson's attention, and the two apparently felt something for each other soon after they first met. Their later life together shows that Jackson genuinely loved her. At the same time, he undoubtedly recognized the benefits of a match with a woman like Rachel. Her family already provided him with the sense of belonging that he had missed since losing his mother and his brothers, but it could also advance his prospects. He had come to Nashville without the prestigious kinship ties that aided other aspiring young men on the frontier, so marriage into the Donelson clan—already regarded as one of the finest in the west—could provide the backing and connections he would need for success. Fortunately, the Donelsons approved of him. Along with his relationship to the widow Donelson, he had become fast friends with Rachel's brothers, who, like Jackson, were striking out to build their own fortunes. Personally, as well as professionally, Rachel seemed ideally suited to become Jackson's wife.[4]

Only one obstacle stood in the way of their union, and it was a major one: Rachel was already married. Her marriage was a troubled one, but in early America, law and custom both considered marriage a lifelong commitment. Rachel's marriage had come while the Donelsons were staying at lands they owned in the western Virginia counties that in 1792 would become the state of Kentucky. There, she met and became infatuated with Lewis Robards, the son of a Virginia planter. Lewis was ten years older than the seventeen-year-old Rachel, but after a brief courtship, the two married in 1785. At first, the newlyweds remained in Kentucky when the Donelsons returned to Nashville, but tension and distrust soon divided the couple. Robards proved financially incompetent, so much so that his father named a younger son, rather than his eldest Lewis, as the executor of his will. Possibly Robards accused Rachel of failing in her duty as a wife when she did not become pregnant. Rachel likely felt betrayed at Robards's rumored affairs and liaisons with slaves, while Robards in turn fumed at her friendliness and easy manner with other men.[5]

The dissension eventually compelled Lewis and Rachel to move to Nashville. Whether Rachel presented Robards with an ultimatum

30   *Andrew Jackson: Old Hickory in Christian America*

demanding that they move closer to her family, or whether Robards sent Rachel back to the Donelsons, then relented and went to reclaim her, remains unclear. In either case, the couple was staying with the widow Donelson when Jackson moved in. At first, he tried to respect their marriage, even though the couple's bickering continued—irritated no doubt by Rachel's friendship with the young lawyer from the Carolinas. When Robards told an acquaintance that Jackson had been "too intimate with his wife," Jackson professed his innocence and, with Overton, moved to another location, but he also confronted Robards and chastised him for mistreating his wife. Robards responded with a threat to whip Jackson, who offered to give him "gentlemanly satisfaction" if necessary. Robards ignored Jackson's hint at a duel, but something must have been going on between Jackson and Rachel. In January 1790, the two ran away together to Natchez, where they apparently began living together as husband and wife. When they returned to Nashville in the fall, friends and family openly referred to Rachel as "Mrs. Jackson."[6]

Laws at this time rarely permitted divorce. The cumbersome process for dissolving a marriage required an act from the state legislature so that a suit for divorce could be brought to a court. Jackson's and Rachel's flight had given Robards ample grounds, though, so in December 1790, the Virginia legislature granted Robards the right to divorce Rachel for abandonment and adultery. Possibly the Donelsons worked out a deal to satisfy Robards's claim to his wife's property, for he neglected to file the required lawsuit against her until spring 1793. Once the court granted the divorce the following September—after Robards himself had already remarried—the Jacksons made their marriage official in a ceremony performed by Rachel's brother-in-law Robert Hays, a justice of the peace, on January 18, 1794.[7]

Despite their marriage's controversial beginning, Andrew and Rachel enjoyed a strong and happy union. In public, they always referred to each other as "Mr. Jackson" and "Mrs. Jackson," but their surviving correspondence reveals an intimate, open, and warm connection in private. Their greatest disappointment proved to be their inability to have children of their own, while Jackson's frequent absences put a strain on their relationship. Still, the two remained close, even when opponents later attacked their marriage as a major political issue. Critics of Jackson's presidential candidacy would label Rachel an

"May the great 'I am' bless and protect you"   31

adulteress and condemn Jackson for stealing another man's wife. John Overton wrote an account of the marriage that became the basis of the Jacksons's defense, in which Overton claimed that Andrew rescued Rachel from an abusive husband before the two fell in love. He likewise contended that the couple fled to Natchez a year later than they actually did, that they married only after they thought Robards had obtained a divorce, and that they quickly remarried once they learned about Robards's delay invalidating their first marriage. Actually, no record exists of a marriage in Natchez, and Overton apparently had to persuade Jackson at the time that, once Robards officially divorced Rachel, the couple needed to marry formally. Overton's story nevertheless would satisfy Jackson voters, while in the 1790s, Nashville society accepted the couple after they returned from Spanish territory. The tendency of Jackson's later enemies to insult his marriage, though, indicated that many in the community, whether openly or quietly, thought the couple had acted improperly. Jackson's sensitivity and angry reactions to their charges likewise suggest that he felt at least some guilt.[8]

Jackson's utility to Nashville's elite dampened much of the criticism of their marriage. Only a few months after he came to the town, he had proven himself to be a dependable, hardworking, and effective ally. With the flourishing of his legal practice, he soon rose to their ranks. By early 1792, he had acquired enough to move with Rachel from the widow Donelson's to their own small farm, which Jackson labeled Poplar Grove. Four years later, the couple relocated to a 640-acre tract—once owned by Lewis Robards—that Jackson named Hunter's Hill. Here he set up one of the region's first cotton plantations, worked within a few years by at least fifteen slaves. Increasing wealth and important connections meanwhile brought political influence. Jackson had always taken an interest in the western settlement's public affairs. Within a few months of coming to Nashville, he had at least some involvement in a plot to threaten the region's secession from the United States, a plan that conspirators hoped would increase trade with nearby Spanish territories and gain the protection from Spanish officials. The ploy failed, but after North Carolina ceded its trans-Appalachian lands to the United States in 1790, William Blount, governor of the newly designated "Southwest Territory," immediately recognized Jackson as a useful associate. Soon after they met, Blount

32 *Andrew Jackson: Old Hickory in Christian America*

named the aspiring young lawyer a justice of the peace for Davidson County, followed with promotions to the Territory's district attorney and then as judge advocate for the county militia. Jackson in turn became one of Blount's chief lieutenants in the district, promoting the governor's interests where he could, well aware that Blount would "attend to" Jackson's own interests as well.[9]

Blount took the Southwest Territory's governorship mainly to protect his investments in western lands, and he likely inspired Jackson's own deepening interest in land speculation. The young attorney had already dabbled in lands, especially when his legal clients sometimes used land titles to pay for his services. After 1794, he so aggressively purchased large tracts that by 1798, with around 50,000 acres, he stood as one of the largest landowners in the west.[10] The need for settlers on their lands brought speculators like Jackson and Blount into direct conflict with the region's Native Americans. Treaties with the Cherokee and Chickamauga nations confirmed the Cumberland settlement's existence, but they also set boundaries that migrants and speculators regularly ignored. The intrusions onto Native lands provoked a series of raids on the settlement that, between 1792 and 1794, killed at least 125 settlers. Counterraids killed a comparable number of Natives, but President George Washington—aware of the settlers' encroachments—ordered officials to fight only in defense. Territorial leaders then took matters into their own hands. John Sevier, commander of the territorial militia, led about 800 men in attacks against several Cherokee bases in the fall of 1793. A year later, Major James Ore led more than 500 volunteers in a series of raids that destroyed Chickamauga's principal towns.[11]

Jackson probably did not participate in either expedition. As the territorial prosecutor, and following Governor Blount's lead, he likely avoided defying direct orders from President Washington. Undoubtedly, he fully approved of the raids, and he had certainly engaged in earlier Indian confrontations. Early historians of Tennessee relate that he participated in a retaliatory expedition against a Native band within a few months after his arrival in Nashville. According to legend, he sometimes also acted as a guard protecting travelers crossing the wilderness to Knoxville, the Territory's capital, and to Jonesborough. These expeditions likely brought him into skirmishes with Natives. Stories claiming that his Indian enemies called him

"May the great 'I am' bless and protect you"   33

"Pointed Arrow" out of respect for his bravery probably exaggerated his experience as an Indian fighter, but like the other Cumberland settlers, he could not conceive of coexisting peacefully with the indigenous nations—"Savage" peoples, he wrote in one of his earliest surviving references to the Natives, "tha[t] will neither ad[here to] Treaties, nor the law of Nations."[12] He thus fully supported Blount's decision to transform the Southwest Territory into a state, which would give local authorities more latitude to deal with the Natives on their own. Blount's political base in the Territory's more populous eastern counties provided ample votes for a referendum that easily approved the move to statehood. Fearing the eastern region's dominance, the Territory's less-populated western counties strongly opposed the proposal, but Jackson, as one of Blount's men in the west, nevertheless became one of Davidson County's five delegates to the convention held in January 1796 to write a constitution for a new state.[13]

Supporters later claimed that Jackson first proposed "Tennessee" for the new state's name and that he took the lead in shaping the state constitution. Actually, William Blount, as president of the convention, played the decisive role in creating Tennessee's first government, with Jackson wholeheartedly backing his political mentor. The convention's journal recorded no speeches or comments from the delegates, but Jackson's votes showed his political views lay more in line with classical republicanism than with the mass democracy he would later champion. While comfortable with widespread suffrage, he seems to have expected voters to defer to their elected officials' leadership. He supported all adult freemen's right to vote, but he also favored landed property requirements for elected officials. When Blount's opponents tried to create a one-chamber assembly, Jackson seconded the successful motion to create a two-chamber legislature, making it more difficult for a popular initiative to quickly become a law. Likewise, he approved giving Tennessee's General Assembly the authority to appoint most of the state's local officers, meaning that the state legislature would appoint the county court justices who would control local affairs.[14]

Jackson's convention votes also offer some of the scant evidence available of his religious views as a young adult. He opposed including in the constitution a provision requiring officeholders to affirm belief in God and an afterlife. At the same time, he favored removing a clause prohibiting clergymen from serving in the state government. These votes indicate that he already held the strong commitment to religious freedom that would characterize his later political career. Boyhood memories of Anglican condescension toward Presbyterians had made him skeptical of a religious establishment, and during the Revolution, the Southern states' disestablishment of their churches furthered a belief in religious liberty as a republican principle. Shortly after the convention, he criticized President John Adams's refusal to appoint federal officials because of their political opinions as something "more dangerous than the establishment of religion." A few years later, when questioning a potential candidate for Congress about his republican principles, Jackson asked for assurance that the aspirant stood, among other points, as "an advocate for freedom of religion." Yet for Jackson, separation of church and state should not prevent clergymen from holding political or military office.[15] Ministers in office presented no threat to religious liberty as long as they served as individuals and not as agents for their particular church. For the rest of his life, Jackson would treat religion as an individual, personal matter, not a concern for a government.

For Jackson himself, matters of faith proved a secondary concern. Though he had abandoned his mother's "rigid" Presbyterianism, he retained the basic Christian tenets he had learned as a child. In his letters, salutations like "May Heaven preserve you" occasionally wished God's blessing on a correspondent. When a good friend's mother died, his assurance that she had "gone to hapier climes than these" may have merely expressed condolences, but he likewise never expressed doubt about an afterlife. He had no trouble identifying his foes as God's adversaries as well, noting for one group that "Heaven" had "some choice curse in store for such Rascals." In contrast to his Calvinist upbringing, though, he never called on God to unleash His wrath on his foes. Instead, he reserved vengeance for himself, stating to a friend in one instance that he would "punish" the "Hellish crew" that had insulted him.[16] Other than these and similar sporadic references, religious allusions or spiritual reflections largely remain absent from his surviving correspondence. In these years, faith for Jackson appeared less about daily devotion to a divine being than about acknowledging the Creator's existence, observing God's standards for right and wrong, and asking blessings on his family and friends. Otherwise, building his

"May the great 'I am' bless and protect you"   35

career and establishing himself in society remained Jackson's main objectives. His letters dealt mostly with business and politics, because men of honor did not share their innermost spiritual thoughts with each other, at least not in print.

Organized religion consequently remained a minor presence in young Jackson's life. Frontier Nashville was a rough and tumble place, characterized more by drunkenness, fights, gambling, and blood sports than by piety. One itinerant minister described the town in 1799 as "a sink of iniquity, a Black Pot of irreligion." Small informal gatherings offered what few religious activities that existed. Before Jackson came west, nineteen early settlers pooled their resources to bring Thomas Craighead, a graduate of the College of New Jersey, to serve as their Presbyterian minister. Craighead set up Davidson Academy, a school for the sons of accomplished men, and he visited families to provide counsel and review children's learning of the Westminster Catechism, just as William Richardson had done for the Crawfords and their kin in the Waxhaws. Jackson probably met Craighead on one of the minister's visits to the Donelsons, and he served on the board of trustees for Davidson Academy from 1791 until 1806. At least once in a while, Jackson may have attended the services that Craighead held when the minister preached from a stump in the front yard of his manse. Yet Nashville remained far from a religious settlement. The migrants to Davidson County with whom Jackson spent most of his time had come from a variety of denominational backgrounds, but no group of worshipers, Presbyterian or otherwise, had the resources or following necessary to set up a church building or form a large congregation. Some town residents openly professed deism, while others rejected orthodoxy for the liberal, Unitarian version of Christianity— fashionable among the young nation's educated elites—that rejected the divinity of Jesus and biblical accounts of miracles.[17]

Rachel probably paid more attention than Jackson to local developments that enhanced Christianity's influence in Nashville society and culture. During the mid-1790s, stirrings among frontier Baptists and Methodists encouraged calls for spiritual renewal. Presbyterian ministers held several outdoor communion services that attracted large numbers and eventually broke out into a wave of revivals in nearby Kentucky, culminating in a massive revival at Cane Ridge in August 1801. Tennesseans participated in these revivals

36 *Andrew Jackson: Old Hickory in Christian America*

and brought their spiritual passions back with them, reinvigorating Nashville's Baptists, Methodists, and Presbyterians and encouraging the formation of several new congregations.[18] Thomas Craighead initially encouraged the revivals, but like other Presbyterian ministers, he became disturbed with the revivalists' preference for ministers who could stir up emotions regardless of their theological training—or lack of it. While sympathetic with the desire for deeper personal commitments to faith, Craighead eventually concluded that the revivals' excessive outbursts would only lead to disorder. He thus approved when his church expelled the revivalists, who later reformed as Cumberland Presbyterians. The split, along with the Presbyterians' growing resistance to the revivals, stunted the church's growth, allowing the Methodist and Baptist churches to emerge in Tennessee, just as nationally, as the most popular denominations.[19]

If Jackson thought much about the revivals, he had little use for them. Their adherents usually came from the small-farming ranks and formed churches as alternative communities to the worldly society in which Jackson was rapidly advancing. More significantly, revivalists' condemnation of material wealth, insistence on strict moral behavior, and calls to abandon practices like gambling and cockfighting directly challenged his understanding of what made him an honorable man. For many of his contemporaries, the revivals "unmanned" their adherents: ministers' insistence on heartfelt repentance and for submission to church discipline weakened a man's authority in his household while compromising his commitment to his peers. The prevalence of female converts and the prominent roles of women and African Americans as spiritual leaders in some churches likewise appeared to threaten placing white men under the authority of their "inferiors."[20] Jackson himself apparently never directly criticized the revivals, nor did he leave evidence of his ridiculing or condemning their advocates. His later relations with white clergymen from various denominations suggest that he typically treated ministers with respect—including Baptists and Methodists associated with revivals, though he usually mingled with them after their commitment to spiritual equality had moved away from its more radical social implications. On the Tennessee frontier, he most likely shared other planters' reservations. He always maintained the mastery of his home, expected women, African Americans, and social inferiors to know their place, and

"May the great 'I am' bless and protect you" 37

remained committed to defending his honor whenever necessary and at whatever cost.

Jackson may have remained quiet because Rachel was likely more sympathetic to the wave of revivals. She left no evidence, though, of disputing her husband's sense of manhood or of opposing his need to vindicate his reputation. Mr. and Mrs. Jackson likewise remained loyal to Thomas Craighead and the Presbyterian church. Gideon Blackburn, who in 1811 would succeed Craighead as the region's Presbyterian minister, held more firmly to strict Calvinist doctrines and had even less respect than his predecessor for untrained ministers. After Blackburn formally organized Nashville's first Presbyterian church in 1814, Rachel attended the services when she could. The ten-mile distance from the congregation's building kept their attendance limited, but Blackburn nevertheless became Rachel's spiritual mentor, her "Father in the Gospel" leading her through a "refreshing" or recommitment to her faith that intensified her devotion. Nothing indicates that Jackson experienced a similar refreshing. He reportedly attended Blackburn's services with his wife, and he promised Rachel that he would join a church at some point in the future. Still, while Rachel absorbed the minister's instruction, Jackson was advising their nephew, who was involved in a dispute with his instructors at West Point, to "suffer death before you will dishonour" and to put "to instant death" anyone—even a superior officer—who might strike or kick him.[21]

Nevertheless, Jackson always considered himself a Christian. Like so many aspiring planters on the Southern frontier, his version of Christianity complemented rather than contradicted his desire to maintain his peers' respect through protecting his dependents while standing up to those who sullied his reputation. Meanwhile, he found his principal spiritual community at the Masonic Lodge. The Masons had emerged in late-seventeenth-century Britain as a fraternal organization promoting morality, benevolence, and civic duty. In post-Revolutionary America, joining a Masonic Lodge became a way for ambitious young men like Jackson to make connections and further their claims to social status. The order's secret oaths and elaborate rituals likewise promoted a sense of brotherhood that connected members across regional and national borders. Jackson probably became a Mason while a law student in North Carolina, and he likely

38   *Andrew Jackson: Old Hickory in Christian America*

sought out Masonic brothers when he came to Nashville, for he was a founding member of the town's lodge when it opened in 1801. For the remainder of his life, he remained a proud Mason, at one point becoming his lodge's Grand Master. Some Americans denounced Masons as heretics. By the 1820s, as he more frequently attended church—and when he no longer needed the social connections the order offered—Jackson let his Masonic activity lapse. Still, he continued to identify with the organization and saw no contradiction between Masonry and orthodox Christianity. The American version, in fact, promoted Freemasonry as the "handmaid" of religion, and lodges often offered free membership to ministers.[22]

As a Mason, a Christian, and, most importantly, a man of honor, Jackson rose quickly in his first years in Nashville. He had arrived with a law degree and a desire to succeed, but little else. Less than a decade later, he stood as one of the most prominent men in a new state despite a controversial marriage that might have hindered the career of someone with less determination. His experience as a youth had taught him that his fortunes could change at any time. Still, his future looked bright. As Congress admitted Tennessee to the Union on June 1, 1796, he remained unaware of the setbacks that awaited him.

Notes

1. Remini, *Course of American Empire*, 37–41; Parton, *Life of Andrew Jackson*, 1:119–24; Booraem, *Young Hickory*, 186.
2. James W. Ely, Jr., "The Legal Practice of Andrew Jackson," *Tennessee Historical Quarterly* 38 (Winter 1979):423–24.
3. Parton, *Life of Andrew Jackson*, 1:135–39; Ely, "Legal Practice of Andrew Jackson, 424–31"; Robert V. Remini, "Andrew Jackson Takes an Oath of Allegiance to Spain," *Tennessee Historical Quarterly* 54 (Spring 1995):2–15.
4. Ann Toplovich, "Marriage, Mayhem, and Presidential Politics: The Robards-Jackson Backcountry Scandal," *Ohio Valley History* 5 (Winter 2005):8.
5. Toplovich, "Marriage, Mayhem, and Presidential Politics," 4–7; Melissa Jean Gismondi, "Rachel Jackson and the Search for Zion, 1760s–1780s" (Ph.D. dissertation, University of Virginia, 2017), 29–32; Kendall, *Life of Andrew Jackson*, 91–92.
6. Remini, *Course of American Empire*, 42–43, 57–66; Parton, *Life of Andrew Jackson*, 1:150–60; Toplovich, "Marriage, Mayhem, and Presidential Politics," 7–9.

"May the great 'I am' bless and protect you"   39

7. Toplovich, "Marriage, Mayhem, and Presidential Politics," 13–14; Kendall, *Life of Andrew Jackson*, 92–97; Opal, *Avenging the People*, 83–84; Gismondi, "Rachel Jackson and the Search for Zion," 33; Cynthia Cumfer, *Separate Peoples, One Land: The Minds of Cherokees, Blacks, and Whites on the Tennessee Frontier* (Chapel Hill: University of North Carolina Press, 2007), 165–71.

8. Toplovich, "Marriage, Mayhem, and Presidential Politics," 10, 15–16; Parton, *Life of Andrew Jackson*, 1:145–53; Remini, *Course of American Empire*, 65–67.

9. Andrew Jackson to Daniel Smith, February 13, 1789, *PAJ*, 1:16–17; Opal, *Avenging the People*, 72–74, 88; Remini, *Course of American Empire*, 51–54, 56, 67–68, 133; Ely, "Legal Practice of Andrew Jackson," 424–27; William H. Masterson, *William Blount* (Baton Rouge: Louisiana State University Press, 1954), 168–69, 190.

10. Parton, *Life of Andrew Jackson*, 1:157–58, 241; Opal, *Avenging the People*, 102; Thomas Perkins Abernethy, *From Frontier to Plantation in Tennessee: A Study in Frontier Democracy* (Chapel Hill: University of North Carolina Press, 1932), 262–76.

11. John R. Finger, *Tennessee Frontiers: Three Regions in Transition* (Bloomington: Indiana University Press, 2001), 138–47; Opal, *Avenging the People*, 85–126; Cumfer, *Separate Peoples, One Land*, 64–69; Kristofer Ray, *Middle Tennessee 1775–1825: Progress and Popular Democracy on the Southwestern Frontier* (Knoxville: University of Tennessee Press, 2007), 10–17.

12. Andrew Jackson to John McKee, January 30, 1793, *PAJ*, 1:40; J.G.M. Ramsey, *The Annals of Tennessee to the End of the Eighteenth Century* (Charleston: John Russell, 1853), 484; A. Waldo Putnam, *History of Middle Tennessee; or, Life and Times of General James Robertson* (Nashville: Printed for the Author, 1859), 316–18; Opal, *Avenging the People*, 74–75; Kendall, 29–35, 88–89, 92.

13. Finger, *Tennessee Frontiers*, 147–50; Abernethy, *From Frontier to Plantation in Tennessee*, 135–36.

14. Parton, *Life of Andrew Jackson*, 1:170–73; Remini, *Course of American Empire*, 75–77; Masterson, *William Blount*, 286–92.

15. Andrew Jackson to John Donelson, January 18, 1798, *PAJ*, 1:168; Jackson to William Dickson, September 1, 1801, ibid., 1:256–57; Thomas S. Kidd, *God of Liberty: A Religious History of the American Revolution* (New York: Basic Books, 2010), 167–86; Matthews, *Religion in the Old South*, 456–58.

16. Andrew Jackson to John Hutchings, March 17, 1804, *PAJ*, 2:16; Jackson to John Coffee, February 28, 1804, *PAJ*, 2:7; Jackson to Coffee, April 9, 1804, *PAJ*, 2:14.

17. Herman A. Norton, *Religion in Tennessee 1777–1945* (Knoxville: University of Tennessee Press, 1981), 3–18, 52; Anita Shafer Goodstein, *Nashville 1780–1860: From Frontier to City* (Gainesville: University of Florida Press, 1989), 14, 58; Gismondi, "Rachel Jackson and the Search for Zion," 39; "Appointment to the Board of Davidson Academy," *PAJ*, 1:29; Thomas B. Craighead to Andrew Jackson, January 14, 1803, *PAJ*, 1:321–22.

18. Matthews, *Religion in the Old South*, 48–55; John B. Boles, *The Great Revival 1787–1805* (Lexington: University Press of Kentucky, 1972), 36–73; Nathan O. Hatch, *The Democratization of American Christianity* (New Haven: Yale University Press, 1989), 49–101.

40 *Andrew Jackson: Old Hickory in Christian America*

19. Norton, *Religion in Tennessee*, 22–27, 35–40; Paul K. Conkin, "Evangelicals, Fugitives, and Hillbillies: Tennessee's Impact on American National Culture," *Tennessee Historical Quarterly* 54 (Fall 1995):250–51; Boles, *Great Revival*, 90–110, 159–63; Gismondi, "Rachel Jackson and the Search for Zion," 76.

20. Matthews, *Religion in the Old South*, 36–46, 58–65; Christine Leigh Heyrman, *Southern Cross: The Beginnings of the Bible Belt* (Chapel Hill: University of North Carolina Press, 1997), 206–52; Anna C. Loveland, *Southern Evangelicals and the Social Order 1800–1860* (Baton Rouge: Louisiana State University Press, 1980).

21. Gismondi, "Rachel Jackson and the Search for Zion," 54, 57–58, 74–84; Goodstein, *Nashville 1780–1860*, 58–62; Andrew Jackson to Andrew Jackson Donelson, December 28, 1818, *PAJ*, 4:263.

22. Goodstein, *Nashville 1780–1860*, 50–51; Booraem, *Young Hickory*, 175–78; "Masonic Minutes," September 5, 1801, *PAJ*, 1:253; Steven C. Bullock, *Revolutionary Brotherhood: Freemasonry and the Transformation of the American Social Order, 1730–1840* (Chapel Hill: University of North Carolina Press, 1996), 137–273; Steven C. Bullock, "A Pure and Sublime System: The Appeal of Post-Revolutionary Freemasonry," *Journal of the Early Republic* 9 (Autumn 1989):359–73.

4

"my reputation is dearer to me than life"

As Jackson approached thirty, he ranked among Tennessee's most prominent men. William Blount now decided to put Jackson's talents to use on the national stage. Even before Tennessee's admission to the Union on June 1, 1796, Blount and his cohorts promoted Jackson's election as the state's first member of the federal House of Representatives. Facing only token opposition, he easily won the contest. That fall he kissed Rachel goodbye and headed for the national capital at Philadelphia.

Once in Congress, Jackson threw himself into his new responsibilities. He secured what he considered his main objective in January 1797 when the House reimbursed the Southwest Territory for the unauthorized expeditions against Natives a few years before. Though he appeared less invested in other legislation, he made a few speeches in the House, and throughout his term he faithfully attended sessions, voted on most roll calls, and wrote letters to keep friends and state officials informed about issues concerning the state. Meanwhile, he identified with the Republican opposition to the Federalist presidential administrations. In one of his first votes, he joined eleven others to oppose a set of resolutions thanking President George Washington for his service to the country. This stance probably reflected his constituents' lingering resentment toward Washington's neglect of Tennessee's Indian troubles, but it also showed Jackson's distaste for the Federalist Party's "British principles," which Republicans claimed had taken over Washington's administration. In letters to supporters back home, Jackson expressed his greatest resentment toward the "unconstitutional" treaty that Federalist diplomat John Jay had negotiated

Andrew Jackson. Jonathan M. Atkins, Oxford University Press. © Jonathan M. Atkins 2025.
DOI: 10.1093/9780191886812.003.0004

42 *Andrew Jackson: Old Hickory in Christian America*

with Great Britain. Perhaps thinking back to his days as a prisoner in Camden's jail, Jackson condemned Jay's Treaty because it submitted American trade with Europe to British restrictions, even though the Royal Navy continued "daily capturing our vessels, impressing our Seamen and Treating them with the utmost Severity and cruelty."[1]

Jackson's course in the House sufficiently satisfied his sponsors so that, after only one session, they promoted him to the Senate. William Blount held one of Tennessee's first Senate seats, but his Senate colleagues expelled him when they learned that, in order to protect his landholdings, he had conspired with Britain to promote a military expedition to seize Spanish territories. William Cocke, Tennessee's other senator, voted for Blount's dismissal, so when Cocke's term expired, Blount's allies in retaliation chose Jackson to succeed him. Jackson duly took his seat in late November 1797. As a senator, he mainly lobbied to get President John Adams's administration to negotiate a land cession from the Cherokees. He also introduced a minor bill designed mainly to increase John Overton's salary as a federal revenue inspector, and, as he did in the House, he tried to keep friends and officials informed about the latest political developments. But in contrast to his diligence in the House, Jackson seemed less engaged in his Senate duties. He attended Senate meetings less regularly, never delivered a speech to the body, and did little to promote his bill for Overton. By the spring of 1798, he had had enough. In April, he received a leave of absence and returned to Tennessee. Once back home, he submitted his resignation.[2]

Jackson attributed his departure from the Senate to his weariness with political affairs. An injury to his knee, caused when he slipped on a patch of ice on a Philadelphia street, confined him for several days and further discouraged him.[3] His main distraction, though, stemmed from a financial crisis. In early 1795, he had set up a new store in Nashville with Rachel's brother, Samuel Donelson. That spring, Jackson went to Philadelphia to purchase merchandise for the store, and he paid for the goods in notes that he had accepted from David Allison, a fellow land speculator. Later that year, he received the unexpected news that Allison had defaulted on the notes, making Jackson responsible for more than $13,000 in debts. To raise cash, Jackson sold his store and much of his land. These deals sufficiently satisfied his creditors so that he seemed safe while serving in the House, but

"my reputation is dearer to me than life"   43

collectors again came after him just as he took his seat in the Senate. William Blount agreed to cosign some of the notes to keep Jackson out of debtors' prison, but Jackson concluded that he could lose everything unless he devoted his full attention to his estate. Thus, he sacrificed his position in the Senate, apparently with few regrets.[4]

For the next several years, Jackson ran a small store on his farm, mainly selling goods to local Indians, while Rachel managed the plantation. For some reason, he did not resume his law practice, which he had ended when elected to Congress. Instead, Blount arranged for the legislature to elect him as a judge on Tennessee's Superior Court, the state's highest tribunal and, more importantly, a position that brought him a salary second only to that of the state's governor. He did seriously consider returning to Congress when friends urged him to run for his old seat in the House, but ultimately, he declined once his comrades found another suitable candidate. Possibly, he feared he might not win the election, but he also could not yet afford to leave his estate. Instead, in February 1802, he formed a partnership to set up a new, larger store with Rachel's nephew, John Hutchings, and with Thomas Watson, a neighbor and fellow planter. The partnership faltered after only eighteen months; Jackson thought Watson failed to collect the firm's fees as aggressively as necessary, and he accused Watson of hiding a cotton shipment from his partners, grumbling that Watson treated him "more cruelly . . . than ever a christian was by a turk." After buying out Watson, he continued the business with Hutchings, and in April 1804, they formed a new partnership with John Coffee, a North Carolina migrant who soon became a close friend and later an important ally in his military campaigns. The new firm prospered for a few years, but Jackson sold his shares in the venture to Coffee when a depression in 1807 drove it to the verge of bankruptcy.[5]

Despite his mercantile setbacks, friends recognized Jackson as "a cool, shrewd man of business," and gradually he regained his financial footing. Sales of cotton, corn, and wheat from his plantation joined returns from his investments in land to help him stay afloat. It would take him twenty years to pay off his obligations from the Allison fiasco, but during the first decade of the new century, debtors' prison no longer appeared a serious threat. Still, finances remained tight. By 1804, he concluded that his judicial salary remained too low. Now in his mid-thirties, the travel across the state that his position on the

44   *Andrew Jackson: Old Hickory in Christian America*

Superior Court required probably no longer appeared as exciting as it once had, so despite his friends' pleas, he resigned his judgeship to concentrate on his businesses. Soon after leaving the bench, though, an accident damaged his cotton shipment to New Orleans. The mishap coincided with the decline in commodity prices that followed a temporary halt to the war raging in Europe. Strapped for cash, Jackson had to sell Hunter's Hill and move with Rachel into a log cabin located about ten miles from Nashville on a smaller, 430-acre farm that he labeled "Rural Retreat."[6]

Within a brief time, Jackson started referring to the new estate with the name that stuck: "The Hermitage," a humble dwelling for a social outcast.[7] The shift may have reflected an awareness that the prestige he enjoyed a few years earlier had slipped away from him. His business reversals undoubtedly damaged his image in the eyes of his peers, but other factors also put him at odds with men who had once welcomed his services. No longer the useful lawyer for Nashville's elite, he had little protection from the resentments that his once-successful practice and rapid advancement had inevitably provoked. William Blount, long his political mentor, died in 1800. John Overton eventually replaced Blount as the state's political manager, but Blount's death nevertheless deprived Jackson of a crucial patron and guide at a critical time. With his status as a leading planter now in question, the controversial circumstances of his marriage and his sudden departure from the Senate appeared less forgivable than before. As he increasingly faced criticism, his commitment to the code of honor produced in him quick and indignant reactions that could lead to violence. Since his mix-up with Waightstill Avery in Jonesborough back in 1788, Jackson's first decade in Nashville had largely remained free of conflict—the encounter with Lewis Robards being the only notable exception. Now, with his status as an honorable gentleman increasingly questioned, he frequently found himself involved in confrontations. Proclaiming that "my reputation is dearer to me than life,"[8] the clashes soon transformed him into Nashville's most controversial figure.

As he fought to defend his name, Jackson never seems to have considered that he might be defying his religion. Christianity remained for him what it had been through the 1790s: a set of beliefs that explained the world to him, a common bond uniting him with Rachel and their family and friends, but a secondary concern to his

"my reputation is dearer to me than life"

career and public image. On occasion, he still wished God's blessing on the recipients of his letters, and he remained on good terms with Reverend Thomas Craighead. Presumably, he still accompanied Rachel to church when possible. Yet he never sensed that his faith might require him to back down from an insult. Instead, his blending of Christian tenets with his social ethic convinced him that religion and honor complemented one another: a good Christian, he concluded, would stand as a man of honor, while an honorable man would act as a good Christian—even when honor compelled him to challenge, fight, or perhaps even kill a rival who had besmirched his reputation. Conversely, an opponent who claimed to be a Christian but acted dishonorably through lying, cowardice, or betrayal only proved himself, to Jackson, to be a scoundrel and a hypocrite.

Faith thus never compelled Jackson to question his commitment to dueling, the ultimate "affair of honor." Legend would later portray him as constantly engaged in as many as one hundred duels. He actually fought only a few—at least one for certain, and possibly one or two more—but he displayed no reluctance about meeting an opponent on the field if a dispute could not be resolved diplomatically. In fact, his involvement in numerous conflicts, either as a participant or as a second for a friend or colleague, gained him a reputation as an expert on the *code duello* whom others could consult in their own quarrels. Many times, too, he physically assaulted social inferiors he deemed in need of discipline but who, in his estimation, lacked the social status worthy of a duel. He well knew about the growing opposition to dueling, including the religious arguments against it. Several states outlawed the practice, including Tennessee in 1801, and James Robertson, a founder of Nashville who had become a devout Methodist, once wrote to discourage Jackson from responding to an insult with a challenge, claiming he "cannot find whare aney honer is attached to dueling." Jackson never replied to his friend's admonition. Instead, more than a decade later, he offered a biblical justification for staunchly upholding his honor. "Blessed is the peace maker," he told a colleague who attempted to intervene in his conflict with East Tennessee politician John Williams, "but even in terms of the Scriptures, where one injureth another he must make reparation before forgiveness & friendship can be restored."[9]

46 *Andrew Jackson: Old Hickory in Christian America*

A disagreement with John McNairy did not lead to violence but did make their friendship an early casualty to Jackson's sense of honor. As Jackson arose to become one of Blount's close associates, McNairy gravitated toward John Sevier, a Revolutionary War hero who was emerging as a rival to Jackson's mentor. At some point, Jackson either forgot about or decided to ignore McNairy's assistance in helping him get his start in Nashville. Early in 1797, McNairy learned from his brother that Jackson had opposed his election both to the state's constitutional convention and to Tennessee's Superior Court. When he expressed his displeasure, Jackson retorted that McNairy had shown himself "not capable of true principles of friendship" and dismissed the complaint as "an ungentleman puppy like Expression." McNairy declared himself ready to defend his conduct "as honor may direct," but rather than face his friend in a duel, he backed off, acknowledging that "it is impossible for me absolutely to determine" the validity of his brother's story. Jackson nevertheless concluded that his "feelings in regard to the violation of our more intimate friendship are not healed," and they never resumed the close relationship they once had.[10]

William Cocke enmeshed Jackson in a more public dispute. A prominent East Tennessean, Cocke had enjoyed a good relationship with Jackson, but he deeply resented Jackson's taking his seat in the Senate. Shortly after the election, Cocke circulated among his friends a private letter that Jackson had sent him. What Jackson actually wrote remains unknown, but whatever he said, he assumed that Cocke expected the letter to embarrass its author. Before leaving for Philadelphia, Jackson wrote to Cocke to protest the "baseness of your heart in violating a confidenc[e] reposed in you in an hour of intimate friendship"; when he returned, Jackson assured Cocke, "you & myself will have an ecclaircisement of the business." As promised, once back in Nashville, Jackson contacted Cocke to demand either "reparation" for the insult or "satisfaction as due from one Gentleman to another." Cocke claimed that an acquaintance had actually shared the controversial letter, and as a fellow Mason, he proposed submitting their differences to a group of their Masonic brothers. Jackson at first resisted, but he relented as the dispute quickly died down, with Cocke's re-election to the Senate in late 1798 no doubt easing the tensions.[11]

John Sevier himself emerged as Jackson's most powerful opponent. As the leader of the victorious American forces in the Battle of

"my reputation is dearer to me than life" 47

King's Mountain during the Revolution, Sevier enjoyed widespread popularity in Tennessee and served as major general in the Southwest Territory's militia. When elected Tennessee's first governor, Sevier resigned the generalship. Jackson knew his election as Sevier's successor could secure his position as one of the state's leading men, so he immediately expressed his interest in the post to the militia's officers, who would elect the next major general. Sevier considered Jackson—not yet thirty—too young and inexperienced for the state's highest military office, so he wrote one of the commanders to express his preference for his friend George Conway. When the officers met for the election, Sevier's ally shared Sevier's choice with his colleagues, and they promptly selected Conway. Jackson deeply resented Sevier's "unconstitutional" interference, especially after he heard that the governor had dismissed Jackson's "Scurrilous Expressions" of his claims as the rants of a "poor pitiful petty fogging Lawyer." Jackson demanded an explanation; Sevier defended his right to state his preference, but he attributed his "petty fogging Lawyer" comment to a rumor that Jackson had insulted his reputation, a story that Sevier said he later learned to be false. The two met in May 1797 to discuss their misunderstanding, and their dispute appeared resolved.[12]

The rapprochement helped Jackson and Sevier maintain a working relationship for the next several years. While serving as Tennessee's representative in the House, Jackson regularly corresponded with the governor to discuss state issues, and their letters displayed a cordial albeit formal relationship. When Conway died in early 1802, though, Sevier—having recently completed his third term as governor—informed the militia that he intended to return to his post as major general. But Jackson still wanted the position; he had spent the last several years cultivating good relations with the militia's officers to ensure their support, and he refused to step aside. This time, the officer's vote ended in a tie. The deadlock left the choice to the new governor, Archibald Roane, one of Jackson's old allies in Blount's circle. To no one's surprise, Roane selected his friend Jackson.[13]

The result infuriated Sevier. The next year, he challenged and easily defeated Roane's re-election as governor, despite Jackson providing evidence of Sevier's fraudulently acquiring land claims from North Carolina. A week after Sevier's inauguration in October 1803, Jackson ran into the governor while crossing a street in Knoxville,

48 *Andrew Jackson: Old Hickory in Christian America*

the state capital. Their verbal sparring led Sevier to charge that Jackson had contributed nothing to the state "except for taking a trip to Natchez with another man's wife." Both men drew their pistols; friends separated them, but Jackson immediately challenged Sevier to a duel. Sevier accepted, but the governor refused to fight in Tennessee because the state legislature had recently outlawed dueling. After a week of bickering over a suitable location, the two finally agreed to fight in nearby Cherokee lands. Sevier's official duties prevented him from reaching the location at the appointed time. Convinced that the governor had backed out, Jackson and his assistants headed back to Knoxville, but on the way, they ran into Sevier's entourage as the governor belatedly traveled to the dueling ground. Because they were back in Tennessee, Sevier again refused to fight; rather than return to Cherokee lands, Jackson accused the governor of cowardice and threatened to beat him with his cane before their associates managed to calm them. As the parties together rode back to the capital, Jackson persistently "damned the Governor for a Coward," while Sevier insisted that "he would not fight him in the State."[14]

After this confrontation, Jackson and Sevier had no further dealings with each other. Labeling Sevier a coward sufficiently satisfied Jackson's honor; for his part, Sevier recorded in his journal that his father visited him in a dream to tell him that Jackson "was viewed by all as a very wicked base man."[15] The fight between a governor and a state court justice meanwhile remained a scandalous topic. Both men's friends published newspaper accounts of the dispute, and in early November, Jackson physically assaulted Tennessee's Secretary of State, William Maclin, for his pro-Sevier version of the encounter. The break with Sevier had political consequences as well. The governor persuaded the legislature to divide the militia, reducing Jackson's authority to the less-populated western portion of the state while making John Cocke, the son of Senator William Cocke, the commander of the larger East Tennessee militia. The dispute likewise probably damaged Jackson's national standing. While in Congress in the 1790s, he had made a modest impression on Republican leaders at best. As president, Thomas Jefferson respected Jackson enough to consider appointing him the governor of the Orleans Territory, the southernmost portion of the Louisiana Purchase. When friends informed him about Jefferson's interest in early 1804, Jackson made a quick detour

"my reputation is dearer to me than life"   49

on a trip to Philadelphia to stop in Washington to display his interest, though he would not call on the president because he did not want to appear "a courteor." In the shadow of Jackson's clash with Sevier, though, Jefferson likely concluded that Jackson was too erratic for an executive position. Despite his availability and lobbying from Jackson's friends in Congress, the post instead went to another Tennessean, William C. C. Claiborne.[16]

Soon after losing this appointment, Jackson's relationship with former vice president Aaron Burr further distanced him from Republican leadership. As Thomas Jefferson's running mate, Burr helped Republicans win the presidential election in 1800. When the votes in the Electoral College unexpectedly ended in a tie between the two Republican candidates, Burr infuriated party leaders because he refused to step aside to let Jefferson assume the presidency. The House of Representatives eventually selected Jefferson; as runner-up, Burr became vice president, but his apparent betrayal made him an outcast in the administration. To avoid a similar near disaster in the future, Republicans ratified the Twelfth Amendment in time for the 1804 election, giving presidential electors separate votes for president and for vice president, rather than two votes for president. Party leaders then refused to nominate Burr for another term, and the disgraced vice president fell further out of public favor when he killed the prominent Federalist Alexander Hamilton in a duel. Once out of office, Burr traveled west with plans to raise an army. His exact designs remain unclear, but he appears to have intended to use this force to seize Spanish Territory in either Texas or Florida. When he came to Nashville, Burr stayed at the Hermitage with Jackson, an acquaintance from their days in Congress. On one visit, Jackson hosted a lavish ball in Burr's honor at a Nashville hotel, and as a general in Tennessee's militia, he discussed Burr's military plans and pledged his full support. Jackson may have believed, as he later claimed, that Jefferson had authorized Burr's expedition. Still, even if Jefferson had covertly given his approval, Jackson's public celebration of the unscrupulous Burr likely irked prominent Republicans.

Recognition of his fading influence probably contributed to the controversy that would permanently scar Jackson both literally and symbolically. The conflict started with a postponed horse race. With John Hutchings and John Coffee, Jackson had built a track near their store,

50   *Andrew Jackson: Old Hickory in Christian America*

and in 1805, he purchased Truxton, a racer that had won several impressive victories in Virginia. Joseph Erwin, another Davidson County planter, offered to challenge Truxton with his finest horse, Ploughboy. Shortly before the scheduled day for the race, Erwin concluded that Ploughboy was not in top form, so he agreed to pay Jackson an $800 forfeiture fee. A brief dispute arose over the fee's payment, but the two met in late December 1805 and quickly cleared up their misunderstanding. A week later, Jackson received a letter from Thomas Swann, a young lawyer and friend of Charles Dickinson, who was Erwin's son-in-law and Ploughboy's part owner. Swann claimed to have heard Jackson tell friends that he thought Erwin was reneging on their original forfeiture agreement. At Jackson's meeting with Erwin, Dickinson asked Jackson about the story, and Jackson proclaimed anyone making the accusation to be a "damn'd Lyar!" Swann, as Dickinson's source, interpreted Jackson's statement as a direct insult and demanded an explanation.[17]

Jackson dismissed the challenge, assuming that Swann lacked sufficient social status to meet him in a duel. When he came across the young lawyer in a Nashville tavern a few days later, Jackson whacked him with his cane, an action showing that he considered Swann socially inferior. Charles Dickinson, rather than Swann, then emerged as Jackson's chief nemesis. Jackson heard a story that Erwin's son-in-law had insulted him by making disparaging remarks about Rachel. When confronted, Dickinson claimed to have no recollection of the comments, attributing any inappropriate statements to drunkenness. Jackson accepted Dickinson's account, but soon afterward, he learned that Dickinson had again publicly ridiculed him. This time, Jackson asked Erwin to intervene, claiming that his enemies—probably Sevier's crew—"*used*" Dickinson to disgrace him. Erwin never responded and apparently did nothing to restrain his son-in-law, convincing Jackson that Dickinson had prompted Swann's demand for satisfaction. In his reply to Swann, Jackson charged Dickinson with stirring up the controversy, referring to Swann's friend as a "*base, poltroon, and cowardly [assassin] tale bearer*" who "*will always act in the [dark] back ground.*"[18]

Furious, Dickinson called Jackson's letter to Swann "replete with equivation" and labeled its author a "*Coward*." He then left for a business trip to New Orleans, reportedly practicing his shooting daily while openly proclaiming his intention to kill Jackson when he "*my reputation is dearer to me than life*" 51

returned. Swann meanwhile published a letter in Nashville's newspaper accusing Jackson of an unprovoked attack. Jackson responded with his own version of their dispute, rebuffing Swann's pretensions to be a gentleman and claiming self-defense because Swann had drawn a pistol before Jackson struck him. His account also provided an explanation, with several supporting affidavits, of his misunderstanding with Erwin, making it clear that he blamed Dickinson for the quarrel. Swann, he wrote, had merely acted as "the puppet and lying valet for a worthless, drunken, blackguard scounderal." When he returned to Nashville, Dickinson in turn published a card condemning Jackson's "scurrilous publication," likewise attacking him as "too great a coward." Concluding that he had no choice, Jackson demanded from Dickinson "that satisfaction due me for the insults offered," and the two agreed to meet on a field in Kentucky on May 30, 1806.[19]

Years later, Samuel Houston told James Parton that Dickinson incited Jackson's hatred with his insulting comments about Rachel.[20] While possible, Jackson never mentioned this offense in his written exchanges with Dickinson. Undoubtedly, Jackson appeared vulnerable to the twenty-seven-year-old Dickinson, who could enhance his prestige by standing up to an old-guard figure no longer worthy of respect. Jackson for his part likely recognized that he had advanced as far socially and politically as he could, and he clearly despised an obnoxious upstart who now wanted to push him aside. He may have determined before the duel that he should kill Dickinson; aware of Dickinson's promise to kill him, he probably recognized that his own survival may have depended on his own willingness to kill his rival. Nevertheless, in their encounter, Jackson let the younger man fire first, despite Dickinson's reputation as the best shot in Nashville. Perhaps he intended to test Dickinson's resolve: if Dickinson intentionally missed, the duel could end with both men claiming satisfaction. Just in case, though, he wore a loose-fitting overcoat to obscure the location of his vital organs. If Dickinson shot to kill, and Jackson survived, Jackson would be permitted his own unchallenged opportunity to finish off his foe.

Dickinson indeed intended to kill Jackson. His shot hit Jackson in the chest and lodged so close to his target's heart that it could never be surgically removed. But Jackson never fell. Steadying himself, he aimed at Dickinson and pulled the trigger. When his pistol failed to

52   *Andrew Jackson: Old Hickory in Christian America*

discharge, both men's seconds inspected the weapon and agreed that it had malfunctioned, allowing Jackson another unchallenged shot. On his second attempt, the pistol fired. The bullet tore through Dickinson's lower abdomen, and after a few agonizing hours, he bled to death.

For the rest of his life, Jackson's wound plagued him as an intensely painful reminder of the encounter. The duel's immediate aftermath, meanwhile, further damaged his public standing. Dickinson had become a popular figure in Nashville, essentially succeeding Jackson as the town's rising young attorney. The fact that he left behind a young widow and an infant son only magnified the tragedy. As stories about the duel reached the town, Dickinson's friends charged Jackson with violating the code of honor because he fired his pistol after his first shot had failed. Recovering at the Hermitage, Jackson fought to defend his name. For the next several months, Jackson responded angrily when anyone questioned his actions in the encounter. In response to a petition signed by seventy leading Nashvillians, the town's newspaper published an issue with black borders in mourning for Dickinson. Jackson immediately demanded to know who had petitioned the paper for the tribute, implying that their request was designed more to insult him than to honor his foe. Dr. Thomas Watkins, the "chief promoter" of the mourning issue, ignored Jackson's challenge to yet another duel, while Thomas Overton and Hanson Catlet, the seconds in the encounter, issued statements affirming that Jackson acted according to the rules that the combatants had agreed to in the contest—though Dickinson's second Catlet later claimed that Overton bullied him into signing his statement. Meanwhile, Jackson secured a letter from the farmer who owned the house where Dickinson died, testifying that no one in Dickinson's party had charged Jackson at the time with violating the terms they had set for the duel.[21]

As the furor over Dickinson's death subsided by the fall of 1806, Jackson's connection with Aaron Burr now brought him under suspicion for treason. When Burr again visited Nashville that September, Jackson provided the former vice president with a list of potential officers for his army. At the same meeting, Jackson accepted $3,500 to purchase five boats to transport Burr's troops to the southwest. Several weeks later, one of Burr's underlings stayed at the Hermitage and revealed that the expedition actually intended to seize New Orleans— now an American city—before invading Texas and Mexico. After

"my reputation is dearer to me than life" 53

probing his guest, Jackson realized "as much . . . as I believe there is a god" that the excursion was really designed to unite Spanish territory with lands detached from the United States in a new, independent western Empire. Jackson immediately wrote to territorial governor William Claiborne in New Orleans, advising him to "put your Town in a state of Defence." While urging his friend Senator Daniel Smith to inform federal authorities about the plot, he then wrote to Burr himself, demanding to know whether the story from Burr's aide was true.[22]

Burr denied any plans to take American territory or divide the United States. Still, when he returned to Nashville in December, Jackson avoided him. When he suspected Burr would call on him, Jackson conveniently was away from the Hermitage; Rachel greeted the former vice president but kept her distance from him, treating him warily and declining to invite him to stay. Burr instead lodged at a nearby tavern, where Jackson finally agreed to meet with him a few days later. Here, Burr's insistence on the patriotic purposes of his mission sufficiently satisfied Jackson. He agreed to deliver the boats and provisions as he had promised, and Burr left with two of the boats shortly afterward. Yet after Burr's departure, word reached Nashville that President Jefferson had issued a proclamation naming Burr the "prime mover" in a conspiracy to seize the American West. Nashvillians who earlier had fawned over the former vice president now rushed to repudiate any connection with a traitor, and rumors circulated that Jackson stood among the conspiracy's leaders.

Among national leaders, suspicions about Jackson's connections passed quickly. In Washington, his friend and Masonic brother, Congressman George W. Campbell, defended Jackson and reported that President Jefferson "declared his intire disbelief" in rumors about his involvement.[23] Jackson bristled at some comments from Secretary of War Henry Dearborn that he interpreted as an accusation, but he nevertheless followed Dearborn's and Jefferson's orders to prepare the militia to march against Burr's force. The action proved unnecessary. Ohio officials easily apprehended Burr's handful of followers. General James Wilkinson, the United States Army's commanding general, arrested several suspects after imposing martial law in New Orleans, while American soldiers arrested Burr himself in the Mississippi Territory in February 1807. Yet as he learned more facts, Jackson became convinced that Wilkinson, rather than Burr, stood as the

54 *Andrew Jackson: Old Hickory in Christian America*

conspiracy's chief instigator. Jackson knew from his earlier meetings with Burr about Wilkinson's involvement in planning the expedition. While he was unaware of Wilkinson's acceptance of bribes to keep Spanish officials informed about American military operations, he always considered Wilkinson an incompetent and corrupt officer. Two years earlier, Wilkinson had ordered the court martial of Jackson's friend Thomas Butler for refusing to cut his hair to satisfy Wilkinson's regulations. Jackson drafted a letter to Jefferson to protest the court martial while warning the president about Wilkinson's "base and vindictive mind." Whether he sent the missive remains unknown, but when the general turned against Burr, Jackson needed little to convince him that Wilkinson actually inspired the plot and now intended to make Burr a scapegoat.[24]

To Jackson's dismay, Jefferson—also unaware of Wilkinson's complicity with Spain—not only stood behind the general but relied on him as the government's chief witness. Summoned as a possible witness to Burr's trial in Richmond, Virginia, Jackson gathered evidence to implicate Wilkinson. But after his testimony before a grand jury, though, neither the prosecution nor the defense would put him on the stand. Attorneys on both sides perhaps feared his hostility toward Wilkinson might damage their case, though his well-known encounters with John Sevier and Charles Dickinson also probably damaged his credibility. Nevertheless, Jackson reportedly "harangued" a crowd in an angry speech in Richmond's Capitol Square, defending Burr and denouncing Jefferson's and Wilkinson's role in the former vice president's prosecution. Once back home, Jackson confessed that he had lost all confidence in Jefferson, dumbfounded at how a man he "adored" as president could now "support such a base man" as Wilkinson "with his present knowledge of his corruption and infamy." Republican leaders, frustrated with Burr's acquittal, concluded that Jackson had acted as a tool for the administration's opponents. The Nashville neighbors who had never forgiven him for killing Charles Dickinson meanwhile continued to suspect him of treason.[25]

As Jackson observed his fortieth birthday, he appeared an angry and bitter man. Only a decade before he had stood as one of Tennessee's promising young men. Since then, his reputation and status had taken devastating hits, due mainly to bad luck, misjudgments, and his obsession with protecting his name. He remained the state's highest

"my reputation is dearer to me than life" 55

military officer, and despite financial difficulties, he still ranked among Tennessee's planter elite. Nevertheless, his days as a social and political leader appeared to be over. Perhaps, when he attended the Reverend Craighead's services with Rachel, he may have wondered whether God had anything in store for his future. He could not foresee that friends and foes alike would soon see him as God's chosen instrument for saving their nation.

Notes

1. Parton, *Life of Andrew Jackson*, 1:196–226; Remini, *Course of American Empire*, 92–100, 102–107; Andrew Jackson to Nathaniel Macon, October 4, 1795, *PAJ*, 1:74; Jackson to Robert Hays, December 6, 1796, *PAJ*, 1:101; Jackson to Hays, December 16, 1796, *PAJ*, 1:103.
2. "A Bill Relating to the Importation of Foreign Goods," January 4, 1798, *PAJ*, 1:162–63; Andrew Jackson to John Overton, February 3, 1798, *PAJ*, 1:174–75; Masterson, *William Blount*, 302–23.
3. Andrew Jackson to John Overton, January 22, 1798, *PAJ*, 1:170.
4. Andrew Jackson to William Blount, January 24, 1798, *PAJ*, 1:198–99.
5. Andrew Jackson to Robert Hays, August 24, 1801, *PAJ*, 1:252–53; Jackson to Hays, September 9, 1801, *PAJ*, 1:254; Nathan Davidson to Jackson, June 3, 1803, *PAJ*, 1:332; Jackson to Boggs & Davidson, September 2, 1803, *PAJ*, 1:357; Jackson to George Rutledge and John Tipton, October 7, 1803, *PAJ*, 1:373; Samuel Meeker to Jackson, October 10, 1803, *PAJ*, 1:378; Kendall, *Life of Andrew Jackson*, 42, 129–35.
6. Andrew Jackson to Robert Hays, August 24, 1801, *PAJ*, 1:252–53; Jackson to George Roulstone, October 8, 1803, *PAJ*, 1:372–74; John Hutchings to Jackson, March 30, 1804, *PAJ*, 2:12; Jackson to John Coffee, May 3, 1804, *PAJ*, 2:21–22; Jackson to Coffee, May 13, 1804, *PAJ*, 2:22–23.
7. Andrew Burstein, *The Passions of Andrew Jackson* (New York: Alfred A. Knopf, 2003), 49–50; Opal, *Avenging the People*, 119–21.
8. Andrew Jackson to William Cocke, June 25, 1798, *PAJ*, 1:204.
9. James Robertson to Andrew Jackson, February 1, 1806, *PAJ*, 2:83–84; Jackson to John Brown, October 8, 1819, *PAJ*, 4:336; Wyatt-Brown, *Southern Honor*, 350–61; Joanne B. Freeman, *Affairs of Honor: National Politics in the New Republic* (New Haven: Yale University Press, 2001), 159–98; C. A. Harwell Wells, "The End of the Affair? Anti-Dueling Laws and Social Norms in Antebellum America," *Vanderbilt Law Review* 54 (May 2001):1813–37; Norton, *Religion in Tennessee*, 15.
10. John McNairy to Andrew Jackson, May 4, 1797, *PAJ*, 1:133–35; Jackson to McNairy, May 9, 1797, *PAJ*, 1:138–41; McNairy to Jackson, May 12, 1797, *PAJ*, 1:143; Jackson to McNairy, May 12, 1797, *PAJ*, 1:144.
11. Andrew Jackson to William Cocke, November 9, 1797, *PAJ*, 1:152–53; Jackson to Cocke, June 24, 1798, *PAJ*, 1:199; Cocke to Jackson, June 24, 1798, *PAJ*, 1:200; Cocke to Jackson, June 25, 1798, *PAJ*, 1:203; Jackson to Cocke, June 25, 1798, *PAJ*, 1:204.
12. Opal, *Avenging the People*, 102, 108–109; Wyatt-Brown, *Southern Honor*, 354–55; Andrew Jackson to John Sevier, May 8, 1797, *PAJ*, 1:136–37; Sevier to Jackson, May 8, 1797, *PAJ*, 1:137–39; Jackson to Sevier, May 10, 1797, *PAJ*, 1:141; Sevier to Jackson, May 11, 1797, *PAJ*, 1:142.

56   *Andrew Jackson: Old Hickory in Christian America*

13. Ray, *Middle Tennessee*, 44–54.

14. Opal, *Avenging the People*, 110, 112–13; "Affidavit of Andrew Greer," October 23, 1803, *PAJ*, 1:490.

15. Editors' note, *PAJ*, 1:381.

16. Parton, *Life of Andrew Jackson*, 1:196; Opal, *Avenging the People*, 114–16; Andrew Jackson to Rachel Jackson, April 6, 1804, *PAJ*, 2:13; Andrew Jackson to John Coffee, April 28, 1804, *PAJ*, 2:19; Jackson to George W. Campbell, April 28, 1804, *PAJ*, 2:18–19; Jackson to Campbell, April 13, 1804, *PAJ*, 2:16; Campbell to Jackson, December 6, 1804, *PAJ*, 2:43.

17. Thomas Swann to Andrew Jackson, January 3, 1806, *PAJ*, 2:77–78; Barbara Stern Kupfer, "A Presidential Patron of the Sport of Kings: Andrew Jackson," *Tennessee Historical Quarterly* 29 (Fall 1970):247–49.

18. Andrew Jackson to Thomas Swann, January 17, 1806, *PAJ*, 2:80; Remini, *Course of American Empire*, 136–38; Parton, *Life of Andrew Jackson*, 1:268–74.

19. Andrew Jackson to Thomas Eastin, February 10, 1806, *PAJ*, 2:84–89; Charles Henry Dickinson to Eastin, May 21, 1806, *PAJ*, 2:97; Andrew Jackson to Dickinson, May 23, 1806, *PAJ*, 2:98; Dickinson to Jackson, May 23, 1806, *PAJ*, 2:99; Wyatt-Brown, "Andrew Jackson's Honor," 8–11.

20. Parton, *Life of Andrew Jackson*, 1:268; Editors' note, *PAJ*, 2:78.

21. Andrew Jackson to Thomas Eastin, June 6, 1806, *PAJ*, 2:101; Jackson to Thomas Gassaway Watkins [c. June 15, 1806], *PAJ*, 2:102–103; "Statements of Hanson Catlet and Thomas Overton re Duel," June 20 & 25, 1806, *PAJ*, 2:104–105; William Harrison to Jackson, June 30, 1806, *PAJ*, 2:105; John Overton to Jackson, September 12, 1806, *PAJ*, 2:108–109.

22. Andrew Jackson to William C. C. Claiborne, November 12, 1806, *PAJ*, 2:116; Jackson to Daniel Smith, November 12, 1806, *PAJ*, 2:118.

23. George Washington Campbell to Andrew Jackson, February 6, 1807, *PAJ*, 2:151.

24. Andrew Jackson to T[homas] J[efferson] August 3, 1804, *PAJ*, 2:33–35; Jackson to Thomas Butler, August 25, 1804, *PAJ*, 2:36–37.

25. Remini, *Course of American Empire*, 153–59; Andrew Jackson to Daniel Smith, November 28, 1807, *PAJ*, 2:176.

5

"the remarkable interposition of Heaven"

Despite the fallout from Charles Dickinson's death and the Burr Conspiracy, Nashville society never completely shunned Andrew Jackson. He continued to interact with the town's leading figures and participate in its public affairs. Though he always reacted swiftly and aggressively to perceived insults, once he resolved a dispute honorably, he could resume good relations with an adversary. Occasional conflicts came up, with one altercation leading to his indictment for attempted murder. A jury quickly dismissed the charge, and he remained an influential man with important connections.[1] Still, his career as a public figure appeared all but over. If he had sought election to an office, he would have lost, and a new president, James Madison, showed little interest in using his services.

The Donelson clan remained Jackson's principal community. He maintained close friendships with several of Rachel's brothers and sisters, often providing them with legal, business, or personal advice. In turn, the Donelsons gave Andrew and Rachel the opportunity to become parents. Rachel's nieces and nephews often stayed with them at their cabins at the Hermitage, and in 1805, the Jacksons took in three of Rachel's nephews after her brother Samuel died. Jackson grew particularly attached to the Donelson boy named after himself, often referring to Andrew Jackson Donelson as his "son," but Jackson never referred to himself as a "father" until he and Rachel adopted another Donelson nephew in December 1809. That month, Elizabeth Donelson, wife of Rachel's brother Severn, delivered twins. The family knew Elizabeth's poor health would prevent her from nursing two children, so on Christmas Day, three days after their birth, the

Andrew Jackson. Jonathan M. Atkins, Oxford University Press. © Jonathan M. Atkins 2025.
DOI: 10.1093/9780191886812.003.0005

58   *Andrew Jackson: Old Hickory in Christian America*

Jacksons adopted one of the boys, naming him Andrew Jackson, Jr. Finally becoming parents at age forty-two, Andrew and Rachel both relished their new responsibility. Andrew Jr. became their pride and joy. Rachel doted on the boy, while Jackson indulged and spoiled his "sweet little andrew." Andrew Jr. apparently felt his adopted parents' love. While Jackson was away on his military campaigns, Rachel wrote about Andrew Jr.'s impatience for his father's return, once taking to bed with him a letter that his mother had just received from her husband.[2]

Military campaigns often took Jackson away from home because he remained a major general in Tennessee's militia. Although he probably sought the position in 1802 to solidify his position as a leading Tennessean, he fancied himself a military man and likely dreamed of military glory. He became a general even though he had no formal training. In an era when soldiers elected their officers, socially prominent men with no knowledge of military affairs were often chosen for command positions. Still, Jackson had a stronger military background than many of his contemporaries. As a boy, his assistance to South Carolina's volunteers during the Revolution exposed him to the basics of training and organizing an army, and he gained early insight on strategy and tactics listening in on his uncle Robert Crawford's meetings with the volunteers' commanders. One of these officers, William R. Davie, apparently became Jackson's model, as he reputedly referred to Davie as the best soldier he ever knew. Once Jackson moved to the west, he likely gained more fighting experience. According to legend, during his frequent crossings through the wilderness between Nashville and Jonesborough, he would defend fellow travelers against Native raids. Also, he likely participated in at least some of the raids against Chickamauga and Cherokee warriors during the wars of the early 1790s.[3]

The possibility remains, too, that he read some of the biographies of military heroes and historical accounts of battles later found in the Hermitage's library, despite James Parton's contention that Jackson "was no great reader of books." To be sure, Jackson only occasionally mentioned books or reading in his correspondence. Several hints, though, suggest that Jackson appreciated the value of books and study. Parton acknowledged that Jackson "was always a devourer of newspapers" and "was particularly fond of hearing an eloquent speech

"the remarkable interposition of Heaven" 59

read aloud in family circles."[4] Years later, while Andrew J. Donelson attended Transylvania University, Jackson commended his nephew for "Having a good library" and encouraged him to "amuse yourself occasionally with history." He particularly recommended that Donelson read up on the life and career of the thirteenth-century Scottish rebel Sir William Wallace, whom Jackson described as "a virtuous patriot, & warrior" and "the best model, for a young man."[5] Jackson likely first learned about Wallace through the legends passed on from his Scottish relatives, but possibly his own reading about Scotland's champion of independence, and about other military heroes, shaped his understanding of how to manage his own armies.

Once Jackson had the opportunity to lead men into combat, he acquitted himself well. While not the great general his devotees claimed, he proved a very good one, as his armies never lost a battle. As historians have usually emphasized, his indomitable will and his determination to fight compelled him to persist through challenges that would have convinced most commanders to give up. Other qualities likewise made him an effective leader. Most importantly, perhaps, he demonstrated an ability to remain calm under fire and make quick decisions without second-guessing himself. Setbacks never paralyzed him or drove him to despair. Rather than brood, he could rapidly assess his position and respond to set up his defenses or regain an advantage. Yet, while decisive, he could change course when necessary. "[N]o man yielded quicker when he was convinced," Thomas Hart Benton recalled, "perfectly illustrating the difference between firmness and obstinancy."[6] He appreciated the importance of good intelligence, relying heavily on information provided by spies and scouts, and though aggressive, he never recklessly ordered his men into a hopeless assault and knew when taking a defensive position presented the wisest course. Impulsiveness sometimes drove his decisions, and at times a failure to ensure that subordinates carried out his orders left his army vulnerable. These flaws might have cost him against a well-trained professional enemy, but he managed to overcome them against smaller, underarmed bands of Native warriors, and against an overconfident European power.

Usually, Jackson enjoyed the widespread loyalty of his men. His strong personality encouraged confidence in his leadership, but he likewise won their favor by treating them with respect—as long as they

60 *Andrew Jackson: Old Hickory in Christian America*

did their duty. In his earliest conflicts, volunteers usually made up the bulk of his troops, and generally he knew how to relate to temporary citizen-soldiers. Praising the militias as "the constitutional *bulwark* of the nation," his proclamations to his men described their cause in strong, passionate language that effectively appealed to their patriotism.[7] He frequently interacted with his men, carefully monitored their conditions, and shared their hardships when in the field. Wisely, he shared credit for his successes with his soldiers and fellow officers, commending them by name in public statements and official reports. But he tolerated no challenge to his authority and dealt sternly with insubordination. His demand for strict obedience, discipline, and total commitment sometimes provoked resistance that he interpreted as mutiny, and by the time he reached the battlefield at New Orleans, he had come to appreciate the qualities of professional soldiers. Victory softened the resentments provoked by his demands, but while on the field, Jackson never let his men forget the lesson he had painfully learned as a youth: war was a serious business that could cost them everything.

Perhaps, as some have suggested, Jackson saw himself as "a divine agent of a sacred national mission." Rachel Jackson, along with others, often interpreted his conflicts in religious terms, seeing natural phenomena and Native hostilities as evidence of God's displeasure.[8] Jackson himself never discussed his campaigns in these terms. Instead, he almost always explained his reasons for taking up arms practically and patriotically: he would do his duty, defend national honor, and protect American independence and self-government. At least once he referred to his army as the "means . . . to punish the impious Britains, for their sacraligious Deeds," but more often he condemned British "depravity" while emphasizing his responsibility to protect women and children from "invasion by the savage foe!" Occasional references to his fate laying in the hands of "the gods" appear less as appeals to a Supreme Being than euphemisms for the uncertainties of war.[9] His correspondence with Rachel showed that he held on to his traditional beliefs, but faith appeared for him a secondary justification for fighting. If Jackson considered himself a holy warrior, the image supplemented his perception of himself as a loyal patriot fighting the enemies of his nation.

"the remarkable interposition of Heaven" 61

Jackson's chief responsibility as the militia's commander involved protecting white Tennesseans from presumably hostile Natives. Throughout his service, American tensions with European powers appeared to lay behind the threat of an Indian war. Since the early 1790s, Great Britain and France had emerged as the principal foes in a clash over the commercial dominance and the political future of Europe. The United States traded extensively with both nations, but with the onset of war in the early 1790s, the British and French navies began seizing American merchant ships that they suspected of carrying goods that would aid their enemies. Presidents George Washington and John Adams managed to avoid war, mainly through diplomatic concessions, and after Napoleon Bonaparte gained power in France, a treaty signed in 1803 appeared to end the conflict. The peace proved temporary, however, and the resumption of war in 1805 brought renewed assaults on American trade. Though far away from Tennessee, the raids disrupted the sale of the corn, wheat, cotton, and other produce grown in the west and south. Tennesseans remained convinced, too, that officials in Britain's colony in Canada used the conflict to justify encouraging and arming Native attacks on the American frontier.

From the war's earliest days, Jackson saw Great Britain as the nation's greatest threat. Few other Tennesseans joined him in his admiration for Napoleon's "energy,"[10] but almost all sympathized with Jackson's lingering resentment toward the atrocities that redcoats had committed in the South during the American Revolution. Now the British appeared to present the most direct challenge to the nation's interest and honor. France no longer had a presence in North America, while Britain's colony in Canada presented a constant threat to American expansion and independence. Likewise, after British warships destroyed a French fleet at the Battle of Trafalgar in October 1805, the greatly reduced French navy captured only a small fraction of the number of ships taken by the Royal Navy. During their raids, too, British commanders frequently insulted the young nation's honor by boarding the merchant ships and impressing crewmen—including American citizens—into service in the British navy.

The opportunity to fight appeared to come in the summer of 1807, when a British warship attacked the U.S.S. *Chesapeake* and apprehended four of its crewmen in American territorial waters off

62   *Andrew Jackson: Old Hickory in Christian America*

the coast of Norfolk, Virginia. In Richmond, for Aaron Burr's trial, Jackson denounced the assault as a "humiliating blow against our independence & sovereignty," and he quickly returned to Tennessee to prepare for a war he now thought "inevitable."[11] Instead of war, Congress imposed an embargo closing the United States' trade with all foreign nations. Though disappointed in President Thomas Jefferson's reluctance to fight, Jackson expected war to follow the embargo, and despite his low regard for the president, at a meeting of the militia's officers in January 1809 that he co-presided with Thomas Swann— the young lawyer at the center of his battle with Charles Dickinson— he delivered a speech calling for unity and promising "to go any length with the government of our country, in defence and support of our nation's rights and independence."[12]

The embargo's attempt to inflict economic pressure on Britain and France failed to stop the raids on American ships. Congress lifted the embargo three days before Jefferson left office in March 1809, but to Jackson's dismay, Jefferson's successor, James Madison, spent three frustrating years trying to resolve the conflict through diplomacy. Through much of this time, Jackson had to deal with lawsuits from disputes brought on by the embargo's closing of foreign trade. Despite the distractions, Jackson paid close attention to developments that might demand a military response. Most disturbing were the reports that Tecumseh, a warrior from the Shawnee nation north of the Ohio River, had visited the South to try to persuade the Southern nations to join a Native alliance that could drive American settlers out of the lands west of the Appalachians. Jackson never doubted that "British agents and tools" lay behind Tecumseh's scheme. Actually, British officials discouraged Tecumseh, and the Shawnee warrior received a lukewarm reception in the South. Still, a portion of the Creek nation—located in the region of the Mississippi Territory that later became the state of Alabama—responded positively to Tecumseh's appeal. Known as "Red Sticks" for the bright red clubs they carried into battle, a handful of these hostile Creeks attacked a farm about eighty miles from the Hermitage, killing seven settlers and taking a woman hostage. Jackson demanded permission to march a force into the heart of Creek territory. The woman's escape and friendly Creeks' execution of the renegades temporarily diffused tensions, but in the meantime, the long-awaited confrontation with Great Britain finally came.

"the remarkable interposition of Heaven"   63

Madison's negotiations broke down in the spring of 1812, and on June 18, Congress formally declared war.[13]

Jackson welcomed the opportunity to fight. Immediately, he offered President Madison the service of 2,500 volunteers. Madison still had no intention of using the controversial Tennessean, but Governor Willie Blount—John Sevier's successor and the brother of Jackson's political mentor—managed to get him into the war. In October, Secretary of War William Eustis asked Blount to provide 1,500 volunteers for the defense of New Orleans. Because Jackson's nemesis, James Wilkinson, commanded the mission, Eustis likely expected Blount to name another Tennessean as the volunteers' leader. Instead, Blount put Jackson in charge of the expedition. Jackson acknowledged that serving under Wilkinson would be "a bitter pill," but he agreed to "swallow" it "for my countries good." Cold weather delayed the volunteers' departure until January 1813, when Jackson headed to New Orleans with a newly painted miniature portrait of Rachel—and with his dueling pistols packed in case of an encounter with Wilkinson. The army arrived in Natchez in mid-February, and for the next month Jackson awaited further instructions. During the delay, he caught a "violent cold" with "a distressing cough," from which a doctor's "free use of the Lancet" relieved him. In the meantime, his frustration with American losses in the north made him "wish we were ordered to upper Canedy—there we could be of service."[14]

Instead, in mid-March, Jackson received a shocking notice from the new secretary of war, John Armstrong. The reasons for the march to New Orleans had "ceased to exist," Armstrong claimed, so he ordered Jackson to dismiss his army and deliver to Wilkinson "all articles of public property which may have been put into its possession." Jackson fumed at Armstrong's directive. If he disbanded his army immediately and gave Wilkinson's men its supplies, his unarmed volunteers would have to make the 500-mile trek home on their own, without provisions, through potentially hostile Indian lands. He suspected, too, that Wilkinson prompted the order to drive Jackson from command and absorb the volunteers into his own army. Jackson expressed his displeasure in a series of indignant letters to his superiors, and he resolved to keep his army together and lead it himself back to Tennessee, at his own expense, "not leav[ing] one of the sick nor one of the detachment behind." With a bullet still lodged near his heart, the month-long

64 *Andrew Jackson: Old Hickory in Christian America*

march drained much of his physical strength. Nevertheless, he made sure the troops had adequate supplies and ordered his officers to let the wounded ride their horses, giving up his own three mounts as he walked alongside his men. By the time he dismissed his army on April 20 at Columbia, Tennessee, his determination to get them home safely had earned for him his long-lasting nickname: "Old Hickory," his soldiers affectionately called him, for the march proved that he was "as tough as hickory," one of the hardest woods found in the west.[15]

Setbacks in the war throughout the Union convinced Jackson that he would need to call his army back into service soon. But while waiting for new orders, the code of honor brought him into his last violent personal conflict—one that, like the Dickinson duel, scarred him permanently. Thomas Hart Benton, one of his military aides, went to Washington and successfully persuaded Congress to reimburse Jackson's expenses for the Natchez expedition. During his absence, Benton's brother, Jesse, found himself in a dispute with another Jackson aide, William Carroll. Their argument eventually led to a duel, for which Jackson agreed to serve as Carroll's second. This encounter resulted in Jesse Benton suffering an embarrassing wound in his backside, and he accused Jackson of invoking confusing and obscure "French" rules in the duel to give Carroll an unfair advantage. The commander's stand against his brother left Thomas Benton bewildered, and his letter demanding an explanation denounced Jackson for acting "in a savage, unequal, unfair, and base manner." Jackson interpreted the letter as a demand for satisfaction, which the younger man denied. Still, the clash between the Bentons's bitterness and Jackson's resentment eventually led to a brawl between the men and their friends in early September at a Nashville hotel. In the fight, Jesse Benton's shot and seriously wounded Jackson in his left arm.[16]

Jackson rejected several surgeons' advice and refused to let them amputate his arm. The shock of the injury and the loss of blood severely weakened him, but he had no time to recover. Just eleven days after his fight with the Bentons, news came to Nashville that, on August 30, hostile Creek warriors had attacked Fort Mims in the Mississippi Territory. The rift in the Creek nation had broken out into a civil war, and in the raid, Red Sticks killed more than 250 Americans and friendly Creeks who had taken refuge at the Fort. Though nearly 400 miles away, the "Fort Mims Massacre" sparked a panic that similar

"the remarkable interposition of Heaven" 65

assaults would soon terrorize the Tennessee frontier. Jackson's old friend, the Presbyterian minister Thomas Craighead, chaired a public meeting in Nashville calling upon the state to raise an army that could march into Creek territory, "exterminate their Nation and abettors, and save thousands of the unoffending women and children. . . ." In Washington, the Madison administration authorized Tennessee and Georgia to raise at least 1,500 men each to cooperate on an offensive mission with the regular army under General Thomas Pinckney's command. Tennessee's legislature went beyond Madison's call and approved enlisting 3,500 militiamen to join the 1,500 volunteers who had served in the aborted Natchez expedition. Though still suffering from his wound, Jackson roused from his bed to lead Tennessee's Second Division.[17]

Jackson must have appeared a pathetic sight when he arrived on October 7 to take charge of his force at Fayetteville, a village eighty miles south of Nashville. Pale and ashen, with his arm in a sling, his coat had to be draped over his shoulder because he could not put his arm through the sleeve. He needed assistance to mount a horse, while the jostling from riding sent sharp pains through his wound. Still, he mustered his strength and gave his men decisive leadership. Moving out with 2,000 volunteers and a band of friendly Creeks, Jackson in late October entered the portion of the Mississippi Territory that is now Alabama. His force quickly saw action. On November 3, a brigade led by John Coffee destroyed a hostile Creek base at Tallushatchee. While his men constructed a stockade that they named Fort Strother, Jackson's scouts informed him that about 1,000 Red Sticks had besieged a village of friendly Creeks at Talladega, only thirteen miles away. With almost his full force, Jackson led a surprise attack that liberated the village and inflicted more than 300 casualties while losing only fourteen of his own men.[18]

Yet Jackson could not follow up on these early victories. His men needed ammunition, supplies, and especially food, so he had no choice but to return to Fort Strother to wait for provisions. The delay brought Jackson to the lowest point of his military career. A few supplies occasionally trickled in, but hunger and cold weather wrecked his men's morale and drove several to attempt to desert. Jackson met these "mutinies" with threats of force. Twice he ordered companies to stand against other units that tried to leave; once he rode in front of an

66 *Andrew Jackson: Old Hickory in Christian America*

unruly brigade while holding a musket with his good arm and threatening to shoot anyone who crossed him. Still, he could not prevent the army's disintegration. Jackson contended that his militia had agreed to serve for six months, but the men insisted that their service would expire after the traditional three months. Meanwhile, the volunteers for the aborted Natchez expedition assumed that their enlistments would expire in December 1813. Jackson countered that their year of service did not include the time between their dismissal in April and their recall in October, so he expected them to remain through the spring. At one point, he ordered a cannon aimed at a brigade and threatened to fire if the men tried to leave. But despite the general's pleas and threats, Governor Blount concluded that the men's enlistment had legally expired, and Jackson had no choice but to let them go.[19]

Still, Jackson refused to abandon the campaign. When Blount suggested that he withdraw, Jackson responded with a frank letter lecturing him on his responsibility to call out more men, even without federal authorization, and warning him about the embarrassment Tennessee would face if the governor feared "taking a little responsibility on himself." Likewise, he pleaded with Gideon Blackburn, Rachel's minister, to use his "great & well-founded" influence "in summoning Volunteers to the defence of their Country—its liberty & its religion."[20] Militia Generals Isaac Roberts and William Carroll went to Tennessee and rounded up about 900 men. Most agreed to serve only sixty days and had little training or fighting experience, but despite their rawness, the short-term enlistments convinced Jackson to resume the offensive while he could. Moving out in mid-January 1814, his army repelled a Red Stick attack at a Creek village called Emuckfau. An unexpected counterattack and heavy casualties convinced Jackson that driving further would prove futile, and while returning to Fort Strother, he nearly met disaster when a band of Red Sticks attacked his men as they crossed Enitachopko Creek. The soldiers at his army's rear fled in terror, but Jackson regrouped his force, held off the assault, and reached the Fort with his army largely intact. Still, the near-defeat and anticipated departure of his army appeared to give his mission little hope for further success.[21]

Finally, Jackson's fortunes changed. Governor Blount—perhaps shamed by Jackson's letter—called for 4,500 new volunteers to reman the militia. Accounts in Tennessee reported the skirmishes at

"the remarkable interposition of Heaven" 67

Emuckfau and Enitachopko as decisive victories, reviving popular enthusiasm for the war and bringing out volunteers to fill the ranks. The raids likewise impressed Jackson's commanding officer, General Thomas Pinckney, who sent a 600-man regiment of regular soldiers to serve as his army's core. By mid-February, Jackson's force totaled about 4,000 men. Before returning to the field, Jackson arranged for a steady delivery of supplies. At the same time, he demanded that his raw recruits become an effective fighting force. Assisted by Pinckney's soldiers, the volunteers drilled regularly, with harsh discipline imposed to prevent further challenges to his authority. Several junior officers suspected of encouraging insubordination were court martialed, along with General Roberts when Roberts sided with his men in a dispute. After Tennessee's First Division arrived to unite with Jackson's forces, its commander, John Cocke, persistently criticized Jackson's severity and Blount's supposedly illegal call for more troops, so Jackson ordered Cocke's arrest for inciting mutiny. In his most controversial decision, Jackson upheld a military court's death sentence for John Wood, an eighteen-year-old volunteer who, in a misunderstanding, had threatened to attack an officer but handed over his weapon once informed of his transgression.[22]

Wood's execution on March 14 shocked Jackson's volunteers, but his strict regimen had successfully turned them into an army. Immediately after the firing squad completed its assignment, Jackson moved out with 3,000 troops, 500 Cherokees, and a hundred friendly Creeks toward a sharp curve on the Tallapoosa River known as Horseshoe Bend, where the Red Sticks had set up their main camp. After crossing through seventy-five miles of wilderness, the army blocked the Red Sticks's access to retreat, and on March 27, launched a devastating attack. The poorly armed and disorganized Creeks proved no match for Jackson's larger and better-equipped army. The assault killed almost 900 Native warriors, while Jackson's army lost fewer than fifty men. Anticipating a counterattack, Jackson moved his force to the confluence of the Tallapoosa and Coosa Rivers about twenty miles away, where his men rebuilt an abandoned French post that they named Fort Jackson in honor of their commander. There, the Georgia militia and General Pinckney's army converged with Jackson's force and prepared for the next battle. The overwhelming American victory at Horseshoe Bend, though, had broken the Red Sticks's spirit. Several

68   *Andrew Jackson: Old Hickory in Christian America*

warriors headed for Spanish Florida to fight another day, but most hostile Creeks surrendered. By late April, the Creek War was over.[23]

A few weeks later, Jackson arrived home at the Hermitage. Though the war with Britain continued, he probably appreciated the respite. Drainage still seeped from the wound in his arm, and on the campaign, he had experienced the first of the periodic bouts of dysentery that would plague him for the rest of his life. Along with the well-needed rest, he was glad to be back with Rachel. He had obviously missed her and their adopted son. Throughout the campaign, he wrote them whenever he could, assuring her that he was safe and—stretching the truth—that his arm was recovering well. When his men threatened to abandon their duty, he expressed to her his fear that "the boasted patriotism of the State was a mere buble, that expires, on the approach of an enemy"; when they succeeded in battle, he provided her with detailed accounts of the conflict. Rachel, for her part, conveyed to him news from home while trusting that "the same God that Led Moses through the wilderness has been and now is Conducting you giving you his aide [and] his protection." Like most soldiers' wives, she prayed for her husband's protection and safe return.[24]

Jackson's replies reassured Rachel of his prayers, and his letters to her presented most of the few religious thoughts he expressed while at the front. The responsibilities of command left him little time to reflect on spiritual matters. On the Natchez expedition, his volunteers sometimes held impromptu services, which they possibly resumed while in Creek country, but Jackson never referred to them and likely did not attend.[25] With Rachel, though, he shared a recognition that he could die in battle and that his fate lay in God's hands. He expounded his thoughts most extensively after he notified his wife that her nephew, Alexander "Sandy" Donelson, "bravely fought and bravely fell" in the clash at Emuckfau. Rachel deeply grieved Sandy's death; fearing for her husband's protection even more than before, she hinted that he should come home at once. "I Cryed aloud and praised my god For your safety. . . My Darling never make me so unhapy for aney Country. . . . you have now don more than aney other man Ever did before[;] you have served your Country Long Enough."[26] In his poignant reply, Jackson reminded her that "I am in the field, and cannot retire when I please, without disgrace, . . ." but he assured her that

"the remarkable interposition of Heaven" 69

I am protected by that same overruling providence when in the heart of the creek nation, as I am at home[.] his protecting hand can Shield me as well from danger, here as there, and the only difference is that his protecting hand is more conspicuous in the field of Battle than in our own peacefull dwellings when we are surrounded, by our boosom friends.

As for Alexander, "The brave must die, in a state of war the brave must face the enemy, or the rights of our country, could never be maintained." Sandy died "like a hero," and "the pleasing thought that we are to meet on high never to part again where we will enjoy happiness unmingled, by the interruption of human depravity & corruption . . ." meant that "we must resign him." "[S]hould it be the will of divine providence to smile upon my honest exertions, . . ." he promised, "I shall return to your arms of love & affection." Until he could leave "with honor and safety to my country, . . ." he admonished Rachel to "summons [*sic*] up your resolution and bear my absence with fortitude."[27]

Jackson's break from the action proved short. The war with Great Britain had entered a new phase. While Jackson was in the field against the Creeks, a coalition of European nations finally pushed Napoleon's armies back into France, leading to the emperor's surrender in early April 1814. Even though Britain agreed to begin peace talks in August in Ghent, located in what today is Belgium, the United States now faced the full brunt of British power undistracted by a war on the continent and with a lingering desire to humble its former colonies. James Madison still had reservations about Jackson, but he could not ignore a national hero, especially after Thomas Pinckney enthusiastically praised Jackson's leadership in his reports. Thus, in June, Madison appointed Jackson a major general in the U.S. Army, in command of the Seventh District. His responsibilities now went beyond defending Tennessee to include the southern regions west of Georgia through Louisiana, so with his commission in hand, Jackson again gathered his strength, kissed Rachel farewell, and headed back to Fort Jackson.

Jackson's first assignment was to negotiate a formal settlement with the Creek nation, but planning for a possible British offensive preoccupied his mind. Reports from Europe indicated that Britain had organized a large force for an invasion somewhere along the Gulf

70   *Andrew Jackson: Old Hickory in Christian America*

coast, which Jackson expected would be coordinated with an attempted Native uprising. He assumed that Britain would use Pensacola, the capital of Spain's colony in West Florida, as the invasion's main base, so he asked the administration for permission to occupy the port while warning West Florida's governor against assisting American enemies. At Fort Jackson, he imposed a harsh settlement on the Creeks, requiring the nation to cede to the United States more than half its lands—including lands held by friendly Creeks who had recently fought with him. He then moved his army to Mobile, which an American force had occupied in 1813, and which he expected to serve as an invasion's main target. A small unit of his men held off an attack from two British warships at Fort Bowyer, an installation at the mouth of Mobile Bay, but then he learned that British soldiers had indeed occupied Pensacola. Though the latest secretary of war, James Monroe, had not yet authorized a move into West Florida, in early November Jackson resolved to "act without the orders of the government" and led 4,000 men to Pensacola. By the time he arrived, the British had withdrawn, but Jackson's men easily defeated a small Spanish garrison and occupied the town.[28]

Jackson remained in Pensacola for only three days. Before the excursion, Monroe notified him that 25,000 British soldiers were now reportedly headed for New Orleans, the Union's most important western port. Jackson still thought an invasion was more likely to come at Mobile. New Orleans, after all, lay more than 100 miles upriver from the mouth of the Mississippi, and swamps limited overland access to the city from the south and east; in contrast, a successful assault on Mobile would give Britain a base from which to incite Native raids and to begin a march toward New Orleans over solid ground. But while at Pensacola, his own intelligence sources confirmed that New Orleans appeared to be the invasion's target. Returning first to Mobile, he secured town's defenses and on November 22 left for New Orleans with 2,000 men, though he stationed another 2,000 troops at Baton Rouge, from whence John Coffee could lead them to either port once Britain's intentions became clear.[29]

Once Jackson arrived at New Orleans on December 1, he found the city more vulnerable than he had anticipated. The Louisiana legislature had provided no funds for the town's defense, leaving the state's militia ill-equipped and poorly trained. Indifference characterized

"the remarkable interposition of Heaven" 71

most of the population, which consisted mainly of descendants of French or Spanish colonists. Nevertheless, Jackson promised the city's residents that he would "drive their enemies into the sea, or perish in the effort." Despite the lingering pain from the wound in his arm, and still suffering from inflammation in his bowels, he spent the next three weeks overseeing construction of the city's ramparts, exhibiting the same ruthless determination that had carried him through the Creek War. Meanwhile, he summoned Coffee's men from Baton Rouge and waited for the 10,000 additional volunteers that Monroe had promised to send him from Tennessee, Kentucky, and Georgia. Even if all these troops arrived, Jackson knew that his army would be decidedly smaller than the invading force, so he scrounged around for any additional men he could find. Against the resistance of the local white inhabitants, he accepted the service of more than 400 *gens de couleur*— free people of color—and reluctantly agreed to cooperate with Jean Lafitte and his band of pirates and slave smugglers. When the legislature refused his request to suspend the writ of *habeas corpus*, Jackson declared martial law, effectively subjecting every man in the city to military service or else face imprisonment.[30]

By then, the invasion had begun. On December 14, British ships captured an American flotilla of five gunboats on Lake Borgne, about twenty miles from New Orleans. Nine days later, Jackson learned that an advanced British guard had crossed the swamps from the lake and was setting up camp on a plantation eight miles southeast of the city. Jackson's force now included more than 4,000 men, but they were mostly untrained volunteers without adequate arms or supplies. Monroe's reports had exaggerated the size of the British army, but its soldiers still outnumbered Jackson's troops, and most were hardened veterans of the Napoleonic Wars. Nevertheless, on the night of December 23, Jackson ordered an attack on the British camp before setting up his main defense line along an abandoned canal that crossed a two-mile plain between the Mississippi River and an impassable marsh. For the next two weeks, Jackson slept and ate little as he oversaw the construction of an embankment behind the canal. When a delegation from the Louisiana legislature encouraged him to consider a surrender, he denounced the representatives and hinted that he would burn the city and fight from its ashes. On December 28, his men drove back an assault on his lines, and on New Year's Day they repelled

72 *Andrew Jackson: Old Hickory in Christian America*

an artillery barrage that destroyed the house that served as his headquarters. As the British awaited reinforcements, the two sides lobbed cannon shells at each other while awaiting what they expected to be a decisive battle.[31]

The final confrontation came on the morning of January 8, 1815. Reinforcements brought Jackson's force up to about 5,000 men, but the British had more than 10,000 and were commanded by General Edward Pakenham, who had won acclaim for his service against Napoleon's armies in Spain. Pakenham had devised a sound plan. The night before the main offensive, Colonel William Thornton's battalion of 1,200 men would cross the Mississippi River, seize a poorly defended battery of American cannons on the west bank, then turn the guns against the right side of Jackson's main line. As they fired, Pakenham would lead 5,000 men in a frontal assault to overtake Jackson's embankment, leaving the British with a clear path to New Orleans. But poor execution and bad fortune turned the battle into a British disaster. Underestimating the strength of the Mississippi's current, Thornton's battalion landed a mile and a half downstream from its target, delaying its attack for eight hours. Despite the lack of cover, Pakenham proceeded with his charge, expecting an early-morning fog to hide his army until it reached the American defenses. Just as his men came within range of the American guns, the fog lifted. Jackson's cannons and riflemen opened fire, killing and wounding scores of British soldiers in a mere twenty-five minutes. By the time Colonel Thornton's men overtook the west bank's battery, Pakenham lay dead, his second and third in command had suffered serious wounds, and General John Lambert, the next highest-ranking British officer, had called off the slaughter.[32]

As his men celebrated, Jackson resisted the temptation to launch a counterattack against the still-larger and better-trained British force. He realized, too, that the loss of the guns across the river left his army vulnerable, so he immediately prepared to defend against another assault. As he barked out orders, he witnessed an eerie scene:

> "I never had," Jackson would say, "so grand and awful idea of the resurrection as on that day. After the smoke of the battle had cleared off somewhat, I saw in the distance more than five hundred Britons emerging from the heaps of their dead comrades, all over the plain, rising up, and

"the remarkable interposition of Heaven" 73

still more distinctly visible as the field became clearer, coming forward and surrendering as prisoners of war to our soldiers. They had fallen at our first fire upon them, without having received so much as a scratch, and lay prostrate, as if dead, until the close of the action."[33]

The expected second attack never came. Instead, Lambert asked Jackson for a ceasefire to bury the British dead and recover their wounded. Within a week, the invading army had begun to withdraw. By the time Jackson visited the enemy's abandoned camp on January 19, all knew that he had won a stunning victory. Lambert counted more than 2,000 British casualties at the Battle of New Orleans, with nearly 300 soldiers killed. Jackson reported losing only seven men killed on January 8, with another six wounded.[34]

New Orleans vaulted Jackson to a prominence few ever attain. The Creek War had made him a national hero; after New Orleans, his countrymen regarded him as the greatest American military commander since George Washington. News of the battle spread across the Union just as word filtered in from Europe that American and British representatives at Ghent had signed a peace treaty on December 24— two weeks before the fight at New Orleans. Despite the timing and the numerous setbacks during the war, Jackson's triumph convinced most Americans that they had won a decisive victory. Quickly, the legend emerged that Jackson had secured the nation's independence when his ragtag army of backwoodsmen humiliated the crack professionals who had conquered Napoleon.

Many concluded that New Orleans signaled God's blessing on the young republic. At the service held soon after the British withdrew, the city's leading Catholic priest, Abbé Guillaume Dubourg, described Jackson as "the worthy instrument of Heaven's merciful designs." Soon afterward, Jesse Denson, a Methodist minister on Jackson's staff, commemorated the general with an account of his triumphs over the "Philistine" Creeks and the "British barbarians" written in the style of the Old Testament Chronicles, praising "Andrew, whose sirname is Jackson" as "a mighty man of war and valiant in fight"—though he acknowledged that the general "blusheth not to take the name of the Lord his God in vain." Even secular celebrants admitted that a divine presence may have aided the general. In Washington, *Niles' Weekly Register*, one of the nation's leading political newspapers, proclaimed

74   *Andrew Jackson: Old Hickory in Christian America*

"Glory be to God that the barbarians have been defeated," while a correspondent to the *Richmond Enquirer* observed that "the finger of heaven was in this thing."[35]

Jackson himself agreed. "If ever there was an occasion on which providence interfered, immediate, in the affairs of men it seems to have been on this," he wrote ten days after the battle. "What but such an interposition could have saved this Country?" He knew he had been fortunate, or perhaps blessed. Outnumbered against a better-trained enemy, his delay in coming to New Orleans and his failure adequately to reinforce the battery on the west bank would have cost him against an efficient and well-executed British offensive. Jackson never acknowledged these missteps, but the confluence of British overconfidence and uncharacteristic ineptitude with the early clearing of the morning fog suggested to him that more than his men's bravery, or his leadership, had determined the outcome. Though he sometimes bragged that he had "defeated the Boasted army of Lord Wellington," more often he credited his victory to, as he told James Wilkinson, "the remarkable interposition of Heaven."[36]

Jackson long referred to a divine contribution to his greatest victory. According to James Parton, years later, the general's conversations with friends and family at the Hermitage "related chiefly to the warlike exploits of himself and his companions. Revolutionary anecdotes . . . were particularly pleasing to him, and he was fond of telling over the story of his own boyish adventures during that conflict." When it came to the Battle of New Orleans, "he usually attributed his success to the direct intervention of Providence in support of the weak against the strong."[37]

Notes

1. "Court Minutes in *State v. Andrew Jackson*, November [9], 1807," *PAJ*, 2:172–74.
2. Rachel Meredith, "'There Was Somebody Always Dying and Leaving Jackson as Guardian': The Wards of Andrew Jackson" (MA Thesis, Middle Tennessee State University, 2013), 32–42, 49–55; Mark R. Cheathem, *Old Hickory's Nephew: The Political and Private Struggles of Andrew Jackson Donelson* (Baton Rouge: Louisiana State University Press, 2007); Andrew Jackson to Rachel Jackson, September 22, 1814, *PAJ*, 3:145.

"the remarkable interposition of Heaven" 75

3. Remini, *Course of American Empire*, 17, 40, 45–47; Booraem, *Young Hickory*, 58; John Buchanan, *Jackson's Way: Andrew Jackson and the People of the Western Waters* (New York: John Wiley & Sons, 2001), 40, 49–50, 227–30; Donald R. Hickey, *Glorious Victory: Andrew Jackson and the Battle of New Orleans* (Baltimore: Johns Hopkins University Press, 2015), 121–24.

4. Parton, *Life of Andrew Jackson*, 2:654.

5. Andrew Jackson to Andrew J. Donelson, March 21, 1822, *PAJ*, 5:163; Meacham, *American Lion*, 19.

6. Benton, *Thirty Years View*, 1:736.

7. Andrew Jackson to Felix Grundy, March 15, 1813, *PAJ*, 2:386; "To the 2nd Division," March 7, 1812, *PAJ*, 2:291.

8. Haselby, *Origins of American Religious Nationalism*, 307; Opal, *Avenging the People*, 151–53; Tom Kanon, *Tennesseans at War, 1812–1815: Andrew Jackson, The Creek War, and the Battle of New Orleans* (Tuscaloosa: University of Alabama Press, 2014), 18–20; Gismondi, "Rachel Jackson and the Search for Zion," 112–20.

9. "To the Tennessee Volunteers," September 24, 1813, *PAJ*, 2:428; Andrew Jackson to Rachel Jackson, January 8, 1813, *PAJ*, 2:354; Jackson to John Coffee, September 23, 1813, *PAJ*, 2:432; Jackson to Thomas Pinckney, March 2, 1814, *PAJ*, 3:36.

10. Andrew Jackson to [William Preston Anderson], January 3, 1807, *PAJ*, 2:135.

11. Andrew Jackson to Thomas Monteagle Bayly, June 27, 1807, *PAJ*, 2:170.

12. "Address to Citizens of Nashville," January 16, 1809, *PAJ*, 2:210–11.

13. Andrew Jackson to Willie Blount, June 4, 1812, *PAJ*, 2:300; Kanon, *Tennesseans at War*, 56–59; Donald R. Hickey, *The War of 1812: A Forgotten Conflict* (Urbana: University of Illinois Press, 2012), 5–48.

14. William Eustis to Willie Blount, October 21, 1812, *Correspondence*, 1:240; Andrew Jackson to George Washington Campbell, November 29, 1812, *PAJ*, 2:344; Jackson to William B. Lewis, March 4, 1813, *PAJ*, 2:378; Jackson to Rachel Jackson, March 7, 1813, *PAJ*, 2:379; Kanon, *Tennesseans at War*, 41–46.

15. John Armstrong to Andrew Jackson, February 6, 1813, *PAJ*, 2:361; Jackson to Armstrong, March 15, 1813, *PAJ*, 2:383–85; "To The Tennessee Volunteers," March 16, 1813, *PAJ*, 2:92; Remini, *Course of American Empire*, 175–80; Kanon, *Tennesseans at War*, 46–47.

16. Remini, *Course of American Empire*, 180–86; Thomas Hart Benton to Andrew Jackson, July 25, 1813, *PAJ*, 2:413–15; Jackson to [Benton], August 4, 1813, *PAJ*, 2:418–22.

17. Kanon, *Tennesseans at War*, 65–70.

18. Kanon, *Tennesseans at War*, 73–79.

19. Willie Blount to Andrew Jackson, November 24, 1813, *PAJ*, 2:460–61; Kanon, *Tennesseans at War*, 73–80.

20. Willie Blount to Andrew Jackson, December 22, 1813, *PAJ*, 2:498–99; Jackson to Blount, December 26, 1813, *PAJ*, 2:505; Jackson to Gideon Blackburn, December 3, 1813, *PAJ*, 2:464.

21. Kanon, *Tennesseans at War*, 83–95.

22. Kanon, *Tennesseans at War*, 95–97.

23. *Tennesseans at War*, 99–107.

76 *Andrew Jackson: Old Hickory in Christian America*

24. Andrew Jackson to Rachel Jackson, December 14, 1813, *PAJ*, 2:487; Rachel Jackson to Andrew Jackson, April 7, 1814, *PAJ*, 3:59.

25. Kanon, *Tennesseans at War*, 42–44.

26. Andrew Jackson to Rachel Jackson, January 28, 1814, *PAJ*, 3:19; Rachel Jackson to Andrew Jackson, February 10, 1814, *PAJ*, 3:28–29.

27. Andrew Jackson to Rachel Jackson, February 21, 1814, *PAJ*, 3:34–35.

28. Kanon, *Tennesseans at War*, 108–10, 124–33; Andrew Jackson to James Monroe, October 26, 1814, *PAJ*, 3:173.

29. Frank L. Owsley, Jr., *Struggle for the Gulf Borderlands: The Creek War and the Battle of New Orleans, 1812–1815* (Tuscaloosa: University of Alabama Press, 2000), 120–26.

30. Robert V. Remini, *The Battle of New Orleans: Andrew Jackson and America's First Military Victory* (New York: Penguin Books, 1999), 22–24, 43; Owsley, *Struggle for the Gulf Borderlands*, 120–32.

31. Remini, *Battle of New Orleans*, 54–127; Hickey, *Glorious Victory*, 89–105.

32. Remini, *Battle of New Orleans*, 127–53; Hickey, *Glorious Victory*, 105–11.

33. Parton, *Life of Andrew Jackson*, 2:208–209.

34. Remini, *Battle of New Orleans*, 169–83; Hickey, *Glorious Victory*, 112–13.

35. Remini, *Course of American Empire*, 246–54; 292–93; John William Ward, *Andrew Jackson: Symbol for an Age* (London: Oxford University Press, 1953), 101–109; Jesse Denson, *The Chronicles of Andrew; Containing an Accurate and Brief Account of General Jackson's Victories in the South, over the Creeks, Also His Victories over the British at Orleans, with a Biographical Sketch of His Life* (Lexington, KY: Printed for the author, 1815).

36. Andrew Jackson to David Holmes, January 18, 1815, *PAJ*, 3:249–50; Jackson to James Winchester, January 19, 1815, *PAJ*, 3:252; Andrew Jackson to James Wilkinson, January 31, 1815, *PAJ*, 3:262.

37. Parton, *Life of Andrew Jackson*, 2:654–55.

6

"God alone is the searcher & judge of hearts"

Andrew Jackson may have credited Providence, but the victory at New Orleans emboldened rather than humbled him. Still a general in the army, he became more convinced than ever that his decisions were not just correct but necessary for the nation's survival. Over the next few years, he would play a decisive role in establishing American control over the South, but his actions provoked divided opinions about him. To most, he remained the nation's savior. To some, he appeared unpredictable at best, a potential despot at worst. The battles with his critics and continuing troubles with his health sparked his desire to retire. Yet he would not leave public life as long as he thought he could serve his country—and as long as he faced any challenges to his character and reputation.

Controversy surrounded Jackson even before he left New Orleans. Within a few weeks after the battle, he started a public argument that lasted for years with the commander of a Kentucky regiment that he blamed for losing the battery on the west bank of the Mississippi. Likewise, his criticism of Louisiana volunteers' "neglect and dereliction from duty" put him at odds with Governor William C. C. Claiborne. His most visible clash challenged the authority of a federal judge. Most Americans thought the battle on January 8 ended the war, but Jackson had to maintain New Orleans' defenses in case the British attempted another onslaught. Rumors about a peace treaty began to filter into the city in early February, but without official notice of peace, Jackson kept New Orleans under martial law. When a French diplomat attempted to help some residents evade compulsory military service, Jackson expelled all Frenchmen from the city and ordered the arrest

Andrew Jackson. Jonathan M. Atkins, Oxford University Press. © Jonathan M. Atkins 2025.
DOI: 10.1093/9780191886812.003.0006

78 *Andrew Jackson: Old Hickory in Christian America*

of Louis Louailler, a representative in Louisiana's legislature who had written a scathing newspaper article urging resistance to Jackson's decree. Judge Dominick A. Hall ordered Louailler's release, but the general then arrested Hall, who spent nearly a week in jail before being exiled to the outskirts of the city.[1]

Official notice of the Treaty of Ghent came to New Orleans two days after Hall's expulsion. Jackson immediately rescinded martial law, and most in New Orleans seemed ready to forget their quarrel with the general. Judge Hall, though, insisted on holding Jackson accountable. Once back in his court, Hall summoned Jackson to appear before him to explain why the general should not be held in contempt. Jackson arrived dressed in civilian clothes, rather than his uniform, but when Hall refused to let him read a prepared statement, he offered no further defense and demanded the judge issue his sentence. Hall then ruled Jackson in contempt and fined him $1,000. Friends and fellow officers collected a fund to reimburse him, but the general insisted the money be given to the families of soldiers who had died defending the city. Meanwhile, he blamed the affair on the "wicked labours of the little malicious *knot*" surrounding Governor Claiborne, and before leaving a week later, he attended two public dinners given in his honor. President Madison expressed his "surprise and solicitude" over the incident and asked Jackson to submit "a full report of the transactions" with Hall, but with the general's popularity still soaring, the administration issued only a mild reprimand.[2]

Jackson's return to Tennessee became a victory tour. Accompanied by Rachel and Andrew Jr., who had joined him in New Orleans in February, the family enjoyed several public celebrations along the way, culminating in a grand banquet in Nashville hosted by Governor Blount. When he finally reached the Hermitage in late May, he was glad to be home. Other than the three-week stay following the Creek War, he had been away for almost two years. Military responsibilities still kept him busy, but he could finally get some rest after the grueling campaign. Now forty-eight, he also enjoyed a financial security that had long eluded him; his salary as a major general provided a steady income, while the postwar boom in American trade with Europe brought good prices for his plantation's crops. These funds allowed him to expand his holdings at the Hermitage to more than one thousand acres and to invest in a second plantation in northern Alabama.

"God alone is the searcher & judge of hearts"   79

Eventually, he felt secure enough to begin construction on a two-story mansion on the Hermitage's grounds. Work on the house started just as a national financial panic in early 1819 again strained his finances, and his persistent health issues convinced him that he would die before he could ever live there. Nevertheless, though still unfinished, in late 1821, the family occupied the mansion that would become Jackson's home for the rest of his life.

Whether in the mansion or in the Hermitage's log cabins, the Jacksons were rarely alone. Friends, relatives, and other guests visited frequently, with several staying for extended periods. Many of the residents were among the general's growing number of wards. In addition to his adopted son and the Donelson nephews, Jackson over his lifetime became either the legal guardian or unofficial caretaker for more than thirty children. At least fifteen of his wards lived for a time at the Hermitage, but regardless of their residence, Jackson took his responsibility for their care very seriously. He displayed a genuine affection for them and tried to manage their estates in their best interests. Like with his troops, he expected obedience from his underlings, but while a soldier's insubordination met stern punishment, a child's or young adult's misbehavior disappointed more than angered him. Usually, the offender received a mild rebuke but then had to listen to Jackson's expressions of sorrow and admonitions for better behavior.[3] Undoubtedly, too, Jackson counseled his dependents on the importance of a good marriage. The Hero of New Orleans had a penchant for matchmaking, but he never attempted to force a partner on his son or a ward. For his dependents, marriage should be, as in his own case, an affair of the heart.

Besides his extended family, friends and members of Jackson's military staff often stayed at the Hermitage. President Madison allowed him to set up his headquarters at his plantation, and he surrounded himself with men he could trust, including younger officers whose career he could promote, just as William Blount had once sponsored him. Other guests included noted travelers passing through Nashville or visitors making a special pilgrimage to meet the Hero of New Orleans. "His house," Thomas H. Benton recalled, "was the seat of hospitality, the resort of friends and acquaintances, and of all strangers visiting the state."[4] Jackson welcomed one guest, Henry Lee of the noted Lee family of Virginia, despite reports of Lee's scandalous affair with his

80 *Andrew Jackson: Old Hickory in Christian America*

sister-in-law. Another, Ralph E. W. Earl, became a permanent resident. A painter by trade, Earl came to the Hermitage from New England to paint Jackson's portrait. Earl particularly amused Rachel, and in 1818, he married Rachel's niece, Jane Caffrey. After Jane died in childbirth less than a year into their marriage, Rachel invited Earl to stay on, and he spent years painting portraits of Jackson and Donelson family members while often accompanying Jackson on his travels. Later, Jackson, while president, provided Earl with a room in the executive mansion to use as a studio, and when Jackson was away the painter would sit in the president's chair "opening your letters and sending them to the Departments, . . ." one associate recalled, "thus playing the part of Sancho panza." Jackson clearly enjoyed Earl's company as a close friend, though most likely he also saw in one of Rachel's favorites a reminder of his departed spouse.[5]

Ministers from various denominations also frequently came to the Hermitage. Though still less devout than his wife, after New Orleans, Jackson seems to have taken his religion somewhat more seriously. To be sure, he never wrote a letter like Rachel's missive to their nephew Andrew Donelson, encouraging him to "fly to his expanded arms, imbibe His spirit, emulate His example, and obey his commands." Jackson did, though, warn Donelson to avoid those "deriding morality & religion as empty hypocritical shows, endeavoring to draw you into little vices & dissapation." References to spiritual matters, while still infrequent, more often appeared in his correspondence. Frustration probably produced his admonition to Governor Claiborne that "God alone is the searcher & judge of hearts," but five years after New Orleans, on his fifty-third birthday, he confessed that he had "some doubts whether I ought or ought not to rejoice, that I was born—or at least whether it would not have been better for me to have not lived to see the 15th of March 1820—but I co[n]clude that it is best, as it is the lords will that I am here." When adhering to the custom of signing a lady's autograph book, he usually wrote "When I can read my title clear," the name of an Isaac Watts hymn that he possibly intended as a tribute to his mother. At least once at the Hermitage, Rachel interrupted her husband's story from his military experiences to ask him to bless the family's dinner; Jackson complied and, after saying grace, returned to finish his profanity-laden tale.[6]

"God alone is the searcher & judge of hearts" 81

Jackson in these years also appeared to reveal a deeper trust in providence. Like most Americans, he had long stated his belief that God controlled all human events, but after the battle—and after surviving his duel with Charles Dickinson and his brawl with the Bentons—he more often expressed a conviction that a divine will directed his personal affairs and worked them together for good. Following the passing of a friend or family member, he usually appealed to providence as a source of comfort. In an era with a much higher infant mortality rate than today, he wrote several touching letters to console young couples coping with the loss of a child. "We ought to rejoice at their change from this world of evil and wo, to those heavenly climes where happiness forever reigns," he reminded Richard K. Call after the death of his former military aide's infant twin daughters; "let us remember '*that god doeth all things well*,' and at the events of providence we ought to be at all times ready to exclaim, 'the Lords will be done.'" At the same time, Jackson more often revealed his belief that God have given the American Union a mission to provide the world with an example of a free, self-governing people. Immediately following the war, he seldom mentioned God's intervention beyond noting the "remarkable interposition" in his greatest military victory, but by the time he became president, he would refer more frequently to the nation's divinely appointed responsibility and his confidence in the Almighty's guidance.[7]

Greater respect for providence and interaction with numerous ministers failed to compel Jackson formally to join a church, but after New Orleans, Christianity clearly had become a more open and important part of his identity. Peter Cartwright, a prominent Methodist itinerant minister, provided some insight into Jackson's Christianity in the years after New Orleans. In his autobiography, Cartwright recalled preaching in Nashville's Methodist meeting house when Jackson entered the building. The general "came to the middle post, and very gracefully leaned against it, and stood, as there were no vacant seats." A fellow preacher whispered "a little loud" to inform Cartwright of Jackson's presence, but the minister "felt a flush of indignation run all over me like an electric shock . . ." and proclaimed, "Who is General Jackson? If he don't get his soul converted, God will damn him as quick as he would a Guinea negro!" Jackson and the congregation "smiled, or laughed right out." Cartwright prepared to face the general's wrath, but when the two met the next day on a Nashville street, Jackson

82 *Andrew Jackson: Old Hickory in Christian America*

warmly greeted the minister and called him "a man after my own heart. . . . I highly approve of your independence; that a minister of Jesus Christ ought to love everybody and fear no mortal man."[8]

On another occasion, after Cartwright "preached on one Sabbath near the Hermitage," Jackson invited the minister to dine at his home "in company with several gentlemen and ladies." One visitor, "a young sprig of a lawyer from Nashville," pestered Cartwright with challenges to orthodox Christian doctrine. As a guest at a social occasion, Cartwright tried to avoid an argument, but the lawyer persisted and challenged him more aggressively. "I saw General Jackson's eye strike fire, as he sat by and heard the thrusts he made at the Christian religion," the minister recalled. "At length the young lawyer asked me this question":

'Mr. Cartwright, do you really believe there is any such place as hell, as a place of torment?'

I answered promptly, 'Yes, I do.'

To which he responded, 'Well, I thank God I have too much good sense to believe any such thing!'

I was pondering in my own mind whether I would answer him or not, when General Jackson, for the first time, broke into the conversation, and directing his words to the young man, said with great earnestness:

'Well sir, I thank God that there is such a place of torment as hell!'

This sudden answer, made with great earnestness, seemed to astonish the youngster, and he exclaimed:

'Why, General Jackson, what do you want with such a place of torment as hell?'

To which the General replied, as quick as lightening,

'To put such d___d rascals as you are in, that oppose and vilify the Christian religion.'[9]

Cartwright acknowledged that Jackson was "no doubt, in his prime of life a very wicked man," and the general's irritation may have stemmed more from his guest's rudeness than from conviction. Still, Cartwright affirmed that the general "always showed a great respect for the Christian religion, and the feelings of religious people, especially

"God alone is the searcher & judge of hearts" 83

ministers of the gospel."[10] Along with the religious references in his correspondence, the minister's observations suggest that Jackson held on to the general doctrines his mother had taught him and that he had at least some degree of Rachel's faith. At the same time, his comments indicate that Jackson never did "get his soul converted"; he neither worried about his salvation nor experienced the type of conversion that Methodists and other revivalists expected of believers.

Though he preferred to stay home, military duties often took Jackson away from the Hermitage. Four months after returning from New Orleans, he traveled to Washington to discuss the army's peacetime reorganization and to defend himself for his conduct with Judge Hall. The trip became another tour celebrating his victories. Numerous communities again honored him with public festivities, with seventy-two-year-old Thomas Jefferson toasting Jackson's service at a banquet in Lynchburg, Virginia. Washington society likewise regaled him. President Madison hosted a reception in his honor. The city sponsored yet another grand public dinner, and leading citizens flooded him with invitations to their homes. The strain of the constant activities took its toll on his health. The wound in his arm still inflicted constant pain, and he caught a bad cold, often coughing up blood. Concern for his survival perhaps stoked his obsession to defend his public image. One of his military aides, Major John Reid, had already begun writing a history of the Creek War and the defense of New Orleans, using documents that the general provided for him. Reid unexpectedly died in early 1816, and Jackson quickly arranged for John H. Eaton, a young Nashville lawyer and another former military aide, to complete the work. When published in 1817, *The Life of General Jackson* served mainly as an account of the military campaigns that Jackson expected would answer his critics. Later editions embellished his personal traits and accomplishments so that it could serve as one of the first presidential campaign biographies.[11]

As commander of the army's Seventh district, Jackson remained preoccupied with defending the southwestern frontier. Though the war had ended, he recognized that future hostilities with Great Britain, or with a different European power, could bring another assault on the Gulf Coast. Even in peacetime, Jackson assumed that British or Spanish agents were inciting Native harassment of American settlers in order to limit the Union's expansion. The key to securing the region,

84 *Andrew Jackson: Old Hickory in Christian America*

he believed, required rapid American settlement to displace the Native population. "This country once settled, . . ." he wrote, "all [E]urope will cease to look at it with an eye to conquest." To his dismay, the Madison administration pursued a more cautious approach. Madison's last secretary of war, William H. Crawford—a Georgian who was not related to Jackson's South Carolina kinsmen—reminded Jackson of his responsibility to clear white settlers from Native lands. Crawford likewise halted the surveys needed to sell the lands that Jackson had acquired for the nation in the Treaty of Fort Jackson, and he dismissed Jackson's proposal to construct a road connecting Nashville to New Orleans. The secretary of war especially infuriated Jackson in March 1816 when he completed a new treaty returning four million acres of Creek lands to the Cherokees and granting to the Cherokees $25,500 for their losses in the war.[12]

Jackson vehemently condemned Crawford's concessions. The general interpreted the partial invalidation of the Fort Jackson treaty both as an insult to the west and as a personal affront. Perhaps as a concession, Crawford placed Jackson on a three-member commission to negotiate new treaties with the major southwestern nations. The war had weakened these nations, and the negotiations took place just as Native leaders were realizing that, with the British seeking better relations with the United States, they could no longer count on European assistance. Jackson dominated the commission, and through intimidation and, he regretted, bribery of native chieftains, over the next two years he concluded agreements that ceded to the United States hundreds of thousands of acres of Cherokee, Choctaw, and Chickasaw land in western Kentucky, Tennessee, and the Mississippi Territory. Still, Crawford's obstructions and delays in approving surveys convinced Jackson that Crawford coveted the general's popularity and wanted to humiliate him. When Crawford opposed the lands' rapid sale because "it would glutt the markett, & the u states would loose by it," Jackson privately noted to John Coffee that the treasury secretary had "better reason[s]": "he does not like us, wishes at the hazard of the safety of the union to cramp our growing greatness . . . and he oposes it because I have recommended it."[13]

Jackson suspected that Crawford lay behind his other disputes. No doubt he knew that Andrew Erwin, who engaged Jackson in a long, bitter lawsuit and was emerging as his most vocal critic in Tennessee,

"God alone is the searcher & judge of hearts" 85

had been Crawford's political ally while the two lived in Georgia. In late 1816, after Crawford had moved from the War to the Treasury Department, George Graham, the acting secretary of war, transferred one of Jackson's officers to another army without first notifying him. The general angrily protested that disregarding the chain of command was "inconsistent with all military rule," and when the administration ignored his objection, he issued his own decree forbidding his soldiers from obeying a directive from the War Department unless it came through him. Several newspapers criticized Jackson's order as insubordinate. The new president, James Monroe, instructed Jackson to revoke the edict but offered to have his new secretary of war, John C. Calhoun, lay down "a few rules" to guide administrative orders in the future. Calhoun promised to notify Jackson before any future transfers, bringing the controversy to an end, but not before Jackson received an unsigned letter accusing another general, Winfield Scott, with authoring an anonymous article condemning Jackson's order. Scott denied writing the article but confirmed that he considered the directive "mutinous," prompting Jackson to propose a duel. Scott declined due to "a sense of religion" and "patriotic scruples," and Jackson dismissed his rival as one of "the intermeddling Pimps & Spies" of Crawford's War Department.[14]

Through these conflicts, Jackson saw an ally in James Monroe. The two likely first met during Jackson's stint in Congress in the 1790s, and Jackson had openly supported Monroe for the presidency over Madison in 1808. Monroe's decision to retain Crawford as his treasury secretary disappointed him, but Jackson heartily approved of his choice of John Quincy Adams for secretary of state. He politely dismissed the new president's suggestion that Jackson himself serve as secretary of war, encouraging instead the appointment of South Carolina's William Drayton, even though he did not know Drayton personally, and despite the fact that Drayton belonged to the rival Federalist Party. Most Federalists "are really monarchists, & traitors to the constituted government," he conceded, but alluding to Jesus's teaching in Matthew 7:16–20, he concluded that "the tree is best known by its fruits." In Drayton's case, "the moment his country was threatened," he "abandoned private ease and a lucrative practice for the tented field. Such acts as these speak louder than words." Monroe rejected the idea, noting that Federalists might interpret the appointment "as an offer of

86   *Andrew Jackson: Old Hickory in Christian America*

compromise" that might "revive that party on its former principles," but the new president expressed his appreciation for Jackson's counsel, urged him to continue writing, and began his administration with the general's loyal support.[15]

Jackson's trust in Monroe likely contributed to the most controversial incident of his military career. The storm arose from the instability along the southern border. After the war, Americans poured into southern Georgia, with many of them squatting on Native lands. The incursion provoked a wave of attacks and counterattacks with the Seminole Nation. The Seminoles also provided a refuge for American and Spanish runaway slaves, as did an abandoned British fort, occupied by fugitives and free African Americans, on the Apalachicola River in Spain's colony of West Florida. Jackson blamed the violence on European powers' inciting Native attacks, and though the Spanish government had agreed in a 1795 treaty to restrain Natives in their colonies, Jackson presumed that officials in East and West Florida instead supplied and sheltered the Seminole raids. The Floridas' governor general denied provoking the attacks but admitted that he lacked enough troops to control the wilderness, so Jackson authorized General Edmund P. Gaines to take an army into Florida in the summer of 1816 to destroy the "Negro Fort." A year later, after Gaines drove Seminoles out of a base that they had set up in Georgia, Natives retaliated with an assault on an American boat carrying forty soldiers and their families, killing all but one woman and four men. In response, Secretary of War Calhoun directed Jackson to take personal command of the army on the frontier and "adopt the necessary measures" to "terminate" the conflict.[16]

Secretary of State Adams and Don Luis de Onís, the Spanish minister to the United States, had already begun negotiations for the American acquisition of East Florida and West Florida. To Jackson, Spain's failure to control the Seminoles justified simply taking the colonies, and he suspected that Monroe would accept gaining them through conquest. He recognized, though, that seizing them might prove controversial and that Monroe might hesitate to issue him a direct order. Instead, before leaving for the front, Jackson wrote a confidential letter to Monroe proposing to occupy the Floridas "in sixty days" and suggesting that the president privately express his approval "through any channel," naming Tennessee Congressman John Rhea

"God alone is the searcher & judge of hearts"   87

as a possible intermediary.[17] Monroe never replied to Jackson's request. Years later, he claimed that he was ill when he received Jackson's letter, so he put it aside and forgot about it for nearly a year. William Crawford later stated that the president discussed Jackson's letter with his Cabinet, suggesting that he did in fact read it soon after its arrival. More than a decade later, when the Florida invasion became a political controversy during Jackson's first term as president, Jackson claimed that Rhea had indeed sent a letter expressing Monroe's approval, but he had destroyed the letter at Rhea's request. Neither Jackson nor Rhea mentioned a letter during the uproar immediately after the invasion, and when Jackson later claimed that it had existed, Rhea—at age seventy and suffering from senility—could not recollect sending anything to Jackson with Monroe's instructions.[18]

Historians have long argued about the existence of a "Rhea Letter," and whether Monroe approved Jackson's conquest of the Floridas. Interpretations range from charges that the general blatantly lied about receiving a message through Rhea to claims that he either intentionally or unintentionally misremembered receiving a letter or that he confused an earlier letter from Rhea as permission to take the colonies.[19] Most likely, Jackson never received direct approval from Monroe through Rhea. He knew that earlier orders from Secretary of War Calhoun allowed General Gaines to pursue the Seminoles into Florida but forbade Gaines from attacking a Spanish fort. Calhoun assumed, he later claimed, that Jackson knew the restriction also applied to him, but the secretary's orders for Jackson to take command of the mission never directly referred to his directive to Gaines.[20] No doubt, too, the general recalled Monroe's tacit approval of his occupation of Pensacola only three years earlier. Given these circumstances, if he did not receive a message he could construe as permission, he could interpret the president's silence as authorization. As he prepared to lead an army into the Floridas, he appeared fully convinced that he had his government's consent.

Jackson entered the Floridas in mid-March 1818, leading about 3,000 soldiers supplemented by an additional 2,000 friendly Creek warriors. Spain had fewer than 500 men stationed in the colonies. Within the promised sixty days, the American army easily occupied St. Marks, a Spanish fort in West Florida, and conducted what historian Robert Remini called "a thoroughgoing campaign of terror"

88   *Andrew Jackson: Old Hickory in Christian America*

on Seminole villages before taking the colonies' capital at Pensacola. Boasting to Rachel that he had "destroyed the babylon of the South," he permitted the Spanish forces to evacuate to Cuba, named one of his colonels the Floridas' provisional governor, and headed home, convinced that he had secured the nation's southern border. But Jackson soon found himself under fire. Aside from seizing the territory of a sovereign nation with which the United States was at peace, during the expedition his men had apprehended two British subjects: Alexander Arbuthnot, a seventy-year-old Scottish merchant, and Robert Ambrister, a former British Marine. Both were court martialed for agitating the Seminole raids against the United States. After Jackson rejected appeals for clemency, Arbuthnot was hanged on the deck of his own ship on April 28, a few minutes before a firing squad disposed of Ambrister.[21]

Even if Monroe had secretly approved the Florida invasion, Jackson had gone farther than anyone could have anticipated. Onís immediately halted his negotiations with Adams. The Spanish government demanded both Jackson's punishment and the American army's withdrawal from the Floridas, while a furious British public demanded retaliation for the executions of Arbuthnot and Ambrister. Meanwhile, despite the diplomatic nightmare, the American public widely celebrated Jackson for occupying the Floridas and suppressing the Seminole raids. In Monroe's cabinet, Secretaries Calhoun and Crawford demanded the administration repudiate the invasion and publicly censure Jackson for waging an unauthorized and unconstitutional war. Only John Quincy Adams defended Jackson. The secretary of state knew that the British government valued its trade with the United States, so he doubted Britain would fight a war over two insignificant subjects, no matter how unjust or tragic their demise. Likewise, he expected the Floridas' occupation to strengthen his hand in his talks with Onís: Jackson's excursion proved that the United States could seize the Floridas at any time, so Adams could push the Spanish minister to accept a small price for the colonies, rather than risk gaining nothing yet still losing them through American conquest.[22]

Ultimately, Monroe decided to stand behind the invasion, though he took a cautious approach. He ordered the return of Pensacola and St. Marks to Spain and avoided endorsing their seizure, but he defended Jackson's occupation of the posts as necessary to stop Spanish officials

"God alone is the searcher & judge of hearts"   89

from providing assistance to the Seminoles. Privately, the president mildly chided Jackson for "transcending" his orders, but he acknowledged that the general had acted in "the honour and interests of your country." Monroe's report to Congress likewise stated that he "duly appreciated" Jackson's reasons for taking the posts and attributed their seizure to "the misconduct of the Spanish officers." Meanwhile, Adams notified the Spanish government that Jackson had acted out of the "purest patriotism" while insisting that Spain needed either to maintain an adequate presence in Florida or to cede the region to the United States. Diplomatically, the responses played out as Adams expected. The British government never formally protested as the outrage over Arbuthnot's and Ambrister's executions subsided. Onís resumed his negotiations with Adams, and they soon concluded an agreement giving the Floridas to the United States in exchange only for assuming payment of $5 million in damages that the Spanish owed to American citizens and for an implicit repudiation of a claim that the 1803 Louisiana Purchase had included Texas—a weak contention that Jackson agreed should be given up.[23]

Monroe's decision to return the posts, and to excuse rather than approve their capture, disappointed Jackson. He denied Monroe's claim that he had "transcended" his order, noting that Calhoun's directive to him "was as comprehensive as it could be." Aware of Monroe's political dilemma, though, Jackson acknowledged that he "must for the present be silent," and the two remained on good terms. Late in 1819, Monroe stayed at the Hermitage during a tour of the Southern states, and at a Nashville hotel the two "entered the ball-room arm-in-arm" at a festivity given in the president's honor. Jackson then accompanied the president as he traveled to Louisville to inspect Kentucky's military installations. Still, the Florida controversy strained their relationship. Monroe initially planned to take Jackson with him on the earlier part of his Southern tour through Southern Georgia and the Gulf Coast region, but the president altered his plans so he would arrive at the Hermitage only after he visited the region associated with Jackson's invasion. For his part, Jackson likely realized that the president wanted to keep a distance from him, at least to some degree.[24]

Meanwhile, Jackson's conduct in the Florida campaign became a national issue. Overall, popular opinion approved his actions, but to many, his apparent independence and disregard for the law raised the

90 *Andrew Jackson: Old Hickory in Christian America*

specter of the type of military dictator that had overthrown republican governments in the past. In Washington, Monroe's rivals saw the invasion as an opportunity to embarrass the president. Kentucky's Henry Clay particularly resented Monroe for choosing Adams rather than himself as secretary of state, and as Speaker of the House of Representatives, he took the lead in attacking the administration through Jackson. Under Clay's oversight, the House took up a series of resolutions denouncing the Spanish forts' seizure and the executions of Arbuthnot and Ambrister. Debate over these proposals dominated the House's business for most of January 1819, with Clay delivering a widely reprinted speech blaming the Indian troubles in the South on "the most severe and humiliating demands" that Jackson had imposed on the Creeks in the Fort Jackson treaty. As he concluded, the Speaker implicitly compared Jackson to Julius Caesar, Oliver Cromwell, and Napoleon—popular commanders who had toppled previous republics—and warned his countrymen against giving "a fatal sanction . . . to military insubordination."[25]

Jackson immediately rushed to Washington to defend his reputation. Arriving in the capital three days after Clay delivered his speech, he concluded that the House Speaker had formed an alliance with Crawford to prevent Monroe's re-election and, in the process, destroy his own reputation. Over the next few weeks, the general met with Adams, Calhoun, and congressional supporters to coordinate their response to the House resolutions. Rumors spread through the city that Jackson threatened to attack his critics physically; one story claimed that he intended to challenge Clay to a duel, while another insisted that he promised to cut off a senator's ears. These tales further promoted his growing reputation as an uncontrollable, raging madman. Actually, Jackson avoided violence and controlled his temper for most of his visit, though he did vent his frustration when Adams brought up Crawford during their meeting. He was away when Clay called at his hotel to explain that, despite his speech, he held no personal animosity toward Jackson, but the general refused to honor Clay with the expected return visit. Instead, he lambasted the House Speaker to Rachel, counting him among those who would "abandon principle & Justice & would sacrafice their country for self agrandizement."[26]

Jackson's vigorous defense may have been unnecessary. Several members of Congress already approved the Florida campaign, and

"God alone is the searcher & judge of hearts" 91

the invasion's widespread popularity made others reluctant to oppose the hero still regarded as the nation's savior. In early February, the House rejected each resolution by solid majorities. While Jackson celebrated at public festivities held in his honor in New York, Philadelphia, and Baltimore, a Senate committee chaired by a Crawford ally submitted a report again condemning the invasion and hinting that the general seized Florida to advance his friends' interests in land speculation. Jackson again hurried to Washington, but most senators had little interest in pursuing the matter further. The committee presented its report two days after Adams had completed his treaty acquiring the Floridas, and in the midst of the agreement's quick ratification and the national celebration of Jackson, the Senate ignored the committee's charges. Still convinced of Crawford's and Clay's intrigue, once home Jackson prepared a forty-seven page "Memorial" to "repel the groundless charges which have been preferred against him." The senators politely received and printed the Memorial, but they never took it up as the furor over the Florida campaign soon faded.[27]

The accolades Jackson received at the public dinners and celebrations given in his honor on his way home provided some compensation for his frustration with Washington politicians. Still, he was ready to step away from public life. He had become "seriously ill" after his return from Pensacola, and though he recovered in time for his trip to Washington, the next summer he suffered a similar attack that again left him bedridden for several days. By the fall of 1819, he had improved enough to travel to Mississippi to impose a treaty acquiring lands from the Choctaw nation, but the national economic collapse joined the costs of keeping his wards to strain his finances. The death of several friends and Donelson family members likewise reminded him of his own mortality. When he returned from the conference with the Choctaws, he asked Monroe to let him know when "in your opinion my services can be dispensed with." He would not resign if his departure offered his enemies "ground for clamouring against me," and he promised to remain in the army as long as the Spanish government's delay in ratifying the Adams-Onís Treaty kept alive the prospect of war. Nevertheless, he told a friend in the summer of 1820 that "my patriotism had a hard struggle, for the first time in my life, to conquer my inclination for retirement."[28]

92   *Andrew Jackson: Old Hickory in Christian America*

President Monroe still had one more task for Jackson. After receiving word in February 1821 that the Spanish government had finally ratified the recent treaty, Monroe asked Jackson to serve as the Florida territories' American governor. Monroe had first brought up the governorship during his 1819 visit to the Hermitage, and though Jackson immediately turned it down, the president renewed the offer after the general wrote that overseeing the Floridas' official transfer "would afford me much pleasure." At first, Jackson again intended to reject the position. Aside from his desire to retire, the governorship would require an extended stay in Pensacola, a prospect that Rachel found "repugnant." Friends in Nashville encouraged him to take the post, hoping that Jackson could advance their investments in Florida lands. He also thought that the Gulf Coast climate might improve Rachel's health, which he noted had been "declining" when Monroe's offer arrived. He assumed, too, that the appointment signified the president's "desire to give evidence to the world that he fully approved my course on the Seminole campaign." Friends at Nashville's post office retrieved his letter turning down the governorship, and he instead told Monroe that he would accept it, "provided . . . that I may resign as soon as the Government is organized and in full operation."[29]

Jackson regretted changing his mind even before his departure. Nevertheless, resolved to do his duty, he headed for Pensacola in April 1821, accompanied by Rachel, eleven-year-old Andrew Jr., and a small entourage of military aides and Donelson family members. Their arrival portended a difficult administration. Spanish authorities in Cuba delayed giving Colonel James G. Forbes the official papers directing the Floridas' transfer, and when Forbes finally arrived with the orders, Governor José María Callava disputed Jackson's insistence that the Spanish army leave the cannons at Fort Barrancas, further postponing the handover. Jackson suspected that Callava and Forbes colluded with merchants to delay American possession so they could bring slaves into Florida—which would be prohibited once under American law—and import as much merchandise as possible before their wares could be subject to federal tariffs. Callava finally agreed to leave the cannons after Jackson threatened to cancel the boats hired to transport the

"God alone is the searcher & judge of hearts" 93

Spanish soldiers to Cuba, and Jackson officially accepted Florida for the United States on July 17.[30]

Once in the governor's office, Jackson found his actual powers limited. He could set up county governments and appoint lower-level offices, and talks with Seminole leaders led to the establishment of a reservation for the nation. To show his respect for the majority's Catholic faith, he dined with Pensacola's priest, whom Rachel described as "a divine looking man," but the Catholic population took offense when Jackson permitted Methodist missionaries to preach on Pensacola's streets. Probably to appease Rachel, he closed theaters and gambling houses on Sundays so the day could be observed as the Christian Sabbath honored by American Protestants. To his disappointment, though, he lacked the authority to confirm the land titles on his associates' investments. More disturbingly, Monroe ignored his recommendations for appointments to territorial offices. Placing young officers on his staff in these positions had provided him with a major reason for accepting the post, and he thought Monroe's appointees lacked the "good character" that "would have given confidence to the people." Some he knew to be allied with William Crawford, and once in Florida, these officials kept their distance from the governor, gravitating instead toward Callava and the handful of Spanish officers who had remained to wrap up their nation's affairs.[31]

Jackson's frustrations culminated in an aggravating confrontation with his predecessor. Despite their earlier standoff, he invited Callava to dine with him at the governor's residence. "The Scripture says return good for evil, . . ." Jackson wrote, "by which," he added with a reference to Romans 12:20, "I will heap coals upon his head."[32] The event went well, but a few weeks later, Callava refused to hand over some official records that Jackson needed to investigate a mixed-race woman's claim that the executor of her father's estate had cheated her out of her inheritance. Distaste for his position and distrust of Monroe's appointees likely intensified his resentment toward Callava, and the dispute quickly degenerated into a two-hour bilingual shouting match that ended with the Spaniard's arrest. Jackson released the former governor-general the next day after acquiring the records he needed, but he ordered all remaining Spanish officials to leave the

94 *Andrew Jackson: Old Hickory in Christian America*

Territory. Callava angrily departed for Washington to lodge a formal complaint, and Jackson once again faced the prospect of a congressional investigation. John Quincy Adams later commented to an acquaintance that he "dreaded the arrival of a mail from Florida, not knowing what General Jackson might do next," but the secretary of state again stood behind Jackson and dismissed Callava's complaint. Monroe's report to Congress attributed the incident to a misunderstanding, an approach that satisfied the lawmakers but frustrated Jackson for once again failing to exonerate him. Though he continued to express support for Monroe, their letters became more formal and less frequent as their mutually beneficial relationship effectively came to an end.[33]

By then, Jackson had abandoned Florida. He never intended to stay long, and the limits on his authority and the skirmish with Callava had worn on him. After only eleven weeks as governor, he concluded that he had accomplished all he could. Rachel's health had improved, but she hated living in Pensacola, despite her husband's upholding the Sabbath. At a farewell banquet hosted for him in early October, he proclaimed that he had tried to ensure for the people of Florida "the protection of their person, property, and religion." The next day, he left with his family, and once back at the Hermitage, he submitted his resignation. Monroe briefly attempted to persuade him to stay on a little while longer, but when Jackson firmly refused, the president bowed to his wishes and dated his resignation effective as of December 1, 1821.[34]

For the first time in nearly twenty years, Jackson held no official position. Perhaps he sincerely intended to stay out of public life and pursue a quiet retirement. Few had done more for his country than he had, yet his actions since his victory at New Orleans—all taken, he thought, because necessary for the Union's security—only involved him in controversies that soured him on politicians and their wiles. Now fifty-four, his health remained precarious, and he expected death to come soon. Yet Jackson also knew that his name had been put forward to succeed Monroe as president. Publicly, he expressed little interest in the nation's highest office. Privately, he did little to discourage those promoting his election. In fact, he often aided them. Only recently had he observed that he still lived because "it is the lords will that I am here."[35] It now appeared that the Lord might have more for him to do.

"God alone is the searcher & judge of hearts"   95

Notes

1. Matthew Warshauer, *Andrew Jackson and the Politics of Martial Law: Nationalism, Civil Liberties, and Partisanship* (Knoxville: University of Tennessee Press, 2006), 30–38.
2. Alexander James Dallas to Andrew Jackson, April 12, 1815, *PAJ*, 3:344–46; Jackson to Edward Livingston, May 17, 1815, *PAJ*, 3:357; Jackson to Dallas, May 23, 1815, *PAJ*, 3:358–59; Dallas to Jackson, August 1, 1815, *PAJ*, 3:375–77; Warshauer, *Andrew Jackson and the Politics of Martial Law*, 38–41.
3. Meredith, "'There Was Somebody Always Dying,'" 1–2, 61–68, 82–88, 104; Cheathem, *Andrew Jackson, Southerner*, 53–57.
4. Benton, *Thirty Years View*, 1:736.
5. Francis P. Blair to Andrew Jackson, July 14, 1836, *Correspondence*, 5:412–413; Parton, *Life of Andrew Jackson*, 2:653–54; 3:603–604.
6. Andrew Jackson to William C. C. Claiborne, February 5, 1815, *PAJ*, 3:271; Jackson to Andrew Jackson Donelson, February 24, 1817, *PAJ*, 4:91; Rachel Jackson to Andrew Jackson Donelson, October 19, 1818, *PAJ*, 4:244; Andrew Jackson to George Gibson, March 15, 1800, *PAJ*, 4:363; Parton, *Life of Andrew Jackson*, 2:652, 655.
7. Andrew Jackson to Richard K. Call, November 21, 1826, *PAJ*, 6:234; Nicholas Guyatt, *Providence and the Invention of the United States, 1607–1876* (Cambridge: Cambridge University Press, 2007).
8. Peter Cartwright, *Autobiography of Peter Cartwright* (New York: Nelson and Phillips, 1856), 192–93.
9. Ibid., 193–94.
10. Ibid., 193.
11. John Reid and John Henry Eaton, *The Life of Andrew Jackson, Major General, in the Service of the United States* (Philadelphia: M. Carey and Son, 1817).
12. Andrew Jackson to James Monroe, January 6, 1817, *PAJ*, 4:80; David S. Heidler and Jeanne T. Heidler, *Old Hickory's War: Andrew Jackson and the Quest for Empire* (Mechanicsburg, PA: Stackpole Books, 2003), 60–62.
13. Andrew Jackson to John Coffee, December 26, 1816, *PAJ*, 4:77.
14. Cheathem, *Andrew Jackson, Southerner*, 93–98; Winfield Scott to Andrew Jackson, January 2, 1818, *Correspondence*, 2:344–45; Jackson to George Graham, January 14, 1817, *PAJ*, 4:85; James Monroe to Jackson, December 2, 1817, *PAJ*, 4:155.
15. Andrew Jackson to James Monroe, October 23, 1816, *PAJ*, 4:69–70; Jackson to Monroe, January 6, 1817, *PAJ*, 4:81; Monroe to Jackson, March 1, 1817, *Correspondence*, 2:276.
16. John C. Calhoun to Jackson, December 26, 1817, *PAJ*, 4:163; Heidler and Heidler, *Old Hickory's War*, 60–70, 100–108.
17. Andrew Jackson to James Monroe, January 6, 1818, *PAJ*, 4:167.
18. Heidler and Heidler, *Old Hickory's War*, 117–21.
19. Daniel Feller, "The Seminole Controversy Revisited: A New Look at Andrew Jackson's 1818 Florida Campaign," *Florida Historical Quarterly* 88 (Winter 2010):309–25.
20. Ibid., 314.

96   *Andrew Jackson: Old Hickory in Christian America*

21. Remini, *Course of American Empire*, 354; Heidler and Heidler, *Old Hickory's War*, 135–76; Andrew Jackson to Rachel Jackson, June 2, 1818, *PAJ*, 4:212.
22. Heidler and Heidler, *Old Hickory's War*, 180–85.
23. James Monroe, "Second Annual Message," November 16, 1818, in James D. Richardson, ed., *A Compilation of the Messages and Papers of the Presidents*, 10 vols. (Washington: Government Printing Office, 1899), 2:612, hereafter cited as *Messages and Papers*; Heidler and Heidler, *Old Hickory's War*, 185–91; James Monroe to Andrew Jackson, July 19, 1818, *PAJ*, 4:225.
24. Andrew Jackson to James Monroe, August 19, 1818, *PAJ*, 4:238; Parton, *Life of Andrew Jackson*, 2:371.
25. *Annals of Congress*, 15th Congress, House of Representatives, Second Session, 634, 654–55.
26. Andrew Jackson to Rachel Jackson, February 6, 1819, *PAJ*, 4:271; Remini, *Course of American Empire*, 373–74; David S. Heidler and Jeanne T. Heidler, *Rise of Andrew Jackson: Myth, Manipulation, and the Making of Modern Politics* (New York: Basic Books, 2018), 109–10.
27. Remini, *Course of American Empire*, 344–47; Parton, *Life of Andrew Jackson*, 2:549–76; "The Memorial of Andrew Jackson, Major General in the Army of the United States, and Commander of the Southern Division," December 14, 1819, Andrew Jackson Papers, Library of Congress, Washington, DC.
28. Andrew Jackson to William McIntosh, July 8, 1818, *PAJ*, 4:220–21; Jackson to Andrew Jackson Donelson, September 17, 1819, *PAJ*, 4:322; Jackson to James Monroe, November 28, 1819, *PAJ*, 4:343; Jackson to George Gibson, July 10, 1820, *PAJ*, 4:374–75.
29. Remini, *Course of American Empire*, 377–79, 392–401; Andrew Jackson to James Monroe, February 11, 1821, *PAJ*, 5:10; Jackson to John Coffee, May 11, 1821, *PAJ*, 5:42.
30. Remini, *Course of American Empire*, 404–406.
31. Andrew Jackson to John C. Calhoun, July 29, 1821, *PAJ*, 5:87; Remini, *Course of American Empire*, 407–10, 417–18; Cheatham, *Andrew Jackson, Southerner*, 94–98; Parton, *Life of Andrew Jackson*, 2:607–10.
32. Andrew Jackson to James Craine Bronaugh, July 15, 1821, *PAJ*, 5:73.
33. Parton, *Life of Andrew Jackson*, 2:639.
34. Remini, *Course of American Empire*, 422–24.
35. Andrew Jackson to George Gibson, March 15, 1820, *PAJ*, 4:363.

7

"providence will spare me untill my enemies are prostrate"

Andrew Jackson first heard his name associated with the presidency soon after his triumph in New Orleans. Only a month after the battle, Virginia legislator John Stokely suggested he "ought to fill the Chair of the Chief magistrate of the Union." The following fall, William Carroll reported that several "leading characters" in Kentucky, Ohio, and Pennsylvania merely awaited a signal from Jackson so they could promote him as a candidate. The hero dismissed these entreaties. James Parton reported that Jackson "laughed at the idea," while Henry Marie Brackenridge, who had served as his secretary and translator during his governorship in Florida, recalled seeing Jackson throw down "in anger," an 1821 New York newspaper mentioning him as a potential candidate. "Do they think . . . that I am such a d___d fool as to think myself fit for President of the United States?" Brackenridge remembered him saying. The general acknowledged that he could "command a body of men in a rough way" but ultimately concluded, "I am not fit to be President."[1]

The calls for him to stand for the presidency must have flattered Jackson. No doubt, he recognized that his election to the nation's highest office would signal the ultimate vindication of his controversial career. Still, in the first few years after his victory at New Orleans, he likely gave the idea little thought. His friend James Monroe stood as the Republican Party's *heir apparent* in the 1816 election, and despite the fallout following his excursion into Florida, he seemed genuinely pleased with Monroe's virtually unanimous re-election in 1820. Also, after returning from his brief stint as the Floridas' governor, a violent cough and severe dysentery once again made him fear for his life. The

Andrew Jackson. Jonathan M. Atkins, Oxford University Press. © Jonathan M. Atkins 2025.
DOI: 10.1093/9780191886812.003.0007

98   *Andrew Jackson: Old Hickory in Christian America*

presidency may have tempted him, but he nevertheless appeared sincere when he protested that he wanted to leave public life and spend his final years at the Hermitage with Rachel, family, and friends.

As the 1824 election approached, Jackson had to consider the presidency more seriously. His nemesis, William H. Crawford, appeared to be Monroe's most likely successor, but Secretary of State John Quincy Adams, Secretary of War John C. Calhoun, and Henry Clay all had valid claims and significant support. With the field wide open, John Overton saw a possible short-term benefit in promoting the candidacy of his longtime friend and sometime business partner. Following William Blount's death, Overton had assumed leadership of the political clique that had long dominated Tennessee politics, but the financial panic that disrupted the national economy in 1819 weakened his grip on the state. In 1821, William Carroll defeated Overton's chosen candidate for governor on a platform calling for relief for debtors hurt by the crisis, and the state legislature subsequently approved several measures challenging the Overton group's control of the state's banking and financial institutions. Recognizing that Jackson's popularity might help return his allies to power, Overton and his associates began aggressively promoting the general for the presidency and arranged for the Tennessee legislature to nominate him formally for the office on July 20, 1822.[2]

Jackson's response revealed that he had greater interest in the position than he ever admitted. He insisted that he had "no desire . . . to be called to fill the Presidential chair, . . ." but he also acknowledged that, if elected, he would "obay the call of the people."[3] While he continued to profess a preference for either Adams or Calhoun, the prospect of confronting Crawford likely stoked his competitive nature. His animosity toward the Treasury secretary went far beyond a personal rift. The republican ideals of Jackson's generation presumed that American independence had established a free government, "the only republick now existing in the world, . . ." as Jackson declared in a military proclamation, making Americans "the only people on Earth who possess rights, liberties, and property which the[y] dare call their own." Foreign conflicts, he assumed, stemmed from European despots' determination to crush Americans' inspiring example to their own suffering peoples, but he also saw internal threats within the republic. If the people lacked virtue, internal discord could produce civil wars, or a military commander, with a loyal army behind him, could establish

"providence will spare me untill my enemies are prostrate"   99

himself as a dictator. The greatest danger, though, came from corrupt politicians who—through bargains, deals, and misleading voters—worked to expand government power, undermine the people's liberties, and establish themselves as an aristocracy. Jackson never doubted the people's virtue, and he bristled at suggestions that he might become a "military chieftain." But after witnessing politicians' extensive "log-rolling business" while in Washington, Jackson became convinced that "corruption" had infected the federal government, with Crawford especially using the Treasury Department's extensive patronage to surround himself with a network of "parasites."[4]

A concern that conspiring politicians threatened liberty had provided a major justification for the colonies' separation from Great Britain. Since then, many American leaders had come to understand cooperation and deals as political realities in a republic; others, like Jackson, clung more tightly to the Revolutionary era's republican principles, even as their nation experienced dramatic changes that undermined their economic and social foundation. By the early 1820s, the Union's population had quadrupled since 1776 to nearly ten million people, while the thirteen states along the Atlantic coast had expanded to twenty-four stretching past the Mississippi River. Thanks largely to Jackson, the United States held the Florida peninsula and the lands west to the foothills of the Rocky Mountains. Thanks also to Jackson's subjugation of the Southern Natives, white Americans had flooded into the southwest after the War of 1812. There, with the labor of African American slaves, they had established the plantations that became the South's "cotton kingdom." During the war, American forces likewise overwhelmed the indigenous populations north of the Ohio River, where white settlement created a region of small but productive commercial farms. Throughout the Union, but especially in the Northeast, manufacturing production also increased significantly. Artisan craftsmen in small workshops still produced most of the country's manufactured goods, and Americans continued to rely on British imports to meet most of their needs for finished products. At the same time, the emergence of some large-scale factories laid the foundation for an economic expansion that would take off during Jackson's last two decades before exploding a generation later in an Industrial Revolution that made the United States one of the world's leading economic powers.[5]

100   *Andrew Jackson: Old Hickory in Christian America*

Perhaps spurred by these changes, the United States meanwhile became a more religious nation. The frontier revivals that began during Jackson's young manhood continued throughout the South and the West, paralleled by similar outbreaks starting in New England and expanding into New York and Pennsylvania. The Methodist and Baptist churches emerged as the nation's most popular denominations, but even among the less zealous, the organization and construction of churches offered ample new opportunities for worship. Some sects withdrew from the larger society to form their own self-enclosed communities, such as the Shakers, an egalitarian and pietistic group that rejected sexual activity while establishing several settlements scattered in the Northeast and the West. Skepticism likewise persisted; though atheism became rare, some, such as the young Abraham Lincoln, continued to hold the deistic views more prevalent during the era of the Revolution. Nevertheless, though less than half of the white population formally joined a church, the large majority of Americans accepted Christian teachings, even if they failed to practice them. Throughout the Union, as the Frenchman Alexis de Tocqueville observed, Christianity "reigns without obstacle, by universal consent," while the historian Richard Carwardine described the evangelical Protestant denominations as "the largest, and most formidable, subculture in American society."[6]

Like millions of his countrymen, Jackson remained among the unchurched believers, at least in terms of formal church membership. He still attended services regularly, especially after the conclusion of his military career, and in 1823, he worked with his neighbors to build a church near the Hermitage, donating three acres of his land, helping to raise nearly $700 for the building's construction, and writing to encourage his friend Samuel Hodge to return to the area and serve as the church's pastor. Rachel formally joined the new congregation, but Jackson resisted her plea that he also join. Most likely, his independence and sense of honor still made him reluctant to submit to a congregation's discipline, but he told his wife that, with his name mentioned for the presidency, affiliating with a church would appear "that I had done it for the sake of political effect." "[I]t is what we all ought to do," he later explained more honestly to John Coffee, "but men in Public business has too much on their mind to conform to the rules of the church, which has prevented me hitherto." Still,

"providence will spare me untill my enemies are prostrate"   101

Jackson continued to attend services with Rachel and promised her that he would become a church member "when once more I am clear of politics."[7]

Religion, in fact, remained one of Jackson's favorite topics. Henry A. Wise, later the governor of Virginia, recalled attending a wedding at the Hermitage and listening to Jackson defend the "some of . . . the most soo-*blime*" concepts of the Swedenborgians, a mystical, non-Trinitarian sect that emphasized the importance of good works and was associated with spiritualism. Only occasionally did he put his thoughts about national religious developments in writing. In 1819, for instance, he observed after visiting a community of celibate Shakers that "the god who rules the universe never intended to put an end to the world of mankind, in that way." Still, after his return from Florida, his letters suggested that his faith was growing stronger. More frequently than before, he commented about the importance of Jesus's atoning sacrifice, and on occasion, he encouraged others to believe as well. Later, after Rachel's death, he admonished her brother that she always "had your *future state*, much at heart . . ." and encouraged him to "put your house in order for the next, by laying hold 'of the one thing needful'—go read the Scriptures," he pleaded; "the Joyful promises it contains, will be a balsame to all your troubles."[8]

Grief from Rachel's passing may have prompted this evangelizing effort, but Jackson had always promoted Christianity when he could. Friends and associates knew that he believed its doctrines were true. James Bronaugh, his personal physician while in Florida, on his deathbed asked George Walton to assure Jackson that he "became religious in his last . . ." and met his death "with resignation and fortitude." More than assurance of an afterlife, Jackson considered Christian principles an important component of a civilized society. "[A] proper respect for character, religion & morality, . . ." he told John McNairy, "lay[s] a solid foundation for the perpetuity of our happy form of Govt. Whenever those are lost sight of [and] party views substituted in their stead, our Government will be changed—it cannot stand, virtue being the only prop which sustains it." His activities in Nashville's Masonic lodge, which he resumed for a few years after returning home from New Orleans, complemented his promotion of Christian behavior; Masonry, he asserted, "brings into active operation, the important principles by which man in his pilgrimage below

102 *Andrew Jackson: Old Hickory in Christian America*

should be guided, and governed." Though he declined an invitation to speak at a meeting of Davidson County's chapter of the American Bible Society, he assured its members that "there is nothing that I can do with propriety that I will not do, to prosper the great & good cause of christianity & the true religion of Jesus christ by the spread of the gospel."[9]

Interestingly, Jackson still never indicated a concern that sin endangered his soul. Nor did he see the need for the dramatic conversion experience demanded by the ministers leading the current wave of revivals. For him, belief and adherence to orthodox Christian principles, and demonstrating them through good works, seemed sufficient. As a result, he maintained an ecumenical faith that took little interest in the theological debates and doctrinal bickering that raged among denominational leaders. His upbringing and his mother's influence gave him a preference for the Presbyterian church, he told Ezra Stiles Ely, a minister in Philadelphia he had known since the 1790s, and when the Presbytery of Transylvania suspended Thomas Craighead for "Pelagian views"—apparently for questioning the doctrine of predestination—Jackson and Rachel stood by him.[10] But Jackson's support derived more from personal loyalty to a friend than from commitment to specific theological principles, for he also told Ely that

> All true Christians love each other, and while here below ought to harmonize; for all must unite in the realms above. I have thought one evidence of true religion is, when all those who believe in the atonement of our crucified Saviour are found in harmony and friendship together.[11]

Ely doubted whether Jackson was "a renewed man, by the power of divine grace," and he admonished Rachel to make her husband "an active Christian." These entreaties likely amused Jackson, for he already considered himself a Christian. Unlike the members of the revived evangelical denominations—but more reflective of American society as a whole—he dismissed theological arguments because of his nonsectarian outlook and commitment to religious freedom. "Amongst the greatest blessings secured to us under our Constitution," he lectured Ely, "is the liberty of worshipping God as our conscience dictates."[12] Several years later, while serving as president, he echoed this sentiment when he told a correspondent,

"providence will spare me untill my enemies are prostrate" 103

Our excellent constitution guarantees to every one freedom of religion, and charity tells us, [(]and you know Charity is the reall basis of *all true religion*[)], and charity says judge the tree by its fruit. all who profess christianity, believe in a Saviour and that by him and through him we must be saved. We ought therefore to consider all good christians, whose walks correspond with their professions, be him Presbeterian, Episcopalian, Baptist, Methodist or Roman catholic.[13]

As a nonchurched believer, Jackson relied both on providence and on republican ideals to help him reconcile his interest in the presidency with his reservations. The era's political principles assumed that voters should distrust a candidate who openly coveted the nation's highest office, so Jackson determined that he would remain "perfectly silent" while leaving the contest in God's hands. Yet when Republicans in Dauphin County, Pennsylvania, asked Jackson in February 1823 whether he would serve, he replied that, though he "had retired from the busy scenes of public life," the office "cannot with propriety be declined when offered by those who have the power of selection"—a statement widely interpreted as an open declaration of his candidacy. Then, while continuing to proclaim disinterest, he closely followed the movements of those who were putting together his presidential campaign. With Jackson's knowledge and approval, William B. Lewis, a neighboring planter and friend, and John H. Eaton, a former military aide now serving as one of Tennessee's senators, took the lead in promoting his candidacy. John Overton soon realized he had tapped into a more powerful force than he had anticipated, and he began meeting frequently with Lewis, Eaton, and other Jackson associates in an informal committee that outsiders labeled the "Nashville Junto," with Jackson himself frequently offering information and advice. Eaton meanwhile published a series of letters under the pseudonym "Wyoming" to promote him as a second George Washington who, like the first, could save his country in its hour of need.[14]

Proponents for the other presidential aspirants at first dismissed him as a serious contender. Adams's supporters floated his name for the vice presidency, while President Monroe's offer to appoint Jackson the American minister to Mexico—which the hero quickly declined—was probably intended to get him out of the way. Nevertheless, his potential impact on the election became clear when, against his wishes, the

104   *Andrew Jackson: Old Hickory in Christian America*

campaign brought Jackson back into public life sooner than he wanted. In the fall of 1823, the Tennessee legislature needed to elect a senator to succeed John Williams, whose term had expired the previous March. Williams wanted to return to the Senate and had the support of most legislators, but he personally despised Jackson. Also, because the senator favored Crawford for president, Williams's re-election would imply that the legislature had nominated Jackson merely as a courtesy, signaling a lack of serious backing in the hero's home state that would effectively end his candidacy. Two staunch Jackson men challenged Williams, but neither could gain the necessary votes from the majority of the legislators. In desperation, Eaton and Lewis put Jackson himself up for the seat. To this point, the hero had resisted appeals to come to the state capital at Murfreesboro to lobby for Williams's rivals, but with his own name now before the legislature, he rushed to the capital "to gratify the state," he claimed, "in prostrating Crawfordism." His nomination and presence in Murfreesboro won over enough legislators to elect him over Williams by a 35-25 margin, keeping his presidential prospects alive—but now requiring him, for the second time, to serve as a United States senator.[15]

Jackson had no desire to return to the Senate. But his letter to Pennsylvania Republicans had proclaimed that a citizen must serve when called by his countrymen, so he could not decline the seat without appearing hypocritical. Thus, despite Rachel's being "more disconsolate than I ever knew her before," in November he again headed for Washington. Just as he had as a young member of Congress, he took his legislative responsibilities seriously. This time, too, Senator Jackson knew that politicians were watching closely to assess him as a presidential candidate. Conscious that he was on display, he stayed up late most nights attending social events and meeting with potential supporters. "[T]he early part of the evening is spent with my friends who visit me," he explained to Rachel; "the latter must be spent in attention to duty and to business." The demands occupied him to the point that he assigned to John Eaton, Tennessee's "senior" senator, the responsibility for keeping Rachel informed about Jackson's activities. Eaton regularly informed Rachel that her husband "is constantly in motion to some Dinner party or other," but he assured her that "every Sunday he takes himself to some one of the churches."[16]

"providence will spare me untill my enemies are prostrate" 105

Jackson especially concentrated on dispelling the notion that he was "a most uncivilized, unchristian man" or that he "could be irritated, thrown from my equilibrium, and prostrated by some act of rashness & impudence." "Great pains had been taken to represent me as a savage disposition," he told John Coffee, "who always carried a scalping Knife in one hand, & a tomahawk in the other; allways ready to knock down, & scalp, any & every person who differed with me in opinion." Turning on the charm that his friends and associates well knew, he set out to show national politicians that, "When it becomes necessary to philosophise and be meek, no man can command his temper better than I."[17] Part of this task involved resolving conflicts with figures from his past. Shortly after taking his seat, he met "on friendly terms" with Winfield Scott, the general who had declined his challenge to a duel for describing one of Jackson's orders as "mutinous." Through their service on the Senate's Military Affairs committee, he came into "harmony & good understanding" with Thomas Hart Benton, now an influential Missouri politician but still the brother of the man who put a bullet in Jackson's shoulder. And, though he remained suspicious of the Speaker of the House, he even agreed to dine with Henry Clay.[18]

The presidential election loomed over the congressional session. When the lawmakers convened in December 1823, Crawford still appeared the frontrunner. The previous August, he had actually suffered a major health setback—probably a stroke—that temporarily left him paralyzed, blind, and unable to speak. By November, he had sufficiently recovered to resume his duties at the Treasury Department, and though he remained weak and with obvious infirmities, his proponents sought to secure his nomination through a congressional caucus. Republican representatives had long used caucus meetings to put forward presidential candidates and unite their party behind a nominee. But Crawford's opponents now condemned the caucus as an outdated, elitist, and aristocratic scheme for selecting a candidate, so when the caucus met on February 14, 1824, fewer than one-third of the Republican congressmen attended. The members who were there duly nominated Crawford, but the meeting's poor attendance, along with a relapse of his illness in April, all but destroyed his prospects. Jackson's cause meanwhile caught fire. Secretary of War Calhoun had expected a state convention in Pennsylvania to boost his own candidacy, but when the conference met in Harrisburg on March 4, the

106   *Andrew Jackson: Old Hickory in Christian America*

delegates instead unexpectedly nominated Jackson. The shocking result convinced Calhoun to accept the convention's nomination for the vice presidency, while the endorsement from an important Northern state now made Jackson's election appear a real possibility.[19]

As a serious contender, Jackson now became the target of direct attacks. Critics charged that his success as a "military chieftain" qualified him more to become a tyrant than to serve as president. Many brought up the controversies that checkered his past, including the dubious circumstances of his marriage and his duel with Charles Dickinson. Jesse Benton—unlike his brother, unwilling to forgive—denounced Jackson as a corrupt and lawless gambler and murderer, while a former Pennsylvania senator brought up the general's recommendation that James Monroe should appoint Federalists to his administration. Jackson's backers continued to portray the hero as an honest republican willing to serve his country whenever called. John Eaton's "Wyoming" letters, now available as a pamphlet for wider distribution, provided the keynote for the campaign, as activists justified Jackson's conduct in each of his controversies while reminding the public that he had saved the nation in its darkest hour. Privately, the nominee fumed at the assaults—he had forgotten that he had indeed encouraged Monroe to appoint William Drayton, a Federalist, as secretary of war—but throughout the summer he largely remained in the background while encouraging the Nashville Junto to respond to the charges.[20]

The election mainly involved the candidates' images. The only substantive issues for Jackson came up when he defended his votes in the Senate to authorize surveys for the construction of roads and canals across the Union and to raise tariff rates on imported goods to increase their prices and encourage Americans to buy American-made products. Many Southern planters feared that the federal government's construction of "internal improvements" threatened state rights. Likewise, they complained that the "protective" tariff compelled British industrialists—the major supplier of the Union's manufactured goods—to retaliate by refusing to buy Southern cotton. Jackson's nationalistic positions apparently had little effect on his strong Southern support.[21] Still, after voters cast their ballots in November, the election's outcome remained uncertain. When the results came in, Jackson had won 41 percent of the popular votes and

"providence will spare me untill my enemies are prostrate"   107

ninety-nine votes in the Electoral College. Adams came in second with 31 percent of the popular vote and eighty-four electoral votes. Despite his illness, Crawford came in third with forty-one electoral votes. Clay actually outpolled Crawford in the popular vote, but the three states he carried brought him only thirty-seven electors. Although Jackson had only won a plurality of the popular vote, the result convinced him that he was indeed the people's choice. Nevertheless, his total fell thirty-two votes short of the required majority in the Electoral College. As directed by the Constitution, the selection of the new president would now go to the House of Representatives, which would choose from the top three candidates, with each state casting one vote.

The representatives' only real choice involved either Jackson or Adams. The physically impaired Crawford obviously could not serve, while Clay's last-place finish in the Electoral College eliminated him from contention. But as Speaker of the House, Clay presumably would have a large impact on the outcome. Given their past dealings, Jackson had little reason to hope for Clay's backing. Acknowledging that he thought Adams's election "most probable," Jackson again pledged "not to interfere in any way." "Situated as I am," he told John Coffee, "patience & fortitude must be exercised, and the will of providence cheerfully submitted to."[22] With Rachel now with him in Washington, Jackson attended to his Senate duties and greeted well-wishers at his hotel, but he made few public appearances other than accompanying Rachel to church. In late January, he fell on a staircase, reopening the wound from his brawl with the Bentons and leaving him bedridden for a week. His infirmity had little influence on the outcome. Clay indeed had no interest in promoting Jackson. The speaker announced his preference for Adams, and when the House voted on February 9, the three states that Clay had carried in the general election, along with at least two more that he influenced, helped to elect Adams, rather than Jackson, as the new president.[23]

The outcome disappointed Jackson. At first, he accepted the result stoically, attending a reception the day after the House's election to congratulate the president-elect and wish him success. Four days later, he learned that Clay had accepted Adams's offer to serve as secretary of state, the most prestigious cabinet post and a position popularly regarded as the steppingstone to the presidency. The news convinced Jackson that "the rights of the people have been bartered for promises

108 *Andrew Jackson: Old Hickory in Christian America*

of office." No evidence exists for an explicit deal—the House Speaker actually stood as the obvious choice for the position—but Jackson never doubted that Adams and Clay had concluded a "Corrupt Bargain," giving Adams the presidency and naming Clay as his successor. Adams's involvement surprised and disappointed Jackson, but Clay, he now concluded, appeared even more than Crawford the most dangerous politician in the Union. "[T]he *Judas* of the West has closed the contract and will receive his thirty pieces of silver, . . ." Jackson fumed. "Was there ever witnessed such a bare faced corruption in any country before?"[24]

Jackson undoubtedly knew that he would challenge Adams in the next election. With four years to wait, he realized that his presence in the Senate could no longer help, but might instead hurt, his candidacy, so after casting his vote against Clay's confirmation as secretary of state, he and Rachel returned to the Hermitage. That fall, after the Tennessee legislature again nominated him for president, he immediately submitted his resignation so he "might be free from the imputation of intriguing for the office."[25] William Lewis and John Eaton, with the cooperation of John Overton and Andrew Donelson, revived the Nashville Junto, which in March 1827 organized more formally as a Nashville Central Committee that, with a similar committee set up in Washington, would direct the campaign. The candidate again convinced himself that he remained above the contest. He made a few public appearances over the next few years, including a visit to New Orleans to commemorate the anniversary of his greatest victory, but most of the time, he stayed at home. Still, he once again frequently consulted with the Nashville Junto to stay informed and help where he could. He now made fewer references than before to leaving the contest in God's hands, but he confidently asserted to John Coffee that "providence will spare me untill my enemies are prostrate."[26]

The backlash over the "Corrupt Bargain" contributed to making the 1828 contest the first modern presidential election. Unlike in 1824, when legislatures still selected presidential electors in six of the twenty-four states, in 1828, all but two states would hold popular elections to choose their electors. With winning public support now more crucial than ever before, two organizations managed national campaigns to appeal for votes across the Union. Jackson's friends in Congress aggressively attacked Adams's administration, while the Nashville and

"providence will spare me untill my enemies are prostrate"   109

Washington committees worked with local organizations to coordinate the campaign's message, distribute funds, circulate information, and promote events like rallies, parades, and barbecues. The candidate's former rivals meanwhile came together to form a coalition committed to ousting Adams and Clay from power. Vice President John C. Calhoun wrote to Jackson in June 1826 to indicate his support, and once sure he could remain as vice president in a Jackson administration, he used his authority as president of the Senate to pack committees with Jackson men while openly calling for the general's election. A few months later, New York Senator Martin Van Buren—William Crawford's principal champion in 1824—likewise offered his services. Van Buren's tour through the south Atlantic states in 1826 successfully brought Jackson's former nemesis and his allies into the general's camp, and with Calhoun, Van Buren quickly emerged as one of the national campaign's chief directors.[27]

Even more than in 1824, the campaigns in 1828 focused mainly on the candidates' images rather than on policies or issues. Jacksonians promoted their man as the defender of the people now determined to cast out the manipulative politicians who had seized control of the government. Harping on the "Corrupt Bargain," the coalition behind him charged that Adams had wasted public money to purchase a pool table for the President's House and manipulated an innocent story from Adams's stint as minister to Russia into a claim that he had once provided a fourteen-year-old American girl to satisfy the lusts of the tsar. For the administration's supporters, Jackson's past again provided ample ammunition for similar attacks. Sensationalizing tales about Jackson's supposed ignorance, unbridled anger, and lawlessness, Adams's men condemned Jackson's order to shoot eighteen-year-old John Wood during the Creek War while a widely reprinted "Coffin Handbill" publicized his rejection of clemency for six volunteers who, under questionable circumstances, were convicted and executed for "mutiny" in 1815. The charges that most infuriated Jackson slandered the two women most important to him. Spokesmen for Adams and Clay claimed that Jackson's mother had worked as a prostitute for the British Army and married a biracial man. Likewise, they brought up the circumstances of his marriage, accused the candidate of stealing another man's wife, and labeled Rachel an adulteress. Privately, Jackson fumed that his inability to punish Elizabeth's and Rachel's

110   *Andrew Jackson: Old Hickory in Christian America*

assailants "is a sacrafice too great to be well endure[*d*]." Aware, though, that a public response would only fuel more charges about his temper and rashness, he reluctantly concluded, "I must bear with it."[28]

More than in 1824, religion proved a notable though secondary theme in the 1828 election. Four years earlier, Jackson stood among the candidates as the most traditional Christian. Crawford, an unchurched believer like Jackson, openly criticized organized religion as hypocritical; Clay had a dissolute reputation for his rakish private life, while many thought Adams subscribed to Unitarianism, a liberal theology that denied Jesus's divinity and rejected biblical accounts of miracles and divine intervention. Jackson's long association with Freemasonry likely hurt him in the Northeast, where an "Anti-Masonic" Party emerged suddenly and condemned the fraternity as a secretive and elitist clique. The candidate himself offered no comments about Anti-Masonry, other than referring to it as a "bubble . . . wasting in the common sense of the people," and his well-known traditional orthodoxy likely reassured devout voters throughout the Union.[29] Several prominent clergymen meanwhile openly preferred Jackson. Shortly before the election, Ezra Stiles Ely published a sermon on *The Duty of Christian Freemen to Elect Christian Rulers*. The text never mentioned Jackson by name, and in the pamphlet's appendix, Ely denied either "advocating the UNION OF CHURCH AND STATE" or promoting Jackson's election. Nevertheless, the pamphlet's implicit endorsement prompted Jackson to remind the minister about the candidate's ecumenical beliefs, and his commitment to religious liberty likely broadened Jackson's appeal among voters outside the mainstream Protestant churches—especially after his proponents discovered disparaging statements that Adams had made years earlier denouncing Roman Catholicism as a "portentous system of despotism and superstition."[30]

More than half of all eligible voters went to the polls in 1828, a higher turnout rate than in any previous presidential election. This time, Jackson scored a solid victory, winning 55 percent of the popular vote while securing a 178-83 majority in the Electoral College. Beyond revulsion against the "Corrupt Bargain" and Jackson's standing as a national hero, several factors contributed to the result.

"providence will spare me untill my enemies are prostrate" 111

The organization behind Jackson proved more effective at stirring up enthusiasm and getting out the vote than did his opponents. His role in defending the frontier and suppressing Native nations helped him carry all of the Southern states, while his image as a pure republican taking on entrenched political interests especially appealed to small farmers in poorer and more remote regions. His appeal as the champion of the people likewise appears to have tapped into the resentments of revived Christians in the Western states against eastern arrogance toward the "uncivilized" frontier. Jackson's association with religious freedom likewise contributed to his strong following among others who perceived themselves as outsiders to the American mainstream, such as Lutheran and Reformed believers in German communities, his fellow descendants of Scots-Irish Presbyterian migrants, and Irish Catholics in New York and Philadelphia. Adams carried New England, his home region, but even in these states, Jackson was the choice of Baptists and Methodists who resented paying taxes to support the established Congregational church.[31] With revivals occurring throughout the nation, too, no doubt at least some voters saw Jackson as God's chosen instrument, divinely called to restore the pure republican principles of the founding fathers.

Jackson himself simply described the result as "a triumph of the virtue of the people over the corrupting influence of executive patronage wielded to destroy the morals of the people." The thrill of competition and a desire for vindication had carried him through the contest. Whether he actually wanted to serve as president remains uncertain. He would take office shortly before his sixty-second birthday, older than any of his predecessors. His health had held up fairly well over the past few years, but he still suffered occasionally from severe headaches, the pains of his wounds, and periodic attacks of dysentery. By this time, too, he had lost most of his teeth, forcing him to wear loose-fitting dentures that made it difficult for him to speak. Nevertheless, he resolved to adhere to the voters' wishes. "[A]ll that I can promise," he assured friends and associates, "is an honest disposition to execute the will of the people, and an earnest reliance on the goodness of providence."[32] When he penned these words, he had no idea what providence had in store for him.

112   *Andrew Jackson: Old Hickory in Christian America*

Notes

1. John Stokely to Andrew Jackson, February 13, 1815, *PAJ*, 3:278; William Carroll to Jackson, October 4, 1815, *PAJ*, 3:386–87; Parton, *Life of Andrew Jackson*, 2:354, 3:18.

2. Donald Ratcliffe, *The One-Party Presidential Contest: Adams, Jackson, and 1824's Five-Horse Race* (Lawrence: University Press of Kansas, 2015), 116–17; Heidler and Heidler, *The Rise of Andrew Jackson*, 136–37, 144–45.

3. Andrew Jackson to James C. Bronaugh, August 1, 1822, *PAJ*, 5:210–11.

4. "To the 2nd Division," March 7, 1812, *PAJ*, 2:291; Andrew Jackson to James C. Bronaugh, January 10, 1822, *PAJ*, 5:136; Jackson to James Gadsden, May 2, 1822, *PAJ*, 5:179; Remini, *Course of American Freedom*, 12–21, 29–35.

5. Daniel Walker Howe, *What Hath God Wrought? The Transformation of America, 1815–1848* (New York: Oxford University Press, 2007), 19–50, 125–42, 211–42, 536–59.

6. Howe, *What Hath God Wrought?*, 164–202, 285–323; Thomas Kidd, *America's Religious History: Faith, Politics, and the Shaping of a Nation* (Grand Rapids, Michigan: Zondervan, 2019), 70–90; Mark A. Noll, *A History of Christianity in the United States and Canada* (Grand Rapids: William B. Eerdmans Publishing Co., 1992), 143–80; Alexis de Tocqueville, *Democracy in America* (New York: Alfred A. Knopf, 1945; orig. pub. 1835), 304–305; Richard J. Carwardine, *Evangelicals and Politics in Antebellum America* (New Haven: Yale University Press, 1993), 44.

7. Edward Ward to Andrew Jackson, August 25, 1823, *PAJ*, 5:291; Jackson to John Coffee, February 20–24, 1828, *PAJ*, 6:419; Parton, *Life of Andrew Jackson*, 3:101–103; James E. Arnold, "The Hermitage Church," *Tennessee Historical Quarterly* 28 (Summer 1969):113–15.

8. Henry A. Wise, *Seven Decades of the Union* (Philadelphia: J.B. Lippincott & Co., 1881), 102; Andrew Jackson to Robert Y. Hayne, October 2, 1819, *PAJ*, 4:333; Jackson to John Donelson, June 7, 1829, *PAJ*, 7:268–69.

9. Andrew Jackson to Andrew J. Donelson, October 11, 1822, *PAJ*, 5:220; Jackson to John McNairy, September 6, 1823, *PAJ*, 5:293; Jackson to William R. Hess and the Masons of Lodge 45, Jackson, Tennessee, September 19, 1825, *PAJ*, 6:102; Jackson to Robert Paine et al., September 30, 1826, *PAJ*, 6:220.

10. Andrew Jackson to Ezra Stiles Ely, July 12, 1827, *PAJ*, 6:358–59; Rev. James Geddes Craighead, *The Craighead Family: A Genealogical Memoir of the Descendants of Rev. Thomas and Margaret Craighead, 1658–1876* (Philadelphia: Sherman & Co., Printers, 1876), 64–70.

11. Andrew Jackson to Ezra Stiles Ely, July 12, 1827, *PAJ*, 6:358–59.

12. Ezra Stiles Ely, *The Duty of Christian Freemen to Elect Christian Rulers* (Philadelphia: William F. Geddes, 1828), 32; Ezra Stiles Ely to Rachel Jackson, October 22, 1819, quoted in Gismondi, "Rachel Jackson and the Search for Zion," 166; Andrew Jackson to Ely, July 12, 1827, *PAJ*, 6:358.

13. Andrew Jackson to Ellen M. Hanson, March 25, 1835, *Correspondence*, 5:333.

"*providence will spare me untill my enemies are prostrate*" 113

14. Andrew Jackson to H. W. Peterson, February 23, 1823, *PAJ*, 5:253; Heidler and Heidler, *Rise of Andrew Jackson*, 132–33; Robert P. Hay, "The Case for Andrew Jackson in 1824: Eaton's 'Wyoming Letters,'" *Tennessee Historical Quarterly* 29 (Summer 1970):139–51; [John H. Eaton], *The Letters of Wyoming, to the People of the United States, on the Presidential Election, and in Favour of Andrew Jackson* (Philadelphia: S. Simpson & J. Conrad, 1824).

15. Heidler and Heidler, *Rise of Andrew Jackson*, 147–51; Ratcliffe, *One-Party Presidential Contest*, 117–18; Andrew Jackson to Richard K. Call, June 29, 1822, *PAJ*, 5:199; Andrew Jackson to [John C. Calhoun], October 4, 1823, *PAJ*, 5:301.

16. Andrew Jackson to John Overton, November 8, 1823, *PAJ*, 5:316; Jackson to Rachel Jackson, January 15, 1824, *PAJ*, 5:339; John H. Eaton to Rachel Jackson, December 18, 1823, ibid., 5:327; Heidler and Heidler, *Rise of Andrew Jackson*, 157–58; Ratcliffe, *One-Party Presidential Contest*, 142–45.

17. Andrew Jackson to Francis Preston, January 27, 1824, *PAJ*, 5:347; Jackson to Andrew J. Donelson, March 19, 1824, *PAJ*, 5:378.

18. Andrew Jackson to Winfield Scott, December 11, 1823, *PAJ*, 5:326; Heidler and Heidler, *Rise of Andrew Jackson*, 158–59; Parton, *Life of Andrew Jackson*, 3:44–48.

19. Ratcliffe, *One-Party Presidential Contest*, 119–24, 149–55; Heidler and Heidler, *Rise of Andrew Jackson*, 164–68, 172–78; Chase C. Mooney, *William H. Crawford: 1772–1834* (Lexington: University Press of Kentucky, 1974), 240–42.

20. Heidler and Heidler, *The Rise of Andrew Jackson*, 141, 181–84; Ratcliffe, *One-Party Presidential Contest*, 165–67.

21. Andrew Jackson to James W. Lanier, May 15, 1824, *PAJ*, 5:409; Jackson to Littleton H. Coleman, April 26, 1824, *PAJ*, 5:400; Heidler and Heidler, *Rise of Andrew Jackson*, 185–88; Ratcliffe, *One-Party Presidential Contest*, 156–63.

22. Parton, *Life of Andrew Jackson*, 3:65; Andrew Jackson to John Coffee, January 5, 1825, *PAJ*, 6:6; Jackson to Coffee, January 23, 1825, *PAJ*, 6:18.

23. Heidler and Heidler, *Rise of Andrew Jackson*, 218–23; Ratcliffe, *One-Party Presidential Contest*, 229–53.

24. Andrew Jackson to John Coffee, February 19, 1825, *PAJ*, 6:36; Jackson to William B. Lewis, February 14, 1825, *PAJ*, 6:29–30.

25. Andrew Jackson to Samuel Swartout, December 15, 1825, *PAJ*, 6:126.

26. Andrew Jackson to John Coffee, February 20–24, 1828, *PAJ*, 6:418; Heidler and Heidler, *Rise of Andrew Jackson*, 247–51, 303–304; Donald B. Cole, *Vindicating Andrew Jackson: The 1828 Election and the Rise of the Two-Party System* (Lawrence: University Press of Kansas, 2009), 39, 50–52, 73–74; Lynn Hudson Parsons, *The Birth of Modern Politics: Andrew Jackson, John Quincy Adams, and the Election of 1828* (New York: Oxford University Press, 2009), 133–40, 147–49.

27. John C. Calhoun to Andrew Jackson, June 4, 1826, *PAJ*, 6:177; Parsons, *Birth of Modern Politics*, 112–40; Cole, *Vindicating Andrew Jackson*, 9–13, 39–40, 45–48, 50–52, 73–74, 141–48; Heidler and Heidler, *Rise of Andrew Jackson*, 312–31.

28. Andrew Jackson to John Coffee, June 20, 1828, *PAJ*, 6:469; Heidler and Heidler, *Rise of Andrew Jackson*, 273–81, 284–86, 348–68; Parsons, *Birth of Modern Politics*, 142–49, 161–62, 167; Cole, *Vindicating Andrew Jackson*, 79–81, 149–53.

29. Mooney, *William H. Crawford*, 16; Cole, *Vindicating Andrew Jackson*, 91–92; Parsons, *Birth of Modern Politics*, 178; Michael F. Holt, "The Antimasonic and Know Nothing Parties," in *Political Parties and American Political Development from the Age of Jackson to the Age of Lincoln* (Baton Rouge: Louisiana State University Press, 1992), 89–112; Andrew Jackson to William B. Lewis, June 26, 1830, *PAJ*, 8:396.

114   *Andrew Jackson: Old Hickory in Christian America*

30. Gismondi, "Rachel Jackson and the Search for Zion," 211–16; Meacham, *American Lion*, 86–88; Parton, *Life of Andrew Jackson*, 3:141; Parsons, *Birth of Modern Politics*, 174–75; Ely, *The Duty of Christian Freemen to Elect Christian Rulers*; Andrew Jackson to Ezra Stiles Ely, July 12, 1827, *PAJ*, 6:358–59.
31. Cole, *Vindicating Andrew Jackson*, 182–203; Parsons, *Birth of Modern Politics*, 175–77; Haselby, *Origins of American Religious Nationalism*, 283–97; Ratcliffe, *One-Party Presidential Contest*, 265, 276.
32. Andrew Jackson to David Corbin Kos, November 20, 1828, *PAJ*, 6:535; Andrew Jackson to Amos Kendall, November 25, 1828, *PAJ*, 6:536.

8

"I find myself a solitary mourner . . ."

The celebration of Andrew Jackson's election overshadowed the fact that Rachel Jackson did not want to go to Washington. While she liked the minister at the city's Second Presbyterian church, she felt that "the pious" in the nation's capital "are not like those at home, they are too much Divided with the world." Beyond leaving the contentment of the Hermitage and her home congregation, Rachel dreaded the innuendo and gossip she expected her presence to provoke. Since her husband's prominence had, against her wishes, brought her onto the public stage, elite socialites and Jackson's foes had ridiculed her appearance, her weight, and her rustic language and ways, including pipe-smoking with her husband. A story later emerged that Jackson had sheltered his wife in the 1828 campaign from the slanders against their marriage. More likely, she was well aware of how the "Enemyes of the Genls hav Dipt their arrows in wormwood & gall & sped them at me."[1] Regardless of what she knew, she no doubt anticipated facing more derogatory and hurtful assaults as her husband's First Lady.

Rachel nevertheless accepted her lot. "[A]s a grateful people have elected my husband [*to*] the highest office in the Union," she wrote, "it is my duty to follow [*him*] without a murmur, & to rejoice at not being separated from him."[2] Through a friend, she ordered two gowns from New Orleans for the inauguration, unaware that Nashville's ladies were putting together a fine new wardrobe to help her fill her new role. The planning and the anticipation, though, strained her health. Over the previous few years, she had increasingly experienced extreme fatigue and heart palpitations. Exhaustion forced her to cut short a shopping trip to Nashville. Shortly after returning home, she felt severe pains in her chest and left arm. Two doctors tried to relieve her discomfort, and a few days later, she appeared to be recovering. Jackson

Andrew Jackson. Jonathan M. Atkins, Oxford University Press. © Jonathan M. Atkins 2025.
DOI: 10.1093/9780191886812.003.0008

116 *Andrew Jackson: Old Hickory in Christian America*

told Richard Call on December 22 that he trusted "in a kind providence, that he will restore her to her usual health in due time to set out for washington."[3] That night, she suffered a relapse. Despite her doctors' efforts and Jackson's frantic pleadings, Rachel died shortly after nine o'clock.

Rachel's death devastated Jackson. During their nearly forty years together, their bond had only grown closer. She had stood beside him throughout his ordeals, and Jackson's regret from having had to leave her so often only compounded his grief. He spent the night of her death keeping vigil next to her body, mourning and searching for any possible sign of life. Two days later, on Christmas Eve, William Hume, the minister at the nearby church Jackson had built for her, preached Rachel's funeral at the corner of the Hermitage's garden, at the spot they had chosen for their burial. Jackson wept openly during the service, but he composed himself sufficiently to express his assurance that "she is now in the bliss of heaven, and . . . can suffer here no more on earth." "Providence knew what was best for her. For myself, I bow to God's will."[4] Anguish long stayed with him. For several weeks, he ate and drank little, and his hand shook so much that he had to dictate replies to letters of condolence. Meanwhile, he arranged for the construction of a domed monument to shelter her burial place. A long inscription carved into the slab over her grave proclaimed that "her piety went hand in hand with her benevolence, and she thanked her Creator for being permitted to do good."[5]

Faith helped Jackson deal with his grief. He took some comfort in Rachel's having lived long enough "to see the countless assaults of our enemies disarmed by the voice of our beloved country." More often, he referred to his need to accept God's will and to his assurance that she had gone to a better place. James Parton concluded that Rachel's death "subdued his spirit and corrected his speech," noting that Jackson avoided profanity for the rest of his life "except on occasions of extreme excitement." Even Reverend Ezra Stiles Ely, who had once exhorted Rachel to encourage Jackson's conversion, noted that he became "a different being in relation to spiritual & eternal matters . . ." and "begun to be one of the humble followers of Christ." Relying on divine grace to assure him that he would one day again be with her in Heaven, he told John Coffee that "as rational beings it behoves us so to live, to be prepared for death when it comes, with a reasonable hope of

"I find myself a solitary mourner . . ." 117

happiness through the atonement made by our blessed saviour on the cross." "Could this world compensate her loss," he lamented, "it might be found in the reflection, that her virtues, her piety & Christianity, has ensured her that future happiness, which is promised to the disciples of Christ, . . ." adding that "the grace which has taken from me the clear partner of my bosom . . . admonishes me by its sudden, solemn, & afflictive influence that I must soon follow her."[6]

Jackson wished he could "spend the remnant of my days" at the Hermitage "& be prepared, when Providence wills it, to unite with her in the realms above." But providence instead determined he should serve as president, "& to his will I must submit."[7] Gradually, he turned his mind back to his public responsibilities. Four weeks after Rachel's death, he left for Washington with an entourage that included Rachel's nephew Andrew J. Donelson, who would serve as his private secretary, and Donelson's wife and first cousin, Emily, who would assume the role of hostess at the executive mansion. Along the way, Jackson sometimes appeared before the crowds that gathered to greet him, but with John Eaton's help, he slipped into the capital on February 11 to avoid a boisterous public celebration planned to welcome him. For the next three weeks, as he met at his hotel with well-wishers, office-seekers, and influential politicians, the demands on his time likely distracted him from some of his grief. Still, the gloom from Rachel's passing remained with him well into his presidency. "I feel the great weight of the late affliction of providence in the bereavement I have been visited with in the loss of my dear wife," he wrote two months after taking office. Francis Preston Blair, who would become one of Jackson's closest advisors, recalled him reading each day a passage that Rachel had marked in her Bible, while Nicholas Trist, who briefly served as his private secretary, remembered Jackson wearing a miniature portrait of Rachel on a cord around his neck and looking at the likeness each night while reading from her prayer book.[8]

The raucous scene at his inauguration on March 4, 1829, contrasted sharply with Jackson's somber mood. Previous inaugurations had been small, dignified affairs, usually held inside the Capitol building and attended mainly by government officials and local elites. The popular campaign for the Hero of New Orleans now brought thousands of visitors to Washington to witness the start of his presidency. To accommodate the crowd, the ceremony was moved outside to the

118   *Andrew Jackson: Old Hickory in Christian America*

Capitol's East Portico, where somewhere between 15,000 and 20,000 spectators gathered to watch Jackson—wearing a simple black suit in mourning—deliver a ten-minute address, take the oath of office, and bow in deference to the crowd after kissing the Bible on which he swore the oath. A mob then rushed upon the new president, hoping to shake his hand and congratulate him personally. Jackson briefly found refuge inside the Capitol, but admirers swarmed around him as he rode a white horse down Pennsylvania Avenue to a public reception at the Executive Mansion. There, the throng overwhelmed him as the overflow of guests packed the house's lower floor. After Jackson again managed to escape the chaos, intruders' rowdy behavior caused thousands of dollars' worth of damage before servants lured the mob out of the mansion by offering liquor on the lawn.[9]

The clamor at his inauguration confirmed for Jackson that "the people" had chosen him to carry out their will. As president, he knew that he served a Christian people—in the sense that the vast majority, like himself, believed in God and accepted basic Christian tenets. His commitment to practicing his faith while in office mostly derived from his own inclination, especially as he mourned for Rachel, but his regular attendance at services—he rented pews at both Presbyterian and Episcopal churches—also displayed his respect for popular piety. Throughout his terms, he often expressed confidence that God would guide him and the nation. An early draft of his Inaugural Address began with an extensive prayer proclaiming his trust in "the smiles of that overruling Providence, 'in the hollow of whose hand,' is the destiny of nations, . . . which shall enable us to steer, the Bark of liberty, through every dificulty."[10] Revisions toned down the appeal to the divine, but the Address still concluded with an affirmation that the "Power whose providence mercifully protected our national infancy . . . will continue to make our beloved country the object of His divine care and gracious benediction." Similar pleas for God's guidance in drafts for his first message to Congress were likewise removed before Jackson submitted the message's final version the following December.[11]

Yet Jackson would not allow his faith to overwhelm what he saw as primarily a secular duty. Reverend Ely's call for the formation of "a Christian party in politics" expected "Christians, of all denominations," to elect rulers who "search the scriptures, assent to the truth, profess faith in Christ, [and] keep the Sabbath holy to God."

"I find myself a solitary mourner . . ." 119

Jackson, without directly repudiating his friend, implicitly rejected Ely's demand. As president, he would "do what my Judgment tells me is right . . . trusting my god to guide & direct me in all things, . . ." but he dismissed admonitions to use his authority to compel a particular Christian practice or viewpoint. He remained silent, for instance, when a "General Union for Promoting the Observance of the Christian Sabbath" flooded Congress with petitions demanding that the government close post offices and stop delivering mail on Sundays. Jackson himself often avoided traveling on Sundays, but unlike when he closed taverns and theaters as the Floridas' governor, he would not compel American citizens to respect Sunday as a holy day. Shortly before Jackson's inauguration, Kentucky Senator Richard M. Johnson—a devout Baptist—responded to the General Union's petitions with a report to Congress noting that "a variety of sentiment exists . . . on the subject of the Sabbath day." Johnson's conclusion that Congress had no authority "to determine what religion is true, or what false," and that "our government is a civil, and not a religious institution," represented the new administration's position.[12]

Throughout his presidency, Jackson tried to avoid the appearance of promoting any specific branch of Christianity. In 1831, William Conway, an attorney in Pittsburgh, protested against Jackson's endorsement for the American Sunday School Union, an interdenominational association formed to promote literacy through Bible reading. The organization represented a "sectarian plot," Conway charged. "*Presbyterianism* is the religion to be inculcated; and *civil ascendency* in the affairs of this government . . . is the grand ultimatum to which its ambitious and fanatical leaders aspire." Jackson assured the lawyer that he considered the Union "a plan for diseminating the Gospel, by a *union of all Christians.*" "I am no *sectarian*; tho a lover of the christian religion, . . ." he reiterated, and should the Union "give ascendency & preference to any sect or denomination, . . . my constitutional notions will compel me to frown down such an attempt because . . . freedom & an established religion are incompatible with each other." The following summer, while a cholera epidemic infected the nation, he rejected a Dutch Reformed Synod's request that he designate a day of national "fasting, humiliation, and prayer." "[W]hile I concur . . . in the efficacy of prayer, . . ." Jackson explained, he could not approve their petition without "transcending" the Constitution's limits on presidential

120 *Andrew Jackson: Old Hickory in Christian America*

authority, "and without feeling that I might in some degree disturb the security which religion now enjoys in this country, in its complete separation from the political concerns of the general government." Congress shortly afterward considered a similar resolution for a day of fasting, but Jackson likewise planned to disregard it, contending that "we ought to seek this alleviation . . . not as a Government but as a people."[13]

Religion had no significant influence on Jackson's selection of the members of his Cabinet. Needing to balance the various political interests that had supported his election, he wanted to appoint men who could work together as a true panel of advisors while avoiding the intrigues that he believed characterized James Monroe's cabinet. Other than John C. Calhoun, who had been re-elected vice president, Martin Van Buren stood as Jackson's most prominent supporter, and though Jackson knew him only casually, he gladly offered Van Buren the Cabinet's most prestigious position as secretary of state. For the other departments, he found his choices limited to men considered second-rate politicians because he refused to appoint anyone who might be promoted as a possible presidential candidate. Ultimately, he chose Pennsylvania's Samuel D. Ingham, a leader of Calhoun's supporters in Pennsylvania, as his secretary of the treasury. North Carolina's John Branch became secretary of the navy, while Georgia's John M. Berrien and Kentucky's William T. Barry accepted offers to serve as attorney general and postmaster general. The appointments underwhelmed Washington insiders, many of whom dismissed his Cabinet as the "Millennium of the Minnows." Jackson nevertheless declared it "one of the strongest . . . that has ever been in the United States, . . ." "a genuine old fashioned Cabinet . . ." that would "act together & form a counsel consultative."[14]

One appointment divided the Cabinet and preoccupied the administration's first two years. Jackson wanted at least one close associate among his official advisors, so for his secretary of war, he selected John Eaton, his former military aide and recent colleague in the Senate. A hint of social scandal followed Eaton into the office. For years, rumors had linked Eaton romantically to Margaret O'Neal Timberlake, the young wife of a naval purser and the daughter of William O'Neal, who owned the hotel where Jackson and the widower Eaton had resided while serving together in the Senate. Little

"I find myself a solitary mourner ..." 121

evidence survives to show the true nature of John's and Margaret's relationship. Eaton had apparently formed a good friendship with her husband, for with Purser John Timberlake's approval, Eaton escorted Margaret—"Peggy" to her detractors—to social events while Timberlake was away at sea. Before embarking on his last voyage, the young officer asked Eaton to take care of his wife should anything happen to him. Whispers rifled through Washington society that Mr. Eaton and Mrs. Timberlake were more than friends. When word came in late spring 1828 that Timberlake had died at sea, a story spread that he had committed suicide over his wife's infidelity. Eaton quickly concluded that he could best defend Margaret's honor by marrying her. Mrs. Timberlake at first resisted, wanting to wait the customary year of mourning for her first husband, but with two small children and her father struggling financially, she finally gave in to Eaton's persistence. A Methodist minister married the couple on January 1, 1829.[15]

Eaton miscalculated the depth of animosity against his new wife. Aside from the circumstances surrounding their marriage, the new Mrs. Eaton long suffered from a scandalous reputation. The accusations against her were likely unfair. Beyond rumors, no evidence exists to indicate that she was sexually active with Eaton or other men either before or during her marriage to Purser Timberlake. Social snobbery provoked much of the criticism. Margaret had attended one of Washington's finest female academies, but as a tavern keeper's daughter, many dismissed her as a social climber. Her marriage at age sixteen to a man holding a low-level position in the navy did little to improve her prospects. More damning was Margaret's disregard for the decorous and reserved behavior expected of ladies. After marrying Timberlake, she still formed friendships with the older male residents at her father's boarding house, often flirting with them more than deemed appropriate. Her forward, witty, and brash personality meanwhile struck many as overbearing. Emily Donelson, now the president's hostess, disliked Margaret's "bad temper" and "meddlesome disposition" and thought John Eaton's elevation to the Cabinet made her "too disagreeable to be endured." Washington society agreed with Jackson's niece and condemned the marriage, and numerous officials in Jackson's administration joined Emily in isolating the pushy and disreputable Mrs. Eaton.[16]

122   *Andrew Jackson: Old Hickory in Christian America*

Several of Jackson's friends and associates tried to discourage Eaton's appointment. After a note about Jackson's decision appeared in the *United States Telegraph*—the newspaper presumed to speak for the administration—a group of supporters from Tennessee called on him to express their disapproval. Reverend Ezra Stiles Ely, still hoping his friend would lead a Christian Party, wrote the new president a long letter listing six reasons why he believed Margaret Eaton "was a woman of ill fame before Major Eaton knew her." A fellow minister, Ely revealed, had told him about Margaret suffering a miscarriage in 1821—at a time when her husband had been away at sea for more than a year—while a "gentleman of high standing" from New York had overheard an associate say—after Margaret failed to respond to his greeting—that "she has forgotten the time when I slept with her." Ely proclaimed that Jackson's own *"dear departed and truly pious wife"* had shunned Mrs. Eaton, and he demanded that Jackson dismiss Eaton and instruct Emily Donelson to refuse *"to return the civilities of Mrs. Eaton."* "I would forgive Mr. and Mrs. E____ and do them all the kindness in my power," the minister concluded; "but forgiveness does not imply that a woman of lewd character for years should on marriage be received, at once, into chaste society."[17]

Eaton offered to decline the appointment, but Jackson declared that he "could not, nay I would not, abandon an old & tried friend." Meanwhile, he vehemently rejected the accusations against Margaret. The president had known Margaret and her family for twenty years. While residing at O'Neal's boarding house, he often joined the family at the services of the Methodist Church, and he enjoyed talking with Margaret and listening to her play the piano. Jackson also knew about Eaton's relationship with Margaret's first husband, and he well remembered giving Richard K. Call a *"severe lecture"* on *"female virtue"* in 1824 after Margaret rejected Call's attempt to seduce her, when the young officer accosted her to the point that she had to defend herself with a pair of fireplace tongs. Besides, Jackson reasoned, Eaton, Timberlake, and O'Neal were all brother Masons, like Jackson himself, which meant that Eaton "could not have had criminal intercourse with another mason's wife, without being one of the most abandoned of men." Jackson thus dismissed the charges against Margaret as nothing more than "the sneers and *tittle tattle* of a set of gossips," and when Eaton informed the president of his intention to marry her, he

"I find myself a solitary mourner . . ." 123

not only approved their union but encouraged the couple to marry as early as possible.[18]

Jackson insisted that he would never force anyone to socialize with the Eatons, but he also made it clear that he expected all members of his administration to pay the secretary of war's family their due respect. When Washington socialites and the wives of several federal officials ignored Mrs. Eaton at the inauguration, Jackson set out to prove her innocence. He dismissed the warnings from his Tennessee friends as "the dupes of my designing enemy," and he wrote a lengthy reply to Ely informing the minister that he had been "badly advised." "Mrs. Jackson," the president insisted, "to the last moment of her life, believed Mrs. Eaton to be an innocent and much injured woman." Had she lived, Rachel would have accepted Mrs. Eaton and stood as one of her leading defenders, for the accusations against her friend's wife were nothing more than *"rumour mere rumour."* That Ely's friend did not "instantly" challenge the "villain" who claimed to have slept with her only dishonored the supposed gentleman, and a clergyman spreading the miscarriage story "seems to me to be so inconsistent with the charities of the Christian religion . . . that it gives me pain to read it." Alluding to John 3:19, Jackson reminded Ely that "falsehood deals in sly and dark insinuations and prefers *darkness* because its deeds are evil," and he concluded by quoting Isaac Watts's version of the 101st Psalm: "the liar's tongue We ever hate, and banish from our sight."[19]

Defending Mrs. Eaton's reputation took up much of the beleaguered president's time. Margaret complicated matters when she and her mother confronted Ely at his home in Philadelphia to demand an explanation for the miscarriage story. The minister finally revealed his source as John N. Campbell, the pastor at the Presbyterian church in Washington that Jackson and the Eatons attended. Aware that his identity would be revealed, Campbell called on Jackson at the executive mansion and claimed he learned about the miscarriage from Margaret's doctor, Elijah Craven, who had passed away in 1823. Jackson asked why Campbell had not taken this *"vile tale"* directly to Mrs. Timberlake to give her an opportunity to "remove this stain upon her character, . . ." thus "pursuing the golden rule of doing to others as we would they should do unto us." The next day, Jackson visited the Eatons's home to review John Timberlake's records to prove that he had indeed been at home when the lost child had been conceived.

124 *Andrew Jackson: Old Hickory in Christian America*

When he presented this information to Campbell, the minister insisted that Jackson "had mistaken *him*, as to the date," though he refused to correct Jackson with a different date. "[P]oor deluded man," Jackson lamented to Ely, "he has forgot that he has assumed the affirmative, and if he do not produce other proof, that his reputation as an embassador of christ is gone forever."[20]

Despite Jackson's efforts, Washington society's rejection of the Eatons infected his administration. Custom dictated that the wives of Cabinet officers and high-ranking politicians pay at least one social call to each other to show their respect. When Mrs. Eaton made her calls, most recipients were away, so in accordance with convention, she left a printed card with her name at each home. Most ladies, though, refused to pay her the expected return visit. The Cabinet members worked with John Eaton in their official capacities, but relations became strained as Samuel Ingham's and John Branch's wives and the widower John Berrien's niece and daughters kept their distance from Margaret. The tensions even divided Jackson's family. Emily Donelson agreed to receive Mrs. Eaton when she called at the executive mansion, but she despised Margaret and refused to visit the Eatons's home. John Eaton condescendingly chastised the "young and uninformed" Emily for listening to a "little nest of inquisitors," and the word that Margaret referred to Emily as a "poor silly thing" further widened the rift. Emily then deeply offended the Eatons. While pregnant with her second child, Emily fainted while on an outing on a steamboat; as she revived, Margaret offered her fan to help cool her, but the president's half-conscious niece rejected Mrs. Eaton's assistance. The incident infuriated the Eatons, but to Jackson's dismay, Andrew Donelson staunchly stood by his wife.[21]

Jackson hoped he could eliminate the Eaton distraction before his first Congress convened in December 1829, so on September 10, he met with Reverends Ely and Campbell, William Lewis, Andrew Donelson, and, except for John Eaton, the members of his Cabinet. There, the president presented his evidence vindicating Margaret Eaton's character. The ministers remained unconvinced. Ely admitted that he had misjudged John Eaton, but when he remained skeptical about Margaret's morality, Jackson shouted, "She is as chaste as a virgin!" Campbell eventually walked out, standing behind his story about Margaret's miscarriage and insisting that Jackson had

"I find myself a solitary mourner . . ." 125

misconstrued its date. The Cabinet officers pledged to continue to work with Eaton, persuading Jackson that the meeting had accomplished its purpose, but the shunning of Margaret continued nevertheless. In late November, Jackson's first official dinner for his administration proved a social disaster. The Cabinet members and their families duly attended, but the guests ate quickly, contributed little to an awkward conversation, and left as soon as they had finished. Over the next several weeks, the Cabinet officers, foreign dignitaries, and other socialites held their own dinner parties, but most neglected to invite the Eatons. When a host did invite the controversial couple, many ladies—supported by their husbands—refused to attend.[22]

At first, Jackson assumed that "the minions of Mr. Clay" had launched the smear campaign against Margaret "in hopes I would be intimidated and drop Eaton" from the Cabinet. By the late summer of 1829, though, he concluded that Vice President John C. Calhoun masterminded the attacks. Calhoun's wife, Floride, committed one of the first notable slights when she declined to return a visit from Mrs. Eaton, but more than social differences encouraged Jackson to suspect Calhoun. Although Jackson had worked well with Calhoun in the past, the two had never developed a close friendship. The president knew, too, that Calhoun expected to succeed him, even though his vice president increasingly appeared to oppose several of his administration's policies. While Eaton loyally upheld Jackson's decisions, the *United States Telegraph*, the administration's newspaper under the editorship of Calhoun loyalist Duff Green, more often presented Calhoun's outlook than Jackson's. Samuel Ingham, one of the Cabinet officers most resistant to Margaret Eaton, had long allied politically with Calhoun, and Jackson increasingly suspected that John Branch and John Berrien joined Ingham in avoiding the Eatons to promote Calhoun's ambitions. Gradually, the circumstances convinced Jackson that Calhoun's allies spread lies about the Eatons to eliminate the vice president's opponents, allow Calhoun to dominate the administration, and possibly push Jackson himself out of office.[23]

As Jackson's faith in Calhoun waned, his confidence in Martin Van Buren grew. In the Cabinet, only William Barry and the longtime widower Van Buren stood by the Eatons. Jackson especially appreciated the kindness his secretary of state extended to Margaret, particularly when Van Buren openly welcomed the Eatons at two successful

126 *Andrew Jackson: Old Hickory in Christian America*

dinner parties that he hosted. Jackson and Van Buren likewise drew closer as they consulted on policy, discovering that they shared similar views on issues and on republican principles. Eventually, the president invited the New Yorker to join him on his daily horse rides around Washington, where they discussed topics like politics, what Van Buren labeled the "Eaton Malaria," and, likely, the grief following the death of a spouse. As a result, the president came to rely on his secretary of state more than he did any other official. Jackson signaled his trust in Van Buren in late 1829, when the president fell ill and feared his end might be near. At William Lewis's urging, Jackson wrote a letter to John Overton declaring Van Buren "not only well qualified, but deserves to fill the highest office in the gift of the people who, in him, will find a true friend and safe depository of their rights and liberty." In case of the president's death, Jackson concluded, Lewis had his "permission to make such use" of the letter "as you may think most advisable."[24]

Jackson's health improved with the New Year, soon before his final break with his vice president. In the spring of 1830, William Lewis showed Jackson a letter, written by Georgia Governor John Forsythe, containing William Crawford's claim that, after the invasion of Florida in 1818, Calhoun, the then secretary of war, had argued strongly in Cabinet meetings for Jackson's punishment. Jackson had always assumed that Calhoun had defended him, but he sent the letter to the vice president and demanded an explanation. Eventually, Calhoun provided a fifty-two-page response acknowledging that, while he "neither questioned your patriotism, nor your motives," he had favored an investigation because Jackson "had exceeded your orders and had acted on your own responsibility." Jackson still insisted that President Monroe had authorized the invasion; comparing Calhoun's duplicity with Brutus's betrayal of Julius Caesar, he tersely informed the vice president, "no further communication with you on this subject is necessary." Politicians loyal to both tried to reconcile the two, but Jackson ignored Calhoun's further overtures while vainly seeking confirmation that his friend John Rhea had sent him a letter conveying Monroe's approval. With the breach irreparable, Calhoun publicized their rift in February 1831 when he published his correspondence with Jackson on the Florida controversy, including comments that implicitly condemned Van Buren for manipulating the issue to eliminate the vice president as a political rival.[25]

"I find myself a solitary mourner . . ." 127

The split with Calhoun had no impact on the cabinet's division over the Eatons. Despite Jackson's demands, Secretaries Ingham, Branch, and Berrien insisted they could work with Eaton, but they made it clear that they would not force their families to accept his wife. The president hoped a visit to Tennessee in the summer of 1830 would allow Nashville society to show Washington how to extend courtesy properly. A crowd of between 300 and 500 guests celebrated the Eatons at a barbecue in Franklin, John Eaton's hometown, and Jackson and John Overton both held successful dinners for the secretary of war at their plantations. Nashville's elite, though, treated the couple coolly and failed to hold the reception for them that the president wanted. Jackson blamed the setbacks on Calhoun's influence on the Donelsons, and he determined that Emily Donelson should remain in Tennessee until she agreed to treat Margaret Eaton as she would any other visitor to the president's house. At the last minute, Andrew Donelson agreed to return to work for his uncle, but once back in the capital, their relationship decayed to the point that, for several days, he and Jackson communicated only through letters, even though both resided in the executive mansion. One of these notes deeply hurt Jackson when Donelson carelessly referred to himself as the president's "guest." "You were my family, my chosen family," Jackson assured his nephew, but he insisted they receive Mrs. Eaton, for, as he told John Coffee, "the nation expects me to controle my household."[26]

Political circumstances appeared to make a satisfactory resolution of the dilemma impossible. John Eaton's resignation would appear to hand his political enemies a victory, but Jackson had so strongly backed his secretary of war that dismissing Ingham, Branch, and Berrien would open him to the charge that Margaret Eaton actually controlled the administration. Finally, Martin Van Buren offered a way to escape the impasse. In the spring of 1831, he proposed to resign as secretary of state, claiming that public discussion of him as Jackson's possible successor had made him a distraction to the administration. Once convinced that his friend was not abandoning him, Jackson joined Van Buren in persuading Eaton to resign as well. The departure of two Cabinet officers would allow Jackson to expect all the secretaries to resign. Since his Cabinet "had come in harmoniously & as a unit, & as a part was about to leave me, . . ." he explained, a "reorganization" would be necessary "to guard against misrepresentation." The

128   *Andrew Jackson: Old Hickory in Christian America*

president could then appoint new heads for each department, without the appearance of having given in to either side. Van Buren and Eaton thus submitted their resignations in early April 1831. Within the next two weeks, Ingham and Branch also resigned, albeit reluctantly, as did Berrien when he returned to Washington after an extended stay at his home in Savannah. Over the summer, Jackson selected a new team of Cabinet officers, with men loyal to Jackson, generally unified, and able to work without the social tensions arising from the Eaton controversy.[27]

For a while, the "Cabinet Purge" produced the uproar that Jackson had wanted to avoid. Margaret Eaton, for one, accused the president of betraying her husband. Shortly after John Eaton's resignation, she received Jackson and Van Buren coldly when they called at her home. Newspapers throughout the Union reprinted Washington papers' accounts of the purge, making the Eaton Affair for the first time a national topic. Jackson's political foes indeed charged that Mrs. Eaton had directed the firings of Ingham, Branch, and Berrien. Calhoun's forces condemned Van Buren's influence on the president, while the three dismissed secretaries complained that they had been unjustly dismissed. John Branch and Samuel Ingham both published accounts claiming they had been ousted merely for refusing to socialize with Margaret Eaton. John Eaton responded to his former colleagues' claims with threats of violence. Branch avoided Eaton's demand for a duel until he could leave Washington, as did Ingham, who before his departure traveled through the capital surrounded by bodyguards. Margaret Eaton later claimed that she overheard a messenger from Jackson advising her husband that he "must kill" Ingham if the former treasury secretary refused to meet him on a field of honor.[28]

With John Eaton no longer in the government, the furor soon subsided. In September 1831, Eaton published his own "Candid Appeal" refuting his detractors' charges, but by then, more substantive issues had pushed the "Eaton Affair" off the public stage. Andrew and Emily Donelson returned to Washington later that month and soon settled back into their roles as the president's secretary and hostess. Jackson still insisted they extend courtesy to Margaret, but his demand became moot after the Eatons left Washington. Meanwhile, Jackson rewarded Van Buren by naming him the American minister to Great Britain. The Senate rejected the appointment when Vice President

"I find myself a solitary mourner . . ." 129

Calhoun broke a tie and voted against his rival's confirmation—infuriating Jackson but setting into motion the movements that culminated in Van Buren's own election as vice president. The president also hoped the Tennessee legislature would send Eaton back to Washington as a senator, but when incumbents Hugh L. White and Felix Grundy both refused to give up their seats, he instead appointed his friend as the governor of the Florida Territory before sending him to represent the United States in Spain in 1836. By then, the Eaton Affair remained little more than a sore memory.

Historians often attribute Jackson's staunch defense of the Eatons to paranoia, stubbornness, and shortsightedness. Misreading social resentment toward Margaret as personal attacks against him, scholars claim, he made acceptance of the Eatons a test of loyalty to his administration, one that could have derailed his presidency before it started. Some biographers presume that he projected onto Margaret his memories of Rachel, comparing the libels against Mrs. Eaton with the charges against his own recently departed wife. Jackson himself always simply explained that, as he told his nephew, he had "never . . . deserted a friend without cause, nor never will, as long as his acts were pure & upright."[29] He likewise long knew Margaret Eaton and never doubted her virtue, and the fact that Eaton and Margaret's father were Masonic brothers only strengthened Jackson's commitment to stand by those who had stood by him. To sacrifice a longstanding friend and comrade, or to abandon an innocent female to slander, would have betrayed the sense of honor that had guided him since adolescence. Dropping Eaton would not only give his rivals a political victory, it would also mean acting in the disreputable and corrupt manner of his enemies.

Historians also usually dismiss religion's influence on Jackson's conduct, stressing instead his fuming at the "meddling" clergymen urging him to dump the Eatons. More recent scholars argue that the "Affair" helped to define women's political and cultural influence in the young American republic.[30] To Jackson himself, defending the Eatons was the moral position, and he often expressed his support for them in Christian terms. He admitted that Margaret Eaton "may have her imprudencies," and he always agreed with the fundamental tenets of Reverend Ely's and Reverend Campbell's faith, including—as an adult far removed from his rambunctious youth—their views on

130   *Andrew Jackson: Old Hickory in Christian America*

the importance of sexual purity for ladies. But Jackson thought her "imprudencies" should be "treated as improprieties" and not lead to her treatment "as a lady without virtue." The ministers may have expected their president to lead a Christian nation, but Jackson resented their hiding under "the hypocritical cloak of religion" and refused to approve their "secrete inquisition" to "decree who shall, & who shall not, come into society."[31] As a result, the Eaton imbroglio widened the breach between those who, like Jackson, considered the United States a "Christian Nation" because a mostly Christian population privately practiced a variety of beliefs, and those who expected a Christian party to elect devout leaders and enforce a distinct branch of the faith. Advocates of government-backed morality would soon openly oppose the administration and become an important wing of an opposition party, while those following Jackson's lead would continue to promote government as "a civil, and not a religious institution."

Jackson always believed he knew the truth about the Eatons and that "truth, being powerful, ever has, & ever will, prevail." In a way, it did. In 1840, John Eaton angrily broke with his friend when the former president recommended his recall as minister to Spain. He returned to Washington to set up a successful law practice, and this time, the capital's ladies accepted his wife as a social peer.[32] Eaton's newfound association with Jackson's political enemies eased their acceptance, for by then, Jackson's presidency had divided the nation into two parties that, among other differences, presented contrasting views on what it meant to be a Christian nation.

Notes

1. Rachel Jackson to Mary Purnell Donelson, January 27, 1825, *PAJ*, 6:21; Rachel Jackson to Elizabeth Watson, July 18, 1828, *PAJ*, 6:367.
2. Rachel Jackson to Mrs. L. A. W. Douglas, December 3, 1828, *PAJ*, 6:538.
3. Andrew Jackson to Richard K. Call, December 22, 1828, *PAJ*, 6:546.
4. Wise, *Seven Decades of the Union*, 114–16.
5. Remini, *Course of American Freedom*, 151–56.
6. Andrew Jackson to Jean Baptiste Plauché, December 27, 1828, *PAJ*, 6:547. Jackson to John Coffee, January 17, 1829, *PAJ*, 7:12; Jackson to Mary Middleton Rutledge Fogg, January 17, 1829, *PAJ*, 7:14; Ezra Stiles Ely to Jackson, July 3, 1829, *PAJ*, 7:322; Parton, *Life of Andrew Jackson*, 3:159.
7. Andrew Jackson to Hardy Murfree Cryer, May 16, 1829, *PAJ*, 7:223.

"I find myself a solitary mourner . . ."   131

8. Remini, *Course of American Freedom*, 158–59, 331–32, 400; Parton, *Life of Andrew Jackson*, 3:602.

9. Remini, *Course of American Freedom*, 172–80; David S. Heidler and Jeanne T. Heidler, "Not a Ragged Mob; The Inauguration of 1829," *White House History* 15 (1997):134–43.

10. "Inaugural Address (draft)," *PAJ*, 7:75.

11. Andrew Jackson, First Inaugural Address, March 4, 1829, *Messages and Papers*, 2:438; "First Annual Message to Congress" (draft), *PAJ*, 7:601–602, 7:629–30.

12. Ely, *The Duty of Christian Freemen to Elect Christian Rulers*, 5–6, 8–9; Andrew Jackson to Ralph E.W. Earl, March 16, 1829, *PAJ*, 7:98; "Transportation of the Mail on the Sabbath," Broadsides, Leaflets, and Pamphlets from America and Europe, Library of Congress, Washington, D.C.

13. William B. Conway to Andrew Jackson, March 31, 1831, *PAJ*, 9:156; Jackson to Conway, April 14, 1831, *PAJ*, 9:166–67; Jackson to John Freeman Schermerhorn, June 12, 1832, *PAJ*, 10:302; "To the United States Congress (not sent)," *PAJ*, 10:355.

14. "Memorandum on Administrative Policy," *PAJ*, 7:69; Andrew Jackson to John C. McLemore, April 26, 1829, *PAJ*, 7:183; Donald B. Cole, *The Presidency of Andrew Jackson* (Lawrence: University Press of Kansas, 1993), 26–32.

15. John F. Marszalek, *The Petticoat Affair: Manners, Mutiny, and Sex in Andrew Jackson's White House* (New York: The Free Press, 1997), 38–48.

16. Marszalek, *Petticoat Affair*, 32–36, 47–53; Cole, *Presidency of Andrew Jackson*, 37–38.

17. Ezra Stiles Ely to Andrew Jackson, March 18, 1829, *PAJ*, 7:101–104; Marszalek, *Petticoat Affair*, 63–66, 77–80.

18. Andrew Jackson to John Coffee, March 22, 1829, *PAJ*, 7:109; Jackson to Richard K. Call, May 18, 1829; *PAJ*, 7:227; Jackson to William B. Lewis, September 10, 1829, *PAJ*, 7:424–25; Jackson to Ezra Stiles Ely, March 23, 1829, *PAJ*, 7:115; Jackson to John C. McLemore, December 25, 1830, *PAJ*, 8:708; John H. Eaton to Jackson, December 7, 1828, *PAJ*, 6:541–42; Jackson to Susan W. Decatur, January 2, 1830, *PAJ*, 8:5; Marszalek, *Petticoat Affair*, 22–23.

19. Andrew Jackson to Ralph E.W. Earl, March 16, 1829, *PAJ*, 7:98; Jackson to Ezra Stiles Ely, March 23, 1829, *PAJ*, 7:113–18; Marszalek, *Petticoat Affair*, 80–82.

20. "Statement of an Interview with John Nicholson Campbell," *PAJ*, 7:405–11; Andrew Jackson to Ezra Stiles Ely, September 3, 1829, *PAJ*, 7:404; Marszalek, *Petticoat Affair*, 22–23, 92–100.

21. Meacham, *American Lion*, 79; Cheatham, *Andrew Jackson, Southerner*, 122–23; Marszalek, *Petticoat Affair*, 85–88, 101–105, 113–14.

22. Marszalek, *Petticoat Affair*, 107–14.

23. Andrew Jackson to Ezra Stiles Ely, March 23, 1829, *PAJ*, 7:116; Jackson to John Coffee, March 22, 1829, *PAJ*, 7:109; Marszalek, *Petticoat Affair*, 52–55, 121–24.

24. Andrew Jackson to John Overton, December 31, 1829, *PAJ*, 7:656; "Note by William Berkeley Lewis," *PAJ*, 7:657–58.

25. Andrew Jackson to John C. Calhoun, May 13, 1830, *PAJ*, 8:255–59; Calhoun to Jackson, May 29, 1830, *PAJ*, 8:306, 310; Jackson to Calhoun, May 30, 1830, *PAJ*, 8:322; Marszalek, *Petticoat Affair*, 126–29, 148–56.

26. Andrew J. Donelson to Andrew Jackson, October 30, 1830, *PAJ*, 8:594–95; Jackson to Donelson, October 30, 1830, *PAJ*, 8:595–96; Jackson to John Coffee, July 20, 1830, *PAJ*, 8:435; Marszalek, *Petticoat Affair*, 129–46.

132 *Andrew Jackson: Old Hickory in Christian America*

27. Andrew Jackson to John Branch, April 19, 1831, *PAJ*, 9:193; Marszalek, *Petticoat Affair*, 157–63.

28. Marszalek, *Petticoat Affair*, 163–76, 186–94.

29. Andrew Jackson to Andrew J. Donelson, May 5, 1831, *PAJ*, 9:230.

30. Remini, *Course of American Freedom*, 205; Catherine E. Allgor, *Parlor Politics: In Which the Ladies of Washington Help Build a City and a Government* (Charlottesville: University Press of Virginia, 2000), 210–38; Kirsten E. Wood, "'One Woman So Dangerous to Public Morals': Gender and Power in the Eaton Affair," *Journal of the Early Republic* 17 (Summer 1997):237–75.

31. Andrew Jackson to Emily T. Donelson, January 20, 1831, *PAJ*, 9:34; Jackson to John C. McLemore, November 24, 1829, *PAJ*, 7:567; Jackson to McLemore, September 28, 1829, *PAJ*, 7:435.

32. Andrew Jackson to Francis Preston, March 6, 1830, *PAJ*, 8:124; Marszalek, *Petticoat Affair*, 221–25.

9

"We want them . . . free from colision with the whites"

Though mourning Rachel and beleaguered by the Eaton Affair, Andrew Jackson aggressively took on his presidential responsibilities. One of his primary objectives involved determining the fate of the more than 100,000 Native Americans living east of the Mississippi River. For these "Indians"—as white Americans referred to them—two centuries of violent conflict with American settlers had largely come to an end. Several small tribes lay scattered north of the Ohio River, while five larger nations—the Cherokees, Creeks, Choctaws, Chickasaws, and Seminoles—spanned across the Southern states. Devastation from the War of 1812 and the withdrawal of British and Spanish support left the Natives in a weak position, making it virtually impossible for them to hold back American expansion. Still, they resisted being completely absorbed into the dominant white culture, adopting European and American goods and technology to their benefit but maintaining their distinct national identities and, as the foundation of their independence, clinging to their ancestral lands.

No direct evidence exists of Jackson's first interaction with Indians. During his boyhood in the Waxhaws, the nearby Catawbas largely kept to themselves, while raids from the more intimidating Cherokees had ended shortly before his parents migrated to the Southern colonial frontier. Undoubtedly, Jackson saw people from both nations when they occasionally came to his community to trade. One North Carolinian recalled that Jackson and his mother were "inveterate haters of the Indians on account of their barbarities." When he first fought against Natives remains unknown. While he perhaps encountered Cherokee warriors as an irregular fighter during the American Revolution, more

Andrew Jackson. Jonathan M. Atkins, Oxford University Press. © Jonathan M. Atkins 2025.
DOI: 10.1093/9780191886812.003.0009

134   *Andrew Jackson: Old Hickory in Christian America*

likely his first confrontations came after his move to Tennessee. Early histories contend that he fought in a retaliatory expedition within six months of his arrival in Davidson County, and several stories—likely embellished—describe clashes with hostile Natives during his frequent early crossings through the wilderness between Nashville and Jonesborough. While he probably did not participate in the Southwest Territory's unauthorized military expeditions against Chickamauga and Cherokee villages in the early 1790s, he almost certainly took part in the raids and counterraids with Natives that plagued the early frontier. One early acquaintance claimed that Jackson was "always ready to pursue a party of Indians that was in doing mischief," and long before he first entered Congress in 1796, he had earned his reputation as an experienced Indian fighter.[1]

Like other white Americans, Jackson considered Indians to be primitive peoples. The Natives he encountered on the Southern frontier actually had well-developed economies and stable social and political systems. They lived in settled communities, grew crops on communal farms, and held elaborate religious beliefs. Neither Jackson nor his neighbors, though, either penetrated into the depths of Native culture or cared much about it. The Natives' rejection of individually owned farms, along with their reliance on hunting and fishing as important sources for food, convinced Americans that Indians wandered aimlessly through their lands, sometimes communed in simple small villages, survived on what their hunters killed and their women gathered, were superstitious, and suffered under the authority of despotic chiefs. Individual Indians, Jackson assumed, were "fickle," with "avarice" and "fear" their "predominant & governing passions." Their rejection of Christianity marked them as uncivilized, and that "depravity, intrigue, cunning, and native cruelty" characterized them as a people. Though Jackson and his men also attacked noncombatants and often exceeded the natives' ferocity in battle, the Indians' vicious brutality in warfare and attacks on "defenceless weomen and children" further proved to him that they were "ruthless savages."[2]

Jackson could show respect for individual Natives, and often he trusted or displayed compassion toward Indians despite their supposed ignorance and simplicity. On military campaigns, he relied heavily on Indian scouts and readily accepted alliances with friendly Natives—though he noted an "inconvenience attending Indian forces" was

"We want them . . . free from colision with the whites" 135

that "you cannot keep them in the field; as soon as they perform an excursion, and take a scalp, they must go home and dance."[3] After the Battle at Horseshoe Bend, he ordered his Cherokee and Creek allies to stop killing their surviving Red Stick enemies. When the East Tennessee militia attacked a village of Hillabee Indians, with whom he had arranged a truce, Jackson ordered the arrest and court martial of William Cocke, the former senator who commanded the troops. Similarly, during the Florida invasion, he arrested a captain in the Georgia militia and demanded the state's governor punish him for leading an unauthorized attack on the Chehaws, a faction of Creeks with whom Jackson had formed an alliance. At the Creek War's conclusion, William Weatherford, the chief responsible for the massacre of Americans at Fort Mims, surrendered voluntarily and appealed for assistance for the tribes' women and children. Weatherford's demeanor so impressed Jackson that the general paroled the chief on the condition he attempt to persuade other warriors to lay down their weapons.

Most notably, Jackson took in three young Indian boys as wards. The circumstances for his taking in Theodore, apparently an infant found on a battlefield during the Creek War, are unknown, and the baby likely died shortly after his arrival at the Hermitage. A second child, called Charley, had been sent to Jackson by a Creek chief. Rachel considered Charley "a fine Boy indeed," and after he grew up, he apparently stayed on to work with the Hermitage's horses. The best-known tale of Jackson taking in an Indian child came after his men retrieved a toddler clinging to his dead mother after the battle at Tallushatchee. "[C]harity and christianity says he ought to be taken care of," Jackson explained to Rachel. "[H]e is a Savage [but one] that fortune has thrown in my h[ands]," noting that "he may have been given to me for some Valuable purpose," and that the toddler's orphaned condition "is so much like myself I feel an unusual sympathy for him." The daughter of one of Jackson's officers gave the child the name "Lyncoya" and took care of him in Huntsville until the Creek War ended, when the general sent the boy to the Hermitage as a playmate and "pett"—a term Jackson often used for young children—for Andrew Jr. Later, Jackson sent Lyncoya along with his adopted son to Davidson Academy in Nashville with the intention of eventually sending the Indian child to the US Military Academy. Once he

136   *Andrew Jackson: Old Hickory in Christian America*

realized that his political enemies would block Lyncoya's appointment to West Point, Jackson instead arranged for his apprenticeship as a saddler—the same trade that Jackson himself was supposed to have learned as a youth.[4]

Still, Jackson never forgot the differences between Native peoples and his own. During the same campaign in which he took in Lyncoya, the general ordered his men to count the number of Indians killed by cutting the noses off their corpses—something he likely never did, and likely would not have considered doing, to the bodies of his European enemies. On the Florida campaign, he ordered the execution of two Seminole chiefs without the trials he accorded to the Britons Alexander Arbuthnot and Robert Ambrister. Andrew Jr. likewise never warmed up to Lyncoya. The Native boy's construction of a bow, despite having "no intercourse with the Indians," intrigued Jackson, but he also frustrated the general when he put on war paint, hid behind furniture, and jumped out screaming to scare other children. A story later emerged that Lyncoya ran away to return to his people, but he was at the Hermitage when he died of tuberculosis at about age sixteen on June 1, 1828. A year later, Jackson's friend Samuel Houston shocked his former commander when he suddenly resigned as Tennessee's governor, left behind his new bride, and took refuge with a band of Cherokees, "Houston must be deranged, or what is worse bewitched," the stunned Jackson wrote. "It cannot be possible you have taken the determination to settle with the Indians and become a savage, . . ." he told his one-time protégé, "unless, indeed, you have determined to study theology and become a missionary amongst them."[5]

Jackson likely intended his comment simply to mock the absurdity of his friend's actions. If serious, he would have had little hope for Houston's missionary efforts. His friend Gideon Blackburn had once established a school in the Cherokee nation, but Blackburn's teaching and preaching produced modest results at best. Still, Jackson insisted, the Indians "must be civilized." Soon after the War of 1812, he contended that their transformation into a modern people offered the best hope both to ensure the Natives' survival and to end the conflicts that had long ravaged the frontier. "The game being destroyed, they can no longer exist by their bows & arrows & Gun," he wrote to the new president on James Monroe's inauguration day. "They must lay them aside and produce by labour, from the earth a subsistence."

"We want them . . . free from colision with the whites" 137

Reducing Indian landholdings, he added, would further their advancement: "circumscribe their bounds—put into their hands, the utensils of husbandry—yield them protection, and enforce obedience to those just laws provided for their benefit, and in a short time they will be civilized." Of course, American possession of Indian lands would benefit speculators like Jackson in his younger days and his current circle of friends. Nevertheless, he insisted that replacing the Natives with "a dense white population" would integrate the frontier more tightly into the Union and—by reducing the chance of an Indian alliance with either the British or Spanish—further secure the republic from its foes. Locating the Indians near "an industrious and virtuous population" would meanwhile "set them good examples" that would influence "their manners habits, and customs."[6]

Congress, Jackson contended, should thus take immediate and direct action to promote the Indians' advancement. More than other American leaders, he rejected claims that the Indians existed within the Union as independent foreign nations. Instead, he insisted, they were "subjects of the United States, inhabiting its territory and acknowledging its sovereignty"; they had "only a possessory right to the soil, for the purpose of hunting and not the right of domain," or ownership. Because they were dependent peoples, Congress could "carry into effect any law . . . necessary and proper to pass for the welfare & happiness of the Indian and for the convenience and benefit of the u. states." Likewise, he argued that negotiating treaties with Natives as if they were independent nations presented "an absurdity not to be reconciled to the principles of our Government." He admitted that the young American Union once had to resort to treaties because it was "too weak to execute any law passed for the regulation of the Indian tribes," but since the recent war's conclusion, "the arm of Government is sufficiently strong" while the Natives stood too weak to resist. Just as the Constitution allowed the national legislature to take a citizens' property for public use, the federal government could regulate and appropriate Native lands for the national welfare. Direct congressional legislation over the Indian peoples, Jackson concluded, would do more to benefit Natives than "the farce . . . of holding treaties with them."[7]

Monroe read Jackson's observations "with great interest," but the new president followed his predecessors' approach and continued to respect treaties with Indians. Jackson likewise avoided challenging

138   *Andrew Jackson: Old Hickory in Christian America*

long-standing national policy. When ordered, he would negotiate with Native leaders. In these talks, he took an aggressive approach, treating the nations less like independent peoples than as the dependents he considered them. Addressing Natives as "Friends & Brothers" under the leadership of "your father the President of the United States," his strategy was to "come out with candor," state explicitly what he wanted from a tribe, and promise "nothing to them, but what you will religiously perform," for "nothing will defeat a negotiation with Indians so soon as the discovery of an attempt to deceive them." After stating his demands, he stood firm, hoping to intimidate tribal leaders into accepting his terms, but he ultimately acknowledged that "a Barter cannot be obtained without giving the Indians Boot"—that is, bribes. Through these tactics, the agreements he concluded after 1815 acquired more than fifty million acres of Indian lands for the United States, earning for him the sobriquet among Natives as "Sharp Knife" while, he insisted, securing the Southwestern frontier and furthering the Indians' advance toward "civilization."[8]

While negotiating with Cherokees in 1817, Jackson for the first time sought to get a Native nation to agree to removal—that is, moving to a region west of the Mississippi River that they would receive in exchange for their lands in the east. Federal officials had begun to promote removal a decade before, even though it contradicted their commitment to "assimilation," the government's long-standing policy of attempting to "civilize" Indians through teaching them to work on individual, privately owned farms while advocating their conversion to Christianity. Thomas Jefferson, while still pursuing assimilation, instructed Indian agents to try to persuade the nations to trade their lands for new homes in the recently purchased Louisiana Territory. In 1808, a band of about 1,000 Cherokees agreed to move to an area that later became part of Arkansas, and Jackson's instructions for his 1817 talks with Cherokee leaders authorized him to encourage more Natives to join their tribesmen in the west. Confident that removal would ensure "Justice" for the Indians, Jackson expected "at least one half of the nation will relinquish their right here and go to the Arkansaw, perhaps the whole with very few exceptions." The nation resisted, but tribal authorities ultimately agreed to trade 2 million acres for an equivalent amount of western land. About 6,000 more Cherokees went west, while those remaining east would receive grants

"We want them . . . free from colision with the whites"   139

of 640 acres each if they agreed to become American citizens, rather than follow the leaders of their tribe.[9]

After these negotiations, Jackson never again spoke of the benefits of surrounding Indians, as he had told Monroe, with "an industrious and virtuous population." Henceforth, he would call for keeping Native and white Americans separate. He assumed, too, that most Indians, "left to themselves, would freely make this election" and choose to move west, but "some whitemen and half breeds," believing that "their income would be destroyed by the removal of the Indians," "overawed" most Natives into resistance.[10] Actually, few Natives wanted either to relocate or to become American citizens, and the Southern Indians especially used the federal government's assistance to counter the appeals to move and show that they were indeed civilized peoples. By the 1820s, many Natives relied on American goods and technology and wore American-style clothing, with some following the paths of their white neighbors and using slave labor to produce cotton for international markets. At the same time, they asserted their distinctiveness by celebrating their cultural traditions. Some converted, but most Natives expressed little interest in Christianity, and while they welcomed the schools that missionaries came to establish, they hoped their children could learn lessons that would help them resist American dominance. The nations likewise continued to farm communally while clinging tightly to their ancestral lands and their claims to national independence. Cherokees most forcefully asserted this claim in 1827, when they adopted their own constitution, created a republican government, and proclaimed their standing as a foreign nation residing within the United States.[11]

Yet while Natives revitalized their nations, removal gained stronger support among federal officials. The Monroe and Adams administrations both encouraged Congress to consider a law to encourage the Indians' movement to the west. The lawmakers never took up their suggestions, partly because other issues took priority, but also because the idea faced more opposition than expected. Religion provided much of the grounds for resistance. Several denominations had sent missionaries to promote the Natives' civilization and conversion. While Baptists especially hoped to encourage the nations to accept removal voluntarily as the surest way to encourage their conversion, Congregationalists and Presbyterians in the Northeast founded the

140   *Andrew Jackson: Old Hickory in Christian America*

American Board of Commissioners for Foreign Missions in 1812 to promote the Natives' civilization in their established homelands as the preliminary step toward their conversion and assimilation into white Christian society. With financial assistance from the federal government, the American Board eventually established several schools among the Southern Natives, and while the Board further encouraged these nations' adoption of white American practices, its missionaries won few converts. Still, several of the missionaries gained the Natives' respect and emerged as the tribes' spokesmen, celebrating the Indians' advancement and strongly defending their right to remain on their lands.[12]

The American Board's missionaries stood among the Natives' leading champions as Indian Removal emerged as a political issue. As the 1828 election approached, a confrontation between the Cherokees and the state of Georgia brought national attention to the Natives' fate. In 1802, Georgia had ceded to the federal government the western lands that would become the Mississippi Territory and, by 1819, the states of Mississippi and Alabama. In the agreement, the Jefferson Administration promised as quickly as possible to extinguish all Indian claims to lands within Georgia. Two decades later, Creeks still occupied a strip along the state's western border, while the Cherokee nation still held the state's northwestern corner. The Natives displayed no interest in leaving, and to Georgia's impatient officials, federal attempts to encourage their removal appeared half-hearted at best. The state government thus took matters into its own hands. In 1825, Governor George M. Troup negotiated a fraudulent treaty to expel the state's remaining Creeks. Soon afterward, the governor and state legislature threatened to assert Georgia's control over the Cherokees' lands, bypassing the nation's tribal government and compelling Cherokees either to accept the state's authority or to leave. Though sympathetic to voluntary removal, President John Quincy Adams rejected Troup's treaty with the Creeks and promised to enforce federal treaties that guaranteed the Cherokees' occupation and governance of their lands. As Adams's term neared its end, Georgians intensified their calls to seize the Cherokee lands by force, while Adams insisted that his Constitutional duty required him to protect Natives from the state's encroachments.[13]

"We want them . . . free from colision with the whites" 141

Jackson vehemently rejected Adams's position. Indians, he maintained, were "a conquered & dependent people," and those living within specific states were subject "not on the Federal power in exclusion to the State authority . . . but to the sovereign power of the State within whose sovereign limits they reside." "[A]n absolute independence of the Indian tribes from State authority can never bear an intelligent investigation," he insisted, because "a quasi independence of State authority when located within its Territorial limits is *absurd.*" A state might choose to respect a tribe's dominion within its boundaries, but once the state determined to assert its sovereignty, the federal government had no right to assist the Indians' resistance. Natives residing in the state would either have to accept, as individuals, the state government's laws or they could leave and continue living as distinct nations, under the federal government's oversight, in a territory outside of any state.[14] At the same time, Jackson dismissed reports about the Southern nations' accepting American goods and practices, contending instead that the Indians still rejected "civilization" and preferred to continue their traditional tribal practices. With white settlement now threatening to overwhelm the Indians, he told Georgia congressman Wilson Lumpkin several months before the 1828 election that "they cannot be long fostered and preserved where they are now—"

> They can only be perpetuated as tribes, or nations, by concentrating them west of the Mississippi upon lands secured to them, forever, by the united States, where its humanity, & liberal protecting care, can be extended to them; and where they can be shielded from the encroachments of the whites, without violation to state rights, or the rights of citizens; where only they can prosper, & be perpetuated—as a nation.[15]

Once in a territory clearly under federal authority, he later added, away from "the mercenary influence of white men, and undisturbed by the local authority of the states . . . the General Government can exercise a parental control over their interests and possibly perpetuate their race." Under this oversight, Indians could advance toward civilization if they chose, or they could continue to practice their "primitive" ways.[16]

142   *Andrew Jackson: Old Hickory in Christian America*

Soon after taking office, Indian removal quickly emerged as one of Jackson's highest priorities. Martin Van Buren later recalled that "There was no measure, in the whole course of his administration, of which he was more exclusively the author."[17] The controversy in Georgia may have spurred him into action. In December 1828, Georgia's legislature declared that, on June 1, 1830, the state would extend its authority over the Indian lands within its boundaries. But Jackson probably would have followed the same course regardless of Georgia's actions. Promising to pursue a "just and liberal policy" toward the Indians, the new president signaled his intentions with the appointments to his Cabinet of John Eaton and the Georgian John M. Berrien, both of whom strongly advocated removal. Two weeks after his inauguration, Jackson wrote to urge the Creek nation to move to "this new country, where you might be preserved as a great nation, and where your white brothers would not disturb you." The following summer, he dispatched Tennessee governor William Carroll—"few men, . . ." Jackson explained, had "more influence with the Indians than he"—to encourage removal among both Creeks and Cherokees.[18] Then, in December, he recommended to Congress "setting apart an ample district west of the Mississippi . . . to be guaranteed to the Indian tribes as long as they shall occupy it." There "they may be secured in the enjoyment of governments of their own choice" while "the benevolent may endeavor to teach them the arts of civilization." Emigration "should be voluntary," he acknowledged, but he warned that those remaining in the east would be subject to the laws of the state in which they lived.[19]

Federal officials already pursued Indian Removal with few questions about its legality; Jackson called for congressional action mainly to get the funds needed for carrying out the policy on a much larger scale.[20] Nevertheless, the implicit endorsement that a federal law would mean now broadened the already-vocal popular opposition. Jeremiah Evarts, a Congregational minister and the corresponding secretary for the American Board of Commissioners for Foreign Missions, published a series of essays under the pseudonym "William Penn" that defended the Cherokees' status as a nation while denouncing Jackson's stance because it dismissed previous treaties with the Natives as "mere waste paper." After proclaiming Christianity "the basis of the present law of nations," Evarts invoked Matthew

"We want them . . . free from colision with the whites"   143

7:12's "Golden Rule" to admonish his countrymen to "*do to others whatever we would desire that they, in like circumstances, should do to us.*"[21] More than one hundred newspapers reprinted the "William Penn" letters as Congregational and Presbyterian ministers in the Northeast took the lead in condemning Jackson's proposal. Town meetings throughout the region publicly demanded justice for the Natives, while opponents flooded Congress with petitions opposing removal. Sensing an opportunity, Jackson's political opponents—most of whom had previously either supported removal or displayed no interest in the Natives' plight—likewise took up the Indians' cause, echoing religious leaders' condemnations and pointing to removal as proof of Jackson's determination to rule as a military tyrant.[22]

To counter the growing opposition, Jackson directed Thomas L. McKenney, head of the Bureau of Indian Affairs, to defend Removal as a humanitarian and Christian response to a difficult national problem. A holdover from the Adams administration, McKenney sympathized with the Native peoples, but he had come to agree that removal offered the Natives their best protection. Working with Dutch Reformed, Episcopal, and Presbyterian ministers in New York, he formed a Board for the Emigration, Preservation, and Improvement of the Aborigines in America to respond to Evarts's charges. McKenney's Board provided newspapers with arguments favoring removal, lobbied members of Congress, and published—with federal funds—pamphlets to refute the American Board of Commissioners' claims. McKenney himself prodded Isaac McCoy—a Baptist missionary who had already published a series of essays promoting the Indians' "colonization"—to make an eight-month speaking tour to defend Jackson's policy as the only hope for the Natives' civilization. Baptist, Methodist, and Moravian missionaries meanwhile preached to Indian audiences about the benefits of relocation and encouraged them to accept removal as inevitable. Downplaying the Indians' strides toward "civilization," removal's advocates insisted that the Natives' "condition is becoming more and more miserable every year." Contact with white Americans would only further degrade Indian peoples, meaning that colonization offered their only hope. "These people are positively perishing, and perishing rapidly," McCoy proclaimed; while no tribe would be forced to move against its will, "They will inevitably be lost in extermination unless we rescue them."[23]

144 *Andrew Jackson: Old Hickory in Christian America*

The rival efforts to win public support shaped the congressional debate over a removal law. Tennessee's Hugh Lawson White introduced into the Senate a bill that would implement Jackson's recommendations and allocate $500,000 for the Indians' relocation. The ensuing arguments focused mainly on the United States' previous treaty obligations with the nations, the Natives' claims to sovereignty, and a state's right to take possession of Indian lands within their boundaries. New Jersey Senator Theodore Frelinghuysen emerged as the bill's leading opponent, earning the label "the Christian Statesman" for his speech denouncing the hypocrisy of those "who covet the Indian lands" while hiding their greed behind claims that "humanity" demanded removal. Frelinghuysen depicted Natives as having made great progress toward civilization; "they have in good earnest resolved to become men, rational, educated, Christian men; and they have succeeded beyond our most sanguine hopes." Removal's proponents countered by pointing to "the only partial success, if it has been only partial," of civilization efforts, and they insisted that all of the tribes were "rapidly diminishing in number." Once in the west, Indians could either pursue civilization or continue their traditional ways, but in either case, Georgia's John Forsyth contended, "We believe their removal will be beneficial to us and to themselves."[24] Jackson's allies managed to carry the bill in the Senate, but the public outcry against removal threatened to defeat it in the House of Representatives. Several representatives from the Middle Atlantic states had supported Jackson and favored his administration's other reforms, but they proved reluctant to counter their constituents' sympathy for the Natives. Ultimately, by making the bill a test of loyalty to the president, enough representatives remained in Jackson's camp to secure the law's approval by a narrow 102-97 vote.[25]

Despite the narrow margin, Jackson moved quickly as if he had a popular mandate to put removal into effect. After signing the Indian Removal Act on May 30, 1830, he invited representatives from the four Southwestern nations to meet with him during his visit to Tennessee that summer. Only the Chickasaws sent a delegation; the Creeks and Cherokees rejected Jackson's request to talk, but after a Choctaw chief proposed his own removal treaty, Jackson dispatched John Eaton and John Coffee to Mississippi to work out an agreement. Through the payment of generous allotments—that is, land grants to tribal leaders,

"We want them . . . free from colision with the whites" 145

many of whom would remain in Mississippi—Eaton and Coffee in September signed what Jackson labeled a "liberal" treaty, swapping Choctaw lands for a region west of the Arkansas Territory. Jackson hoped that the Choctaws' relocation would provide a model for other nations' removal. Instead, poor planning, corruption and bickering among the agents sent to oversee the move, and cost-cutting efforts ended up inflicting severe hunger, cold, and hardship on the migrants. Alexis de Tocqueville, witnessing the first wave of Choctaws as they passed through Memphis, noted that, though "it was then the middle of winter, and the cold was unusually severe, . . . they possessed neither tents nor wagons, but only their arms and some provisions. . . . [N]ever," the Frenchman lamented, "will that solemn spectacle fade from my remembrance." The odyssey meanwhile proved much more expensive than Jackson had anticipated. By 1833, more than half the Choctaw nation resided in the Arkansas Territory, but the horrendous ordeal of their removal had cost the government more than $5 million—over $2 million more than Jackson had estimated for removing all of the eastern Natives.[26]

Notwithstanding the costs and the persisting public criticism, Jackson pressed on. He devoted more than one-tenth of his 1830 Message to Congress to defending the legality, liberality, morality, and justice of removal, emphasizing again how separating the Indians from the white population would "retard the progress of decay, which is lessening their numbers." Francis P. Blair meanwhile published a series of essays in the Washington *Globe* denouncing removal's critics as "hypocritical politicians," while Jackson continued to insist that "evil counsellors"—"Chiefs and leading men" who were "unwilling to risk their present places and power"—had "mislead" the "common Indians" into resisting relocation. After Eaton resigned as secretary of war, Jackson replaced him with Lewis Cass, the longtime governor of the Michigan Territory and one of the Union's strongest proponents of removal. Meanwhile, the president halted federal funding for the American Board's schools on Indian lands and ordered previously promised payments to Native leaders to be withheld until they agreed to accept removal. Ignoring complaints about improper treatment, Jackson dismissed McKenney when his head of the Bureau of Indian Affairs accused agents responsible for overseeing removal with corruption.[27] Still, the president defended his policy as resting on high moral

146 *Andrew Jackson: Old Hickory in Christian America*

ground. "[W]e want them in a state of safety removed from the states & free from colision with the whites," he persistently declared. The popular opposition he attributed to misguided "religious enthusiasts" while blaming the political attacks on the "malignity" of Henry Clay and John C. Calhoun. "They would . . . overturn heaven & earth, to prostrate me," he grumbled, "but providence athwarts all their wicked designs, and will turn it to the benefit of our happy country."[28]

Pressure, bribery, and military force left the Native nations with no choice. By the end of his first administration, Jackson had secured removal treaties with the Chickasaws, Creeks, and several Northern tribes. He sent an army to fight a short war in Illinois after Chief Black Hawk's small band of Sauks attempted to return to their homeland, while the Seminoles' resistance sparked a war that eventually lasted seven years and cost the federal government more than $20 million. William Wirt, the attorney general for James Monroe and John Quincy Adams, filed a lawsuit for the Cherokees seeking a federal injunction to stop Georgia's attempts to take control of their lands. The Supreme Court dismissed the case in March 1831, ruling that Indian nations could not sue because they were not "foreign states." Instead, Chief Justice John Marshall declared, they were "domestic dependent nations . . . under the sovereignty and dominion of the United States." Wirt nevertheless filed a second lawsuit after Georgia authorities arrested two American Board missionaries residing in Cherokee lands. In this case, the Court upheld the Cherokees' right to govern themselves within Georgia as "a distinct community occupying its own territory," a decision that implicitly reprimanded Jackson for failing to protect the Cherokees from state legislation. Legal technicalities, though, prevented the Court from directly ordering the president to act; Jackson pronounced the decision "still born" and dismissed the Court's reasoning as "unsound both in law, & in facts." Eventually, he compelled a group of unauthorized Cherokee leaders to sign a removal treaty of dubious legality at best. The vast majority of tribesmen rejected the agreement, but the treaty provided enough legal basis for the next administration to force most Cherokees west on a horrendous trek that became known as the "Trail of Tears."[29]

Long before then, public protests over Removal had largely faded. Jeremiah Evarts's death in May 1831 deprived the Natives of their most passionate white champion. During Jackson's campaign for

"We want them . . . free from colision with the whites" 147

re-election in 1832, supporters of Henry Clay—who had once told John Quincy Adams that the Indians' "disappearance from the human family would be no great loss to the world"—publicly denounced removal as evidence of Jackson's cruelty, brutality, and disregard for the Constitution and the law, but by then, other issues had come to the forefront and pushed aside concerns about the Indians' fate. With removal widely popular among white Americans in the South and West, Jackson's determination had made removal seem inevitable. When he left office in 1837, the Second Seminole War dragged on, the costs of removal had escalated, and the actual movement of the major Southern nations remained to be completed. Nevertheless, he had already overseen the transplantation of approximately 46,000 Natives to the west, opening up about 100 million acres of eastern lands to white settlement. Eventually, a total of about 90,000 Indians would be displaced, and Jackson always insisted that he had humanely solved a long-standing national problem. "[T]his unhappy race, . . ." he boasted in his Farewell Address, "are now placed in a situation where we may well hope that they will share in the blessings of civilization and be saved from that degradation and destruction to which they were rapidly hastening."[30]

Indian Removal remains the darkest stain on Jackson's presidency, and Jackson himself bears primary responsibility. Explanations for his obsession with removal range from attributing to him a sincere concern for the Natives' fate, condemning him for a ruthlessness contempt for Indians, and psychoanalytically claiming that he projected onto Natives a supposedly unreconciled rage against his mother and the father he never knew.[31] The truth is complicated. Whether at war or peace, Jackson—like the vast majority of white Americans in his age—always regarded Indians as primitive "savages." He fought them relentlessly when he thought the British and Spanish provoked their attacks on the frontier, though he did acknowledge his fellow countrymen's responsibility in aggravating the conflicts. "Every war . . . we had with the Indians was brought on by frontier ruffians, who stole their horses, oppressed, defrauded, or persecuted the Indians," he later told a visitor to the Hermitage. "This caused them to unbury the hatchet, and their massacres of the whites plunged innocent people in all the horrors and cruelties of war."[32] Once Native nations no longer appeared a threat to American independence, the possibility of

148   *Andrew Jackson: Old Hickory in Christian America*

persisting clashes—wars that might lead to the Indians' annihilation—still remained a concern for him. Removal, he concluded, offered the best solution to a perplexing national dilemma. He did not originate the policy, but he pursued it more aggressively than his predecessors and took it in a new direction when he insisted that the federal government lacked both the resources and authority to protect Native nations within the states.

Jackson's consistent professions of Indian Removal's benefits for the Natives seem sincere, and there is no reason to doubt that he believed them. Still, the policy provided the white American majority with a highly self-serving solution. Throughout his presidency, concern for the Indians' well-being appeared for Jackson to be a secondary motivation at best. Other forces drove him to pursue the Natives' relocation, among them his Southern and Western compatriots' land hunger, the expectation that white encroachment would lead to further bloodshed, and—though now highly unlikely—a lingering concern that the Natives might once again ally with the Union's European enemies. The bottom line for him, though, was that the Natives' presence blocked American progress. With the Indians in a weak position—and recognizing his opponents' defense of the Natives as disingenuous political opportunism—he saw an opportunity to eliminate that obstruction. Contrary to modern accusations, he never advocated genocide, and historian Stuart Banner notes that, because of army records and press coverage, we have more evidence for the calamities that occurred during the removals in Jackson's era than for previous relocations that likely also produced tremendous suffering.[33] Nevertheless, Jackson's heavy-handed pursuit of what later generations would call an ethnic cleansing gutted his promise to implement a "just and humane policy towards the Indians." He could not foresee that, within a generation after his death, American expansion would again surround the nations that he had moved west or that government officials would more aggressively confine Indians on reservations. But his administration's clumsy implementation of removal while proclaiming its "paternal care" reinforced a precedent for future generations of federal mistreatment.[34]

While spokesmen who promoted or challenged removal often avoided presenting their arguments in religious terms, religion nevertheless provided much of the motivation for both sides. The national

"We want them . . . free from colision with the whites"   149

debate over the policy, after all, divided white Americans as Christian people. Proponents and detractors both always expressed a desire for the Indians' welfare. Jackson himself only occasionally discussed the Natives' fate as part of a Christian mission, such as when he asserted that preventing the Indians' "colision" with white Americans might allow them "gradually . . . to cast off their savage habits and become an interesting, civilized, and Christian community."[35] Adherence to their traditional beliefs provided Jackson and his fellow countrymen with ample evidence of the Indians' persisting primitivity, and Jackson never realized—or cared—about how expulsion and abuse, especially when conducted by agents who were ministers, further alienated Natives from Christianity. No easy answer existed to resolve the conflict between Native and white American civilizations. Jackson's solution, while perhaps well intentioned, never acknowledged that removal contradicted the principles of his own faith, and he chose to remain blind to its tragic outcome.

Notes

1. Cheathem, *Andrew Jackson, Southerner*, 6–7, 9, 20, 25–26; Parton, *Life of Andrew Jackson*, 1:121–24, 142–45; Booraem, *Young Hickory*, 194.
2. Andrew Jackson to Thomas Jefferson, April 20, 1808, *PAJ*, 2:192; Jackson to William H. Crawford, June 9, 1816, *PAJ*, 4:44; Jackson to John Coffee, September 19, 1816, *PAJ*, 4:64; Jackson, D. Meriwether, & J. Franklin to William H. Crawford, September 20, 1816, *PAJ*, 4:66; Robert V. Remini, *Andrew Jackson and His Indian Wars* (New York: Penguin Books, 2001), 26, 56–57, hereafter cited Remini, *Indian Wars*.
3. Andrew Jackson to James Monroe, November 20, 1814, *PAJ*, 3:192.
4. Andrew Jackson to Rachel Jackson, December 19, 1813, *PAJ*, 2:494–95; Andrew Jackson to Rachel Jackson, December 29, 1813, *PAJ*, 2:516; Andrew Jackson to Rachel Jackson, February 21, 1814, *PAJ*, 3:35; Editors' Note, *PAJ*, 11:766; Meredith, "'There Was Somebody Always Dying and Leaving Jackson as Guardian,'" 42–46; Gismondi, "Rachel Jackson and the Search for Zion," 122–53.
5. Andrew Jackson to John C. McLemore, May 3, 1829, *PAJ*, 7:200; Jackson to Samuel Houston, June 21, 1829, *PAJ*, 7:294; Editors' Note, *PAJ*, 11:766; Gismondi, "Rachel Jackson and the Search for Zion," 62–74.
6. Andrew Jackson to James Monroe, March 4, 1817, *PAJ*, 4:96; Jackson to John Coffee, September 2, 1829, *PAJ*, 6:200.
7. Andrew Jackson to James Monroe, March 4, 1817, *PAJ*, 4:95–96; Jackson to John C. Calhoun, September 2, 1820, *PAJ*, 4:388.

150 *Andrew Jackson: Old Hickory in Christian America*

8. Andrew Jackson to John Williams, May 18, 1814, *PAJ*, 3:73–75; James Monroe to Jackson, October 5, 1817, *PAJ*, 4:147; Jackson to Pathkiller et al., January 18, 1821, *PAJ*, 5:7–8; Jackson to John Dabney Terrell, July 29, 1829, *PAJ*, 6:192; Jackson to John Coffee, September 2, 1826, *PAJ*, 6:200; Remini, *Indian Wars*, 80–92, 108–29; Anthony F.C. Wallace, *The Long, Bitter Trail: Andrew Jackson and the Indians* (New York: Hill & Wang, 1993), 18–21, 53.

9. Andrew Jackson to Robert Butler, June 21, 1817, *PAJ*, 4:119; Jackson to John C. Calhoun, September 2, 1820, *PAJ*, 4:388; Remini, *Indian Wars*, 114–16, 120–29; Ronald N. Satz, *American Indian Policy in the Jacksonian Era* (Norman: University of Oklahoma Press, 1974), 1–2; Francis Paul Prucha, *The Great Father: The United States Government and the American Indians* (Lincoln: University of Nebraska Press, 1984), 30–34, 179–80; Stuart Banner, *How the Indians Lost Their Land: Law and Power on the Frontier* (Cambridge, MA: The Belknap Press of Harvard University Press, 2005), 191–98; Guyatt, *Providence and the Invention of the United States*, 174–80.

10. Andrew Jackson to Robert Butler, June 21, 1817, *PAJ*, 4:119.

11. Wallace, *The Long, Bitter Trail*, 56–62; Howe, *What Hath God Wrought?*, 342–46; William G. McLoughlin, *Cherokee Renascence in the New Republic* (Princeton: Princeton University Press, 1986), 350–66.

12. Banner, *How the Indians Lost Their Land*, 206–209; Guyatt, *Providence and the Invention of the United States*, 181–82; Haselby, *Origins of American Religious Nationalism*, 296–98.

13. Wallace, *The Long, Bitter Trail*, 39–40, 63–64; Banner, *How the Indians Lost Their Land*, 198–201; Prucha, *The Great Father*, 186–91; Howe, *What Hath God Wrought?*, 346–48.

14. Andrew Jackson to Lewis Cass, December 1831, *PAJ*, 9:789–90.

15. Andrew Jackson to Wilson Lumpkin, February 15, 1828, *PAJ*, 6:418.

16. Andrew Jackson to James Gadsden, October 12, 1829, *PAJ*, 7:491–92.

17. "Autobiography of Martin Van Buren," *Annual Report of the American Historical Association for the Year 1918*, volume 2 (Washington: Government Printing Office, 1920), 295.

18. "First Inaugural Address of Andrew Jackson," March 4, 1829, *Messages and Papers*, 2:438; "To the Creek Nation," March 23, 1829, *PAJ*, 7:112; Andrew Jackson to John Overton, June 8, 1829, *PAJ*, 7:271; Wallace, *The Long, Bitter Trail*, 64–66; Prucha, *The Great Father*, 191–95; Satz, *American Indian Policy*, 12–13; Banner, *How the Indians Lost Their Land*, 215–16.

19. Andrew Jackson, "First Message to Congress," December 8, 1829, *Messages and Papers*, 2:458; Remini, *Indian Wars*, 226–33.

20. Banner, *How the Indians Lost Their Land*, 217.

21. [Jeremiah Evarts], *Essays on the Present Crisis in the Condition of the American Indians; First Published in The National Intelligencer, under the Signature of William Penn* (Philadelphia: Thomas Kite, 1830), 95, 101.

22. Satz, *American Indian Policy*, 23–24, 27–28; Prucha, *The Great Father*, 200–206; Howe, *What Hath God Wrought?*, 349–50.

23. Isaac McCoy, *Remarks on the Practicability of Indian Reform, Embracing Their Colonization* (Boston: Lincoln & Edmands, 1827), 12, 18; Satz, *American Indian Policy*, 14–18; Prucha, *The Great Father*, 198–200; Guyatt, *Providence and the Invention of the United States*, 181–83; Banner, *How the Indians Lost Their Land*, 206–209.

"We want them . . . free from colision with the whites" 151

24. United States Congress, *Register of Debates*, 21st Congress, 1st session, 318–19, 339, 376.

25. Howe, *What Hath God Wrought?*, 350–52; Satz, *American Indian Policy*, 20–31; Remini, *Indian Wars*, 233–38; Cole, *Presidency of Andrew Jackson*, 71–78.

26. Andrew Jackson to Martin Van Buren, October 23, 1830, *PAJ*, 8:571; Tocqueville, *Democracy in America*, 1:340; Satz, *American Indian Policy*, 64–87; Wallace, *The Long, Bitter Trail*, 76–81; Remini, *Indian Wars*, 239–43; Prucha, *The Great Father*, 215–19; Howe, *What Hath God Wrought?*, 352–53.

27. Andrew Jackson, "Second Annual Message" to Congress, December 6, 1830, *Messages and Papers*, 2:520; Andrew Jackson to Wilson Lumpkin, April 30, 1833, *PAJ*, 11:278; Andrew Jackson to George R. Gilmer, July 15, 1831, *PAJ*, 9:386; Richard B. Latner, *Presidency of Andrew Jackson: White House Politics, 1829–1837* (Athens: University of Georgia Press, 1979), 96; Guyatt, *Providence and the Invention of the United States*, 195–96; Wallace, *The Long, Bitter Trail*, 41–48, 73–75, 81–82; Satz, *American Indian Policy*, 78, 151–56; Cole, *Presidency of Andrew Jackson*, 109–12; Banner, *How the Indians Lost Their Land*, 212.

28. Andrew Jackson to John Coffee, November 6, 1832, *PAJ*, 10:554; Jackson to Coffee, April 7, 1832, *PAJ*, 10:225.

29. Satz, *American Indian Policy*, 44–52, 98–108, 113–14; Banner, *How the Indians Lost Their Land*, 218–25; Remini, *Indian Wars*, 254–71; Wallace, *The Long, Bitter Trail*, 86–87, 90–101; Howe, *What Hath God Wrought?*, 354–56, 412–13, 417–20; Andrew Jackson to John Coffee, April 7, 1832, *PAJ*, 10:226; Jackson to Henry Baldwin, March 6, 1832, *PAJ*, 10:151.

30. Prucha, *The Great Father*, 207–208; Cole, *Presidency of Andrew Jackson*, 116–17; Remini, *Indian Wars*, 272–96; Andrew Jackson, "Farewell Address," March 4, 1837, *Messages and Papers*, 3:294; Cole, *Presidency of Andrew Jackson*, 146–51.

31. Francis Paul Prucha, "Andrew Jackson's Indian Policy: A Reassessment," *Journal of American History* 56 (December 1969):527–39; Heidler and Heidler, *Old Hickory's War*; Michael Paul Rogin, *Fathers and Children: Andrew Jackson and the Subjugation of the American Indian* (New York: Alfred A. Knopf, 1975).

32. Parton, *Life of Andrew Jackson*, 3:634.

33. Banner, *How the Indians Lost Their Land*, 225–26.

34. Andrew Jackson to James Gadsden, October 12, 1829, *PAJ*, 7:491; Jackson, "Farewell Address," *Messages and Papers*, March 4, 1837, 3:294; Wallace, *The Long, Bitter Trail*, 117–20.

35. Jackson, "Second Annual Message," December 6, 1830, *Messages and Papers*, 2:520; Guyatt, *Providence and the Invention of the United States*, 197–98.

10

"My negroes shall be treated humanely"

The institution of slavery lay deeply entrenched in Andrew Jackson's world. Slaves worked in the close-knit community of his boyhood, with possibly at least one present in James Crawford's household, where he spent his earliest years. His uncle Robert Crawford possessed several servants, teaching the young Jackson early that slave-ownership characterized a successful gentleman. At least once he oversaw the sale of some of Uncle Robert's enslaved persons, and Jackson may have acquired at least one slave of his own before his first known purchase— a young black woman named Nancy—when he was twenty-one. Establishing himself as a planter required investing heavily in slaves. An inventory taken shortly before he began his presidency counted ninety-five slaves at the Hermitage, ranking him among the largest slave owners in Tennessee. By the time of his death, his estate included one hundred ten slaves at the Hermitage and another fifty-one at a Mississippi plantation that he jointly owned with his adopted son.[1]

The adult Jackson, in fact, dwelt almost constantly in the presence of enslaved people. Household slaves worked at the Hermitage and at other homes and public buildings he visited. From his early adulthood, undoubtedly, he usually had a manservant with him. George, the son of Rachel's personal servant Hannah, filled this role while Jackson served as president. A young man about twenty years old when Jackson's administration started, George slept on a pallet near Jackson's bed and remained in Jackson's service until his owner's death. Jackson's carriage driver through his first term, Charles, had been his personal servant during his military campaigns. "[H]e is 'a favorite of mine,'" Jackson later stated; "it could not be otherwise, as he has passed thro

Andrew Jackson. Jonathan M. Atkins, Oxford University Press. © Jonathan M. Atkins 2025.
DOI: 10.1093/9780191886812.003.0010

154   *Andrew Jackson: Old Hickory in Christian America*

so many privations, & dangers, with me."[2] The identities of Jackson's previous manservants are unknown, but like other elite Southerners, he and Rachel almost certainly had personal servants close at hand as soon as they could afford them.

Despite slavery's pervasiveness, Jackson's writings only occasionally mentioned either the institution or the presence of slaves. These references usually came up when inquiring about the condition of his property or when slaves or slavery provoked a specific problem or concern. He never offered a comprehensive justification for holding humans in bondage, nor did he ever question slavery's morality. Unlike Thomas Jefferson and others in the founding generation, Jackson left no account about wrestling with the contradiction between his ownership of slaves and the proclamation in the Declaration of Independence that "all men are created equal." A comment from one of Rachel's nephews, that an overseer treated Jackson's servants "as humane and kind to them as the nature of slavery will admit," offers a possible hint that Jackson and his circle might have discussed the paradox among themselves. Still, the denial of African American freedom never appeared to be a major concern for him. As James Parton concluded, he "took slavery for granted." Slavery existed, and he used the institution to his advantage.[3]

Jackson's writings also said little about race. Likely he accepted the arguments that other Southerners used to justify holding African Americans as slaves, assuming that black people, like Indians, existed as a different category of people. Interestingly, racial epithets rarely appear in his papers. He never wrote that all black persons should be slaves, and he sometimes employed free African Americans. While defending New Orleans and desperate for soldiers, he shocked the city's residents when he not only accepted the services of a volunteer regiment of *gens de couleur*—free men of color—but also when he promised that, as "sons of freedom," they would be paid "the same bounty in Money and lands, now received by the white Soldiers of the United States." Perhaps because of their race, he confessed some concern about the regiment's ability to fight, but he assured Louisiana's governor that, "If their pride and merit entitle them to confidence, they can be employed against the Enemy." Soon afterward, he reprimanded his reluctant paymaster for questioning his order to pay the soldiers "without enquiring whether the troops are white, Black, or red."[4] Still,

"My negroes shall be treated humanely" 155

as president, he ended the practice of hiring free African Americans as messengers when white workers complained, and he rejected the idea that emancipated slaves and white Americans could live together as equals in the same society. Shortly before his death, he insisted that the Southern states "would have taken measures to have introduced an amelioration of their Slaves" if agitation had not provoked fears of "Servile War," and he asked, if slavery were abolished, "Where are they to live; are they to amalgamate with the Whites[?]"[5] For Jackson, as for the vast majority of his fellow countrymen, that option was unacceptable.

Jackson also knew that slaves constituted an important property and that their value and production contributed significantly to their owners' wealth. Whenever he could, he upheld slaveowners' property rights. In the Creek War, he recovered, and eventually returned to their owners, several slaves taken in the Fort Mims massacre. After the battle at New Orleans, he attempted to recover slaves who had taken refuge with British forces, though he angered Louisiana planters when, following protocol, he waited for the official peace before requesting their return. Ultimately, he chose to let the slaves go—and hasten the enemy's withdrawal—when the British commander refused to force them to go back to their American masters. A few years earlier, he had angrily defied Silas Dinsmore, the federal agent to the Choctaw nation, because Dinsmore enforced a usually overlooked regulation requiring him to confiscate slaves on a road crossing through Choctaw territory if their owners failed to present state-issued passports for each. Jackson accused Dinsmore of using the slaves' labor for his own benefit and charging the expenses for their upkeep to their owners. With no sense of irony, Jackson thundered, "are we free men or are we slaves[?]," and when he transported twenty-six slaves through the Choctaw country on their way to New Orleans for sale, he purposely left behind the slaves' passports so he could provoke an encounter with Dinsmore. The Indian agent's absence from his post prevented a confrontation, but after the general became a national hero, he blocked a petition for a land grant to compensate the agent for his losses during the war.[6]

As he did with the soldiers under his command, Jackson expected absolute obedience from his slaves. Because American slavery ultimately rested upon force, including violence, he disciplined his bondsmen, sometimes harshly, when he thought it necessary. Runaways especially

156   *Andrew Jackson: Old Hickory in Christian America*

infuriated him. In September 1804, he posted a now-infamous advertisement in a Nashville newspaper offering a $50 reward for the recapture of "a Mulatto Man Slave, about thirty years of age . . ." who had fled from his farm, and he promised to pay whoever apprehended the fugitive "ten dollars extra, for every hundred lashes . . . to the amount of three hundred." Jackson apparently never recovered the runaway, and possibly he mellowed somewhat in his treatment of his slaves as he grew older, as he never again made such an extreme offer. Still, despite his claim two decades later to "hate chains," he ordered runaways bound in iron when he concluded he had to, and he accepted the need for his slaves' corporal punishment "whenever any of them depart from proper conduct." While serving as the Florida Territories' governor, he ordered Betty, the Hermitage's cook, to be given fifty lashes at "the public whipping post" if she continued to act with "a great deal of impudence" toward her mistress Rachel. "She is capable of being a good & valluable servant," he noted, "but to have her so, she must be ruled with the cowhide."[7]

Interactions with his enslaved people, though, brought a human dimension to the institution that eased somewhat the strict line dividing master and slave. Dealing with servants reminded Jackson that, despite their racial differences, black people were not beasts but were indeed humans. He strongly rejected political charges that he invested in and profited from slave trading, a disreputable business notwithstanding its prevalence in the antebellum South. The accusations annoyed him, partly because some of his business dealings as a younger man gave them a degree of truth, but also because he associated the idea of "making a fortune of speculating on human flesh" with his dishonorable enemies. Instead, Jackson envisioned himself a just and kind master—stern when necessary, able to inflict harsh punishment when he thought discipline called for it, but usually gentle and forbearing. Numerous times he insisted, as he told his adopted son, that "My negroes shall be treated humanely," adding on a later occasion that he "could not bear the idea of inhumanity to my poor negroes."[8] His letters home often sent greetings to "Tell the negroes *all* howde, for me" and to "tell them I send my prayers for their health & happiness. . . ." At least verbally, his bonds people responded with appreciative remarks that suggest, to at least some degree, a personal connection. During one of Jackson's long absences, Old Sampson, the Hermitage's

"My negroes shall be treated humanely"   157

gardener, felt sufficiently comfortable to joke with his owner when, through John Eaton, Sampson expressed to the president "a strong desire, that you may be *beat next time*, because then you would *come home*." If Jackson picked up on the implicit double-entendre, the remark provoked no repercussions. Eaton simply but smugly commented, "How pleasurable to be thus recollected, & kindly cherished by old & faithful servants."[9]

Several motives encouraged Jackson to provide his slaves with adequate accommodations and what he considered fair treatment. Presumably, a contented labor force would work harder and present fewer discipline problems. Jackson's self-image as an honorable man likewise required him to offer paternal direction and compassion to those under his authority. He appears, too, to have actually liked and wished the best for the people he owned. Religious sentiments also contributed to his desire to act benevolently. As cotton's expansion across the South revived slavery as a crucial source of labor, and as converts in the late-eighteenth and early-nineteenth century revivals became more economically secure and socially respectable, churches in the South that had once directly challenged slavery abandoned calls for its abolition. Over the next generation, Southern clergymen would take the lead in presenting slavery as a divinely ordained practice that had brought the gospel to "heathen" Africans. Citing passages in the Pauline Epistles that masters should treat their servants justly, ministers admonished Christian slave owners to deal kindly with their bondsmen and encourage their conversion. Jackson's own Presbyterian church long wrestled with slavery's presence. Gideon Blackburn, Rachel's spiritual mentor, would eventually leave the South at least partly because of his antislavery views, and differences over the institution would contribute to the denomination's division in 1837. Jackson left no comments on these developments; the vast majority of sermons that he heard have long been lost, and he apparently never brought a minister to the Hermitage to preach to his hands. Still, at a time when Southern churches were shifting from questioning to upholding slavery, his religious activities likely reinforced his assumptions about a Christian master's duty to his slaves.[10]

Whatever he heard at church, Jackson took seriously his Christian obligation to treat his slaves well. Several of his servants did identify as Christians. Hannah recalled years later that, despite the Jacksons'

158   *Andrew Jackson: Old Hickory in Christian America*

Presbyterianism, she and Alfred, another favorite, were proud Baptists. Meanwhile, Jackson tried to make sure that his slaves had sufficient provisions. Archaeological digs at the Hermitage indicate that the slaves possessed ceramic and glass dishes—likely given to them after the white family no longer used them—and that they could supplement their diets through fishing and hunting, as trusted servants were allowed to possess firearms. No Southern state legalized slave marriages, but Jackson encouraged families among "his" people, with at least two slave weddings—Hannah's marriage to Aaron and Alfred's marriage to Gracey—taking place in the plantation's mansion. Two inventories taken during the 1820s grouped Jackson's slaves according to the cabins they lived in, listing them by a male slave's name "& wife" with their children. Both counts indicate that the vast majority belonged to nuclear family units. When he could, Jackson proved willing to purchase or sell slaves to unite families—though in at least one case he approved an effective divorce when he agreed to Charlotte's request, with her husband George's consent, to sell her to another local planter. Hannah recalled that Jackson never sold children away from their parents, and once when facing financial constraints, he rejected a business associate's advice to sell his "too great a quantity of Negroe property."[11]

No evidence exists, either, of Jackson's raping or sexually abusing his slaves. Possibly Jackson did make nocturnal visits to the slave quarters or summon an enslaved woman to share his bed. Across the South, owners often sexually assaulted their slaves, while friends and neighbors usually maintained a code of silence about slave mistresses as well as about biracial children produced in those unions. A century and a half after his death, one woman leveled an unsupported claim to be Jackson's descendant through a child born to him by Hannah in 1826. The fact that Jackson and Rachel had no offspring raises the question of whether he could father children, though Rachel's barrenness with her first husband suggests she likely was unable to conceive. Nicholas P. Trist, who briefly served as President Jackson's private secretary, observed that the elderly Jackson displayed "a womanly modesty and delicacy, as respects the relation of the sexes. . . . [C]haste would be the right word as to him." Trist's comment, of course, refers to Jackson's treatment of white women, and hypocrisy in a public figure would hardly be shocking. He infuriated Rachel once when he

"My negroes shall be treated humanely"   159

said nothing as one of the junior officers staying at the Hermitage "led one of the young colored girls off."[12] If Jackson himself forced a relationship on any slave, these encounters probably occurred when he was a younger man, before his often-frail health and the wear on his body from his wounds likely made sexual activity difficult for him, if not impossible. The bitterness of his political campaigns and personal battles probably would have produced at least whispers, if not direct charges, if his opponents suspected his own children lived among the Hermitage's slaves.

Like most planters, Jackson relied on hired overseers to run the daily operations at the Hermitage. Finding someone who could balance the slaves' proper treatment with maximizing the farm's profits proved a persistent problem. During his absences, news about insufficient production and improper handling of the slaves compelled him frequently to send instructions threatening an overseer's dismissal, and most ended up working at the Hermitage for only a few years. The death of the field hand Gilbert from the actions of one overseer deeply disturbed Jackson. Gilbert had attempted to escape three times, and though at one point Jackson was determined to sell him, he instead punished Gilbert by having him whipped "moderately with small rods." Ira Walton, the Hermitage's overseer at the time, complained that Jackson's "indulgence" encouraged Gilbert's insolence and that Gilbert stirred dissent among the other hands. Shortly before Jackson became president, Walton stabbed Gilbert when the slave tried to choke him. Gilbert died from the wounds, and Jackson requested a coroner's inquest to determine whether Walton should be charged with murder. The inquest accepted Walton's claim that he had killed Gilbert in self-defense, but Jackson then consulted with a state prosecutor about possibly filing an indictment against his overseer. "I have no wish to prosecute Mr Walton should you think justice does not demand it," he explained, "but being the guardian of my slave, it is my duty to prosecute the case so far as justice to him may require it." Jackson then fired Walton and swore out a warrant for his arrest, but a grand jury eventually dismissed the case.[13]

The need to find a reliable overseer remained a problem for Jackson throughout his presidency. While in office, he hired and fired three different managers. The plantation's poor performance, the overseers' defiance of his instructions, and their failure to communicate with

160   *Andrew Jackson: Old Hickory in Christian America*

him regularly provided the main reasons for the dismissals, but in each case their supervision of his slaves undermined Jackson's confidence in them. After sacking Walton, Jackson hired Graves Steele on a four-year contract, but shortly into the first year, reports about Steele's "severe" treatment and "neglect of my negroes when taken sick" worried him. When he fired Steele after only three years, he had concluded that Steele "poisoned my servants with his bad advice, and conduct." Burnard Holtzclaw replaced Steele, but once Holtzclaw took charge, Jackson soon learned about the deaths of several Hermitage slaves. Visitors to the Hermitage praised Holtzclaw's management of the farm and its workforce, but Andrew Donelson noted that "the negroes appear as tho they were entirely abandoned . . . and in a state of despair." Holtzclaw's successor, Edward Hobbs, likewise proved disappointing. Not only did Hobbs ask for a raise despite a bad harvest, he neglected to purchase the slaves' "shews and warm cloathing so as to give them in due time when the frost came, that they might be able to go to their work early." In each case, Jackson assumed that poor conditions limited the slaves' productivity, and none of his overseers satisfactorily followed their absentee employer's instruction to "treat them with great humanity, feed & cloath them well, & work them in moderation."[14]

Once back home after his presidency, Jackson could watch his overseers' handling of his slaves more closely. Still, neither he nor other owners could monitor the servants constantly, and one incident among unsupervised slaves showed the potential costs of acting as a paternal master. During a Christmas gathering among slaves near the Hermitage in 1838, a fight broke out that led to the death of a bondsman named Frank. Jackson "more than once in a friendly manner" urged Frank's owner, Rachel's nephew Stockly Donelson, "to hear the testimony . . . that the[re] were many in the riot," but Donelson nevertheless took out a warrant for murder against four of Jackson's slaves—George, Alfred, Jacob, and Squire. Officials dropped the charge against George—possibly because he was the former president's personal servant—but then scheduled the other three to be tried in late January 1839. Jackson could have left their fate in the hands of a court-appointed defender; instead, he spent about $1,500— slightly more than the three slaves' approximate value—to hire three leading Nashville attorneys to take the case. The defense team secured

"My negroes shall be treated humanely"   161

their acquittal, but Jackson had to borrow $1,000 and sell some of his land "to clear me of this unexpected expence." An estrangement from Donelson might have prompted Jackson's determination to protect his slaves, but he maintained that he acted "so that the lives of my negroes may not be jeopardised by false and perjured witnesses," adding that "it was a constitutional right, that all men"—apparently including slaves—"by law are presumed to be innocent until guilt is proven."[15]

Alfred, Jacob, and Squire faced execution if convicted of murder, so they no doubt appreciated Jackson's assistance. Whether they considered him a good master remains unknown. After Jackson's death, several servants long spoke highly of him. Hannah reminisced about the kindness, especially toward children, of the man she sometimes referred to as "father." In an 1880 interview, given when she was likely in her eighties, she insisted that "Ole Master was gold to us." One of the acquitted slaves, "Uncle Alfred," remained at the Hermitage with "Aunt Gracie" long after slavery's abolition, giving tours of the grounds and being buried in the Hermitage garden near the Jacksons' tomb after his death in 1901. The frequent number of runaways among fieldhands, on the other hand, provides a reminder that, no matter what Jackson's intentions, slavery included harsh treatment and the denial of basic human rights. Most of Jackson's enslaved persons probably considered him a decent owner while they played the roles expected of them. Suppressing their dissent, they expressed affection toward "Ole Master" and—like Hannah and Alfred—said what they thought white people wanted to hear. Roeliff Brinkerhoff, a tutor hired to teach Andrew Jr.'s children at the Hermitage, recalled a revealing conversation with Alfred around the time of Jackson's death. One day, upon finding Alfred "unusually reticent and gloomy" and "full of discontent with his lot," Brinkerhoff reminded him that freedom had its burdens and that Jackson had taken good care of him. Alfred quickly acknowledged that "Massa Andrew is always very kind" but then simply asked, "How would you like to be a slave?"[16]

Alfred and Jackson's other enslaved people undoubtedly recognized that their master expressed no antislavery sentiments. At no point in his life did Jackson openly favor an effort to bring slavery to an end. The American Colonization Society, an organization that promoted emancipation through purchasing slaves and transporting the freed people to Africa, named Jackson an "officer" at its founding in late

162   *Andrew Jackson: Old Hickory in Christian America*

1816, but he never participated in or endorsed its activities. While visiting Rhode Island as president, he ignored a petition handed to him by a representative from the Providence Antislavery Society calling for slavery's abolition. At the same time, Jackson never vocally defended slavery or described the institution as a "positive good." In 1819, in fact, he advised the Methodist itinerant Peter Cartwright on how to enforce a church rule requiring ministers to emancipate slaves they might inherit from family members. Whenever slavery-related issues came up in national politics, he always blamed selfish politicians for stirring up emotions and threatening disunion merely so they could promote their ambitions. In 1819, for instance, when Congress angrily debated whether to admit Missouri as a slave or free state, he attributed the controversy to the "wicked design of Demagogues," both Northern and Southern, "who talk about humanity, but whose sole object is self agrandisement regardless of the happiness of the nation." His alliance with John C. Calhoun in 1828 marked the first and only time that slaveholders ran on the same ticket for president and vice president, and some Southerners promoted their election as necessary to preserve the institution. But Jackson himself never explicitly linked his candidacy to a need to defend slavery.[17]

Nevertheless, as president, Jackson always upheld slavery and owners' "right" to hold slave property. His administration refused to challenge state laws that required the temporary imprisonment of free black sailors when their ships stopped in Southern ports, and though he approved helping 120 recently captured slaves return to Africa after a Spanish ship ran aground near Florida, he rejected cooperation with British efforts to suppress transporting more Africans to the western hemisphere as slaves.[18] When his presidency faced one of its most significant challenges, though, Jackson refused to concede to prominent slaveholders' demands. Federal tariff policy actually provoked the Nullification Crisis, but historians have persuasively shown that concerns for slavery's future lurked beneath the controversy. The crisis stemmed from the nation's adopting the policy of placing high taxes on imported goods in order to "protect" American manufacturers from foreign competition. Higher prices on imports—coming mainly from Great Britain—would encourage Americans to buy cheaper American-made products; manufacturers would then presumably invest their profits to expand their businesses, reduce the nation's

"My negroes shall be treated humanely" 163

dependence on foreign imports, and eventually make the Union economically self-sufficient. Many Southerners favored tariff protection at first, and Congress in 1816 and 1824 approved laws that significantly raised tariff rates. In the decade after the Panic of 1819, however, cotton prices remained low, and planters charged that British manufacturers retaliated against the exclusion of their wares by purchasing less Southern cotton. Protective tariffs, they now insisted, were unjust because they favored Northern-based manufacturers while harming Southern planters; moreover, they were unconstitutional because they benefited one section of the Union at the expense of another.[19]

Though a cotton planter himself, Jackson while in the Senate had voted for the Tariff of 1824. During the 1828 presidential campaign, his supporters in Congress tried to reassure Southerners by proposing a bill that would reduce tariffs on goods that competed with products made in New England—a region that Jackson men expected to lose—while raising the duties on raw materials and goods produced in the western and Middle Atlantic states. Proponents never expected the bill to pass, but their strategy backfired. After a confusing series of bargains, deals, and logrolling, Congress instead transformed the bill into a law that raised tariff rates to levels higher than ever before. Most Southerners remained loyal to Jackson, and many presumed that John C. Calhoun, who would remain as vice president, could control Jackson and direct the aging new president toward eliminating protection. Still, Southerners condemned the 1828 law as the "Tariff of Abominations," and in South Carolina—Calhoun's home state—some threatened secession if Congress continued to protect Northeastern industries. When South Carolina's legislature asked Calhoun to prepare a statement explaining the state's position on the tariff, the vice president proposed instead that a state could invalidate a federal law. In his anonymously published *South Carolina Exposition and Protest*, Calhoun argued that a specially elected state convention could review an act of Congress; if the delegates determined the law to be unjust, they could declare it unconstitutional by proclaiming it "null and void" within the state's boundaries. And while the *Exposition and Protest* focused primarily on the tariff, Calhoun acknowledged privately that Nullification also offered Southerners a constitutional way to

164   *Andrew Jackson: Old Hickory in Christian America*

defend itself if a hostile Northern majority ever attempted to abolish slavery.[20]

Calhoun would not reveal his authorship of the *Exposition and Protest* until 1831, but Jackson likely heard Washington rumors about his vice president's association with nullification soon after he took office. From the outset, Jackson vehemently rejected Calhoun's theory as "jesuitical" and "absurd." Low cotton prices hurt his interests as well, but he had long accepted the need for higher tariff rates to provide the income necessary to pay off the national debt; he likewise held a more nationalistic perspective than Calhoun and agreed that "a careful and judicious tariff" could protect American industries and encourage the nation's economic independence. More ominously, nullification struck Jackson as a threat to the Union of states—to him, the foundation of American nation. "Without union our independence and liberty would never have been achieved," he later proclaimed; "without union they can never be maintained." As nullification appeared to gain strength, Jackson warned that disunion would "end in colonial dependence on a foreign power," and he disputed Calhoun's contention that the Union existed as a voluntary compact among the states. "[T]he whole people" of the United States, he insisted, had bypassed the state governments and collectively given the federal government full power to accomplish its purposes, making "the Constitution and the laws . . . supreme and the Union indissoluble." If one state could obstruct the execution of a federal law, Jackson insisted, "then indeed is our constitution a rope of sand," and though he upheld the states' rights to perform their duties—as in Georgia's clash with the Cherokees—he charged nullification's advocates with intending "to destroy the union, & form a southern confederacy." Because the theory "leads direct to civil war, . . ." he concluded, "the other states have a perfect right, to put it down."[21]

Calhoun's connection with nullification, along with his apparent snub of Margaret Eaton, further disgraced the vice president in Jackson's eyes. Meanwhile, the *United States Telegraph*, edited by Calhoun's ally Duff Green, gave the impression that Jackson supported nullification, compelling the president to deal the doctrine a stinging rebuke. The organizers of a dinner to commemorate Thomas Jefferson's birthday on April 13, 1830, planned to conclude the festivities with a series of after-dinner toasts that would denounce the tariff and implicitly

"My negroes shall be treated humanely" 165

endorse nullification. After listening to nullifiers' harangues, Jackson, as president and according to custom, offered the first voluntary toast. Staring at Calhoun, he stood, raised his glass, and stated simply, "Our Union—it must be preserved!" Calhoun replied with his own rambling toast, defending liberty over Union. With their differences now openly confirmed, Jackson spent the next year eliminating Calhoun's influence in the administration while blocking his vice president's presidential aspirations. Reluctantly, Jackson allowed Francis P. Blair to announce in the Washington *Globe* that, if re-elected, he would serve a second term. The "purge" in the spring of 1831 then forced Calhoun's associates out of the Cabinet, and when Calhoun, as vice president, cast the deciding vote in the Senate to reject Van Buren's appointment as minister to Great Britain, Jackson insisted that his supporters redress "the insult offered to our government" by promoting Van Buren to the vice presidency. The following May, the first national Democratic convention formally nominated the former secretary of state, solidifying his position as Jackson's *heir apparent*.[22]

South Carolina meanwhile moved forward with Nullification. Following Jackson's recommendation, Congress enacted a new tariff law lowering rates in July 1832, but because the Tariff of 1832 still provided protection for Northern manufacturers, Nullifiers vehemently condemned the law. That fall, after Nullifiers won clear majorities in the state elections, the state legislature quickly approved a convention that on November 24 put Calhoun's theory into practice, declaring both the 1828 and 1832 tariff laws null and void within the state. No tariffs, the delegates proclaimed, were to be collected in South Carolina after February 1, 1833, and 25,000 volunteers responded to the governor's call to resist if the federal government attempted to enforce the law.[23] Jackson prepared to meet South Carolina's defiance with force. Insisting that "*the union will be preserved*, & the laws duly executed," on December 10 he issued a Proclamation denouncing nullification and secession and promising to enforce the tariff. The Nullifiers' "object is disunion," he warned, "but be not deceived by names; disunion, by armed force, is TREASON." Over the next several weeks, as he planned a military operation against the state, he asked Congress to approve a law, soon popularly known as the "Force Bill," that would authorize his ordering the army and navy into South Carolina to

166   *Andrew Jackson: Old Hickory in Christian America*

collect the tariff in Charleston. To many, a war between the federal government and a state appeared inevitable.[24]

At the same time, Jackson sought a peaceful resolution to the crisis. While he admonished commanders to avoid provoking a confrontation, Treasury Secretary Louis McLane moved Charleston's customs houses to military posts on islands at the mouth of Charleston Harbor. There, ships importing foreign goods could pay the duties before reaching the town. A New York congressman meanwhile introduced into the House of Representatives a bill that McLane drafted to reduce tariff rates significantly. The prospect of compromise convinced South Carolina to postpone nullification past the February 1 deadline, but McLane's bill met resistance both from Northeastern manufacturers and from Calhoun, who now represented South Carolina in the Senate. Calhoun agreed instead to support a proposal from Henry Clay—now also in the Senate, representing Kentucky—to cut rates gradually over the next nine years, maintaining protection for the present but effectively ending the policy in 1842. Jackson resented his two leading political foes' replacing his administration's proposal, but he also realized that Clay's bill had the backing needed to bring the crisis to an end. He insisted that Congress still give him the authority to use military force if necessary while signaling that he would approve Clay's proposal, and he signed the Force Bill and Clay's Compromise Tariff into law the day after Congress passed both on March 1, 1833. South Carolina's Nullifiers meanwhile found themselves isolated. Nullification won modest support across the South, but no other state attempted to nullify the tariff, with several formally condemning Calhoun's theory. With nowhere else to turn, South Carolina's convention repealed its Nullification ordinance in March 15, though in a final act of defiance, the delegates then nullified Jackson's now-moot "Force Bill."[25]

Throughout the crisis, Jackson never publicly associated Nullification with anxieties over slavery's future, but he likely sensed the connection. Soon after approving the Compromise, he observed that "the tariff was only the pretext" for nullification; "disunion & a southern confederation" was "the real object," and he expected "the next pretext" to be "the negro, or slavery question." Several recent developments had heightened sectional tensions while stoking fears of slave rebellion. Only a decade earlier, South Carolina officials had

"My negroes shall be treated humanely" 167

thwarted Denmark Vesey's plan to launch an uprising in Charleston. In 1827, Charleston's Robert J. Turnbull published a pamphlet, under the pseudonym "Brutus," warning that Northerners intended to use the tariff and internal improvement issues to justify expanding federal power so they could abolish slavery. Two years later, David Walker, a free African American in Boston, published his own scathing condemnation of slavery and white racism while calling for black people to rise up and claim their freedom. Then, in January 1831, the appearance of the first issue of *The Liberator* marked the onset of the abolitionist movement. Unlike previous antislavery activists, abolitionists denounced the institution as a moral evil because it contradicted Christian teachings about the brotherhood of all men. Slaves should be emancipated immediately rather than gradually, abolitionists argued, with no compensation for "manstealers" and, some contended, without separating the races. Eight months after *The Liberator*'s debut, Nat Turner, a Virginia slave, led an uprising that, before its brutal suppression, killed about sixty white civilians. Southerners widely believed that the impassioned harangues of the paper's editor, William Lloyd Garrison, had incited the nation's largest and most deadly slave rebellion—and that Garrison and other "fanatics" heartily approved the insurrection.[26]

Jackson regretted the increasing tensions over slavery and saw in the Abolitionist movement the same treasonous motivations that had produced Nullification: "mischievous and intrigueing individuals," he presumed, intended "to stir up amongst the South the horrors of a servile war" so they could "disturb and shake our happy confederacy" and further their own political ambitions.[27] This presumption guided him when explicit arguments over slavery irritated sectional tensions late in his presidency. After forming the American Anti-Slavery Society in December 1833, abolitionists attempted to mail antislavery pamphlets to every slaveowner in the South. When their first mailings arrived in Charleston in July 1835, a handful of men broke into the post office, seized the pamphlets, and led a raucous demonstration around a bonfire that burned the booklets along with effigies of leading abolitionists. The Antislavery Society then flooded Congress with petitions demanding slavery's prohibition in areas clearly under federal authority, including the District of Columbia. By rule, petitions were to be read aloud to the House or the Senate, but the documents' damning rhetoric enraged slaveholding Southern congressmen who demanded

168   *Andrew Jackson: Old Hickory in Christian America*

that their colleagues reject the petitions. During these controversies, a riot in Washington in August 1835 heightened tensions after a drunk slave's threat to murder a white woman incited a mob to try to lynch a doctor suspected of possessing abolitionist literature; when thwarted in their initial attack, the crowd instead destroyed a restaurant owned by Beverly Snow, a free African American. In the uproar's aftermath, a deputation insisted that Jackson fire Augustus, another free African American who worked in the Executive Mansion, for supposedly distributing antislavery tracts to "persons of color."[28]

Jackson refused to hand over Augustus. "My servants are amenable to the law if they offend against the law," he told the delegation, "and if guilty of misconduct . . . they are amenable to me." Most likely, Jackson imposed no discipline on Augustus, who continued to work for the president through the completion of his second term. An appeal from the threatened woman meanwhile persuaded Jackson to pardon the young black man whose actions had provoked the Snow Riot.[29] Still, Jackson's worries about antislavery agitation and its threat to the Union drove him to skirt the law and employ questionable tactics to get abolitionist controversies out of politics. Although the Charleston riot directly defied the federal government's legal responsibility to deliver the mails, Jackson backed the decision of Postmaster General Amos Kendall to allow local postmasters to refuse to deliver "inflamatory papers" unless an addressee requested them—but he also suggested that postmen "take the names down" of those who took the pamphlets "and have them exposed in the publik journals," for their "patronizing these incendiary works" would bring them "into such disrepute with all the South, that they would be compelled to desist, or move from the country." Likewise, with Jackson's approval, administration supporters in Congress provided the crucial votes to secure passage of what became known as the "Gag Rule." According to this provision, representatives would formally receive antislavery petitions, but the petitions would then immediately be "tabled," without being read or printed and with no further action taken on them.[30]

Clashes over slavery continued to disturb Jackson after he left the presidency. He worried less about the fate of slavery than about how abolitionist activism might incite slaves "to insurrection and to massacre," and how Northern and Southern demagogues could selfishly use the issue to dissolve the Union. His commitment to the institution

"My negroes shall be treated humanely" 169

meanwhile never wavered. When he died, he liberated none of his slaves in his will, and he apparently passed away thinking that the institution would long survive him. Throughout his life, he had benefited from slavery and never questioned the distinction between master and slave. At the same time, he recognized that, though legally considered property, the slaves he owned were humans. Witnesses at his deathbed recalled servants saying their tearful goodbyes, with Jackson encouraging them "to look to Christ as their only Savior" and promising that they would all meet again in Heaven. Hannah recalled him assuring them that "Christ has no respect to color."[31] But while he could accept enslaved African Americans as his brothers and sisters in Christ, this acceptance failed to lead him to challenge slavery's existence. Instead, he acted on the presumptions he had learned as a youth, reinforced by the teachings he likely had heard at church: because God had ordained the institution, he should discipline his slaves—severely if he thought it necessary—but he was also to act as a just and kind master. Racial presumptions, economic interests, and the realities of human bondage, though, kept him from becoming the paternal Christian patriarch he considered himself to be.

Notes

1. Booraem, *Young Hickory*, 16, 136–38, 185–86, 232–33n.31; Cheatham, *Andrew Jackson, Southerner*, 14–15; "Record of Slave Sale," November 17, 1788, *PAJ*, 1:15; "Inventory of Hermitage Slaves and Property," January 5, 1829, *PAJ*, 7:8–10.
2. Callie Hopkins, "The Enslaved Household of President Andrew Jackson," *White House Historical Association*, https://www.whitehousehistory.org/slavery-in-the-andrew-jackson-white-house; Matthew Warshauer, "Andrew Jackson: Chivalric Slave Master," *Tennessee Historical Quarterly* 65 (Fall 2006):214–15; Parton, *Life of Andrew Jackson*, 3:602; Andrew Jackson to Sarah Yorke Jackson, January 26, 1833, *PAJ*, 11:72.
3. John Donelson to Andrew Jackson, May 8, 1833, *PAJ*, 11:301; Parton, *Life of Andrew Jackson*, 1:249.
4. "To the Free Coloured Inhabitants of Louisiana," September 21, 1814, *Correspondence*, 2:58–59; Andrew Jackson to William C. C. Claiborne, October 31, 1814, *Correspondence*, 2:88; Jackson to Waters Allen, December 23, 1814, *PAJ*, 3:216.
5. Edward de Krafft to Andrew Jackson, March 5, 1832, *PAJ*, 10:150; Cheatham, *Andrew Jackson, Southerner*, 190–91.

170   *Andrew Jackson: Old Hickory in Christian America*

6. Andrew Jackson to George W. Campbell, October 15, 1812, *PAJ*, 2:334; Parton, *Life of Andrew Jackson*, 1:349–60, 2:301–302, 576–81.

7. "Advertisement for Runaway Slave," September 26, 1804, *PAJ*, 2:40–41; Andrew Jackson to James Bronaugh, July 3, 1821, *PAJ*, 5:66; Jackson to Andrew J. Donelson, June 28, 1822, *PAJ*, 5:195; Warshauer, "Andrew Jackson: Chivalric Slave Master," 204–205, 209–210.

8. Andrew Jackson to Thomas Eastin, June 1806, *PAJ*, 2:106; Jackson to Andrew Jackson, Jr., July [1]4, 1829, *PAJ*, 7:333; Jackson to Andrew J. Hutchings, June 2, 1833, *PAJ*, 11:374; Warshauer, "Andrew Jackson: Chivalric Slave Master," 203–204.

9. Andrew Jackson to Andrew J. Hutchings, June 13, 1829, *PAJ*, 7:280; John H. Eaton to Jackson, April 16, 1832, *PAJ*, 10:238; Jackson to Sarah Yorke Jackson, July 11, 1832, *PAJ*, 10:412.

10. Kidd, *America's Religious History*, 131–33; Mathews, *Religion in the Old South*, 66–80, 136–84; Ernest Trice Thompson, *Presbyterians in the South*, 3 vols. (Richmond, VA: John Knox Press, 1963–1973), 1:323–412; Mitchell Snay, *Gospel of Disunion: Religion and Separatism in the Antebellum South* (Cambridge: Cambridge University Press, 1993).

11. James Jackson to Andrew Jackson, October 10, 1814, *PAJ*, 3:158; "Memorandum of Slaves and Land in Davidson County, Tennessee," January 1, 1825, *PAJ*, 6:34; "Inventory of Hermitage Slaves and Property," January 5, 1829, *PAJ*, 7:8–10; Andrew Jackson to Robert J. Chester, November 7, 1830, *PAJ*, 8:611; Andrew Jackson to Robert J. Chester, November 25, 1830, *PAJ*, 8:636; Warshauer, "Andrew Jackson: Chivalric Slave Master," 206–207, 219–22; Mark R. Cheatham, "Hannah, Andrew Jackson's Slave," *Humanities* 35 (March/April 2014): https://www.neh.gov/humanities/2014/marchapril/feature/hannah-andrew-jacksons-slave.

12. Mark R. Cheatham, "Andrew Jackson, Slavery, and Historians," *History Compass* 9 (2011):332–33; Cheatham, "Hannah, Andrew Jackson's Slave"; Parton, *Life of Andrew Jackson*, 3:602–603.

13. Andrew Jackson to William Faulkner, August 28, 1827, *PAJ*, 6:384; Warshauer, "Andrew Jackson: Chivalric Slave Master," 206, 210–13.

14. Andrew Jackson to Charles Jones Love, December 17, 1829, *PAJ*, 7:639; Jackson to William Donelson, October 8, 1829, *PAJ*, 7:481; Jackson to Andrew Jackson, Jr., July [1]4, 1829, *PAJ*, 7:333; Jackson to Andrew J. Donelson, September 1832, *PAJ*, 10:507; Jackson to Andrew Jackson, Jr., September 2, 1833, *PAJ*, 11:583; Jackson to Andrew Jackson, Jr., November 5, 1836, *Correspondence*, 5:436.

15. Andrew Jackson to John A. Shute, January 3, 1839, *Correspondence*, 6:1–2; Jackson to Andrew J. Hutchings, March 18, 1839, *Correspondence*, 6:7; Warshauer, "Andrew Jackson: Chivalric Slave Master," 216–18.

16. Warshauer, "Andrew Jackson: Chivalric Slave Master," 221, 224, 228n74; Roeliff Brinkerhoff, *Recollections of a Lifetime* (Cincinnati: The Robert Clark Company, 1900), 61.

17. Andrew Jackson to Andrew J. Donelson, April 16, 1820, *PAJ*, 4:367; Henry Martin et al. to Andrew Jackson, June 16, 1833, *PAJ*, 11:387–89; Henry Noble Sherwood, "The Formation of the American Colonization Society," *Journal of Negro History* 2 (July 1917):227; Latner, *Presidency of Andrew Jackson*, 141–42.

18. Andrew Jackson to John Branch, June 30, 1829, *PAJ*, 7:308; Howe, *What Hath God Wrought?*, 362.

"My negroes shall be treated humanely" 171

19. Howe, *What Hath God Wrought?*, 274–75; William W. Freehling, *Prelude to Civil War: The Nullification Controversy in South Carolina, 1816–1836* (New York: Oxford University Press, 1965), 136–40.

20. [John C. Calhoun], *Exposition and Protest, Reported by the Special Committee of the House of Representatives, on the Tariff* (Charleston: D.W. Sims, 1829); Howe, *What Hath God Wrought?*, 395–98; Freehling, *Prelude to Civil War*, 154–76, 254–59; John Niven, *John C. Calhoun and the Price of Union* (Baton Rouge: Louisiana State University Press, 1988), 158–62.

21. Andrew Jackson to Littleton H. Coleman, April 26, 1824, *PAJ*, 5:400; Jackson to John Stoney et al., June 14, 1831, *PAJ*, 9:308; Jackson to William B. Lewis, August 9, 1832, *PAJ*, 10:450; Jackson to Joel R. Poinsett, December 2, 1832, *PAJ*, 10:630; Jackson to Anthony Butler, December 4, 1832, *PAJ*, 10:658; Jackson to John Coffee, December 14, 1832, *PAJ*, 10:723; Jackson to Maunsel White, December 22, 1832, *PAJ*, 10:745; Jackson to John Coffee, April 9, 1833, *PAJ*, 11:235; Andrew Jackson, "Second Inaugural Address," March 4, 1833, *Messages and Papers*, 3:4; Latner, *Presidency of Andrew Jackson*, 140–41; Freehling, *Prelude to Civil War*, 221–27.

22. Andrew Jackson to William B. Lewis, August 25, 1830, *PAJ*, 8:500; Editors' Note, January 22, 1831, *PAJ*, 9:54; Jackson to James A. Hamilton, January 27, 1832, *PAJ*, 10:57; Latner, *Presidency of Andrew Jackson*, 125–39; Howe, *What Hath God Wrought?*, 372–73, 398–99.

23. Cole, *Presidency of Andrew Jackson*, 150–54; Freehling, *Prelude to Civil War*, 252–54, 260–64, 274–78.

24. Andrew Jackson to Anthony Butler, December 4, 1832, *PAJ*, 10:658; Andrew Jackson, "Proclamation," *Messages and Papers*, December 10, 1832, 2:654; Freehling, *Prelude to Civil War*, 264–70, 278–86; Cole, *Presidency of Andrew Jackson*, 159–60.

25. Freehling, *Prelude to Civil War*, 280–81, 286–97; Howe, *What Hath God Wrought?*, 406–408; Cole, *Presidency of Andrew Jackson*, 162–80.

26. Andrew Jackson to Andrew J. Crawford, May 1, 1833, *PAJ*, 11:285; Freehling, *Prelude to Civil War*, 53–61, 127–33, 250–52; Howe, *What Hath God Wrought?*, 402–404, 423–28.

27. Andrew Jackson to Amos Kendall, August 9, 1835, *Correspondence*, 5:360; Jackson to Roger B. Taney, October 13, 1836, *Correspondence*, 5:429.

28. Freehling, *Prelude to Civil War*, 340–51; Cole, *Presidency of Andrew Jackson*, 226–28; Parton, *Life of Andrew Jackson*, 3:584–85.

29. Cheatham, *Andrew Jackson, Southerner*, 172–75; Remini, *Course of American Democracy*, 268–70; Parton, *Life of Andrew Jackson*, 3:606–607.

30. Andrew Jackson to Amos Kendall, August 9, 1835, *Correspondence*, 5:360–61; Freehling, *Prelude to Civil War*, 346–48, 351–53; Remini, *Course of American Democracy*, 259–63, 405–407.

31. Andrew Jackson to Amos Kendall, August 9, 1835, *Correspondence*, 5:361; Cheatham, *Andrew Jackson, Southerner*, 201; Parton, *Life of Andrew Jackson*, 3:677–78.

11

"Providence . . . has chosen you as the guardians of freedom"

Andrew Jackson entered his presidency committed to "reform." Few knew what he thought "reform" actually meant. The campaign that elected him in 1828 wisely avoided committing him to specific positions, and his proponents' broad assurances and vague promises reinforced his popularity while winning him a widespread coalition of support. "Jackson men" would hold clear majorities in both chambers of his first Congress, but the loose alliance behind him represented a diverse range of conflicting interests. Through two terms, Jackson's conduct and decisions as president made him the Union's most controversial figure, separating his followers from his detractors into the rival parties that would dominate the next generation of American politics.

Jackson indeed entered the presidency with clear goals in mind: he intended to sweep out the corruption that he believed had infiltrated Washington after the War of 1812—he would, as he stated himself, "bring back the Government to what it was in the days of Jefferson" and "restore the administration to the original reading of the constitution." Once in office, he moved quickly, as he often put it, to "cleanse the augean Stables." Directing his cabinet secretaries to cut expenses, he stunned Washington by dismissing a large number of federal officeholders, many of whom had held their positions for more than twenty years. His predecessors rarely dismissed government officials, but Jackson embarked on a thorough purge of vital positions, dismissing in his first year alone more than 900 appointees— far more than previous presidents had removed during their entire administrations. Opponents charged that Jackson fired competent public servants merely so he could replace them with men subservient

Andrew Jackson. Jonathan M. Atkins, Oxford University Press. © Jonathan M. Atkins 2025.
DOI: 10.1093/9780191886812.003.0011

174 *Andrew Jackson: Old Hickory in Christian America*

to his will, but the new president defended the removals as necessary to "perpetuate our liberty." "[R]otation in office," or regularly replacing federal officials, he explained, reminded appointees that they were public servants with no "vested right" in a position. The discovery that some of Adams's officials had embezzled funds strengthened his case, but William L. Marcy—a Van Buren ally—confirmed critics' point when he remarked in the Senate that there was "nothing wrong in the rule, that to the victor belong the spoils of the enemy." Jackson always contended that he replaced sycophants with men deemed "honest, fit, & capable," but as political circumstances increasingly influenced his selections, he never acknowledged—or perhaps realized—that his "Spoils System" closely resembled the "corruption" he claimed to eliminate.[1]

While replacing officeholders and dealing with society's rejection of Margaret Eaton, Jackson also devoted considerable time in his first year in office to preparing his first annual message, which he would submit to Congress in December 1829. The Constitution required the president to report periodically on "the State of the Union," and Jackson designed the message to show the course he intended for his administration to pursue. He prepared the document following the same process he would use when putting together most of his presidency's major public statements: he would jot down the points he wanted the message to get across, share them with associates, and prepare his own rough version while asking his colleagues likewise to draft either specific sections or the entire paper. After receiving their input, Jackson himself would then produce a longhand draft before meeting with his co-writers to shape its final version. In these discussions, as in his sessions with his Cabinet, he expected his advisors to speak honestly and directly, accepting disagreement and wanting frank discussion and counsel to help him make informed decisions. Those decisions, however, he accepted as his responsibility alone. Unlike predecessors who worked with their Cabinets as a team to develop national policy, Jackson used his official advisors as a panel of consultants to help him form positions that he alone determined. Rarely did he poll his cabinet on an issue, and once he came to a conclusion, he expected full cooperation from his administration to carry it out.[2]

With some notable exceptions, Jackson usually worked amicably with his official counselors. Perhaps because of his first cabinet's

"Providence . . . has chosen you as the guardians of freedom" 175

estrangement over the Eatons, he also came to rely heavily on friends and associates dedicated, he believed, to his administration's success. Rumors about the influence of various individuals—forerunners of later presidents' political consultants—provoked accusations that a "Kitchen Cabinet" controlled him, taking over the duties that were supposed to be performed by the official "Parlor Cabinet." In reality, the label "Kitchen Cabinet" implied a more fixed institution than actually existed. Jackson himself always remained in charge, and the men he relied on most closely fluctuated throughout his presidency. William B. Lewis's leverage waned by the start of Jackson's second term, for instance, even though he remained a reliable friend, while Martin Van Buren's influence ebbed and flowed. Two men eventually emerged among his closest confidants. Amos Kendall, an editor who had led the Jackson party in Kentucky in the recent presidential election, so impressed Jackson that he gave Kendall an important position in the Treasury Department so the editor could remain in Washington and consult regularly with the president. Two years later, after Jackson decided to replace the pro-Calhoun *United States Telegraph* as the administration's newspaper, Kendall encouraged the president to bring Francis P. Blair to Washington to edit the Washington *Globe*. Jackson and Blair quickly formed a strong friendship, and with Van Buren and Kendall, the *Globe*'s editor became one of the president's most trusted allies.[3]

Long before Blair's arrival in Washington, Kendall, with Van Buren and John Eaton, provided the major assistance in preparing Jackson's First Message. In its final form, the message reflected Jackson's persisting resentment toward the "corrupt bargain." After opening with a long review of the Union's generally "pacific and friendly" foreign relations, Jackson insisted that "*the majority is to govern*" and recommended the elimination of the Electoral College, proposing to hold a run-off if no presidential candidate received a majority of the popular vote in a general election. A constitutional amendment, he added, should also limit presidents to a single term "of either four or six years," and members of Congress should be excluded from being elected president or appointed to federal office. After defending his recent removals of federal officials, Jackson presented several recommendations on the important issues he saw facing the Union while reminding the representatives that the Constitution created "a

176 *Andrew Jackson: Old Hickory in Christian America*

government of limited and specific, and not general, powers" and that "the great mass of legislation relating to our internal affairs was intended to be left . . . in the State governments." Finally, Jackson concluded with an appeal to his fellow citizens to trust "the guidance of Almighty God, with a full reliance on His merciful providence for the maintenance of our free institutions."[4]

Congress never seriously considered Jackson's proposals for term limits or for changing the presidential election process. Nor did the lawmakers move on his recommendation for "gradual and certain" tariff reductions, despite the looming threat of nullification. Passage of the Indian Removal Act in May 1830 marked the only significant legislative accomplishment of his first congressional session. The day before Jackson signed the act, though, he again shocked Washington when he vetoed a law to fund construction for a road linking Maysville to Lexington in Kentucky. Sponsors justified the act as an extension of the National Road, a thoroughfare that the federal government had begun in 1811 in order to connect the eastern states to the trans-Appalachian west. Jackson's veto message—written mostly by Van Buren—proclaimed the president "sincerely friendly" to internal improvements, and the message encouraged Congress both to devise a plan for routes that would "promote harmony between different sections of the Union" and to approve a constitutional amendment that would clarify the federal government's role in constructing improvements. But the Maysville Road bill, Van Buren through Jackson contended, clearly exceeded the Constitution's boundaries: because it existed in only one state, it conferred only "partial instead of general advantages" that would benefit a state but not the entire nation. Privately, Jackson fumed that unnecessary internal improvements wasted the public's money and represented the worst of a "corrupt log rolling system" of deals among legislators. The fact that the Maysville Road crossed through Henry Clay's home state also likely influenced his decision. Still, over the next few weeks, Jackson vetoed three additional internal improvement acts, signaling that he would uphold a stricter constitutional standard when determining what constituted a legitimate national project.[5]

The flurry of vetoes coming at the end of the congressional session garnered as much attention as did Jackson's strict constructionism. In the Union's first thirty years, six presidents had issued nine vetoes.

"Providence . . . has chosen you as the guardians of freedom"   177

Jackson vetoed four laws passed by his first Congress, and he eventually rejected twelve congressional acts. With each, he contended that Congress had exceeded its authority, but he also implicitly claimed that the president had a larger role to play in the lawmaking process than his predecessors had assumed. This assertion of presidential authority opened him to charges that he acted as a dictator. Criticizing his vetoes as "executive tyranny," supporters of Adams's administration increasingly coalesced behind Henry Clay as "National Republicans" and rejected Jackson's limited-government principles, countering that an energetic federal government could best promote the public welfare. Anti-Masonry meanwhile remained a potent force in the Northeast, and though Anti-Masons remained leery about Clay, they joined with National Republicans in condemning the president's "usurpations." Most Jackson men remained loyal, with many relying on the president's popularity to boost their own electoral prospects. Still, his unprecedented wielding of the veto, along with the sense of where his "reforms" might go, led some now to question quietly whether they could always trust his leadership.

Jackson's "War" against the Bank of the United States proved his presidency's most divisive issue. Congress first created a central bank in 1791 to hold the federal government's money and to assist with its financial affairs. Jeffersonian Republicans contended that the Constitution had not given Congress the authority to charter corporations, and the First Bank closed after a Republican majority refused to renew its charter in 1811. The Union's disastrous finances during the War of 1812 persuaded most political leaders of the need for a national bank. Setting aside their constitutional scruples, Republicans established the Second Bank of the United States in 1816. Some blamed the Bank for causing the Panic of 1819, but after Nicholas Biddle became its president in 1822, the Bank helped to stabilize the economy. Under Biddle's direction, the Bank also provided an important national service by regulating state banks' issuances of paper money, providing the economy with a stable national currency. The Supreme Court meanwhile satisfied most Americans' constitutional reservations when it ruled in 1819 that Congress indeed had the authority to charter a bank. As trade and commerce thrived, reservations about the Bank's existence all but disappeared. By the time Jackson took office, the Bank

178 *Andrew Jackson: Old Hickory in Christian America*

stood as a popular institution that most considered essential for the nation's well-being.[6]

Jackson thus surprised politicians when his first message to Congress included a claim that "the constitutionality and the expediency of the law creating the bank are well questioned by a large portion of our fellow citizens" and that the Bank had "failed in the great end of establishing an uniform and sound currency."[7] In 1820, Jackson had opposed both the Bank's establishment of a branch in Nashville and the Tennessee legislature's creation of a new state bank, but otherwise, he had never gained a popular reputation for crusading against banks. Perhaps, as many historians have concluded, Jackson's brush with bankruptcy after endorsing David Allison's notes in 1795 stirred in him a distrust of all paper money and banks. He later told Thomas H. Benton that he had "always been opposed" to the Bank of the United States "upon constitutional grounds as well as expediency and policy." After he took office, he stated directly to Biddle that he did "not dislike your Bank any more than all banks."[8] Still, Jackson's hostility appeared to stem mainly from his commitment to reform. The Bank had close ties to his political foes and, he firmly believed, had used its resources against his election. The institution likewise mainly served the wealthy and ambitious politicians, he presumed. Under the control of "all the sordid & interested, who prised self interest more than the perpetuity of our liberty," the Bank's ability to buy off legislators potentially made it more powerful than the people's representatives. As president, Jackson concluded, he thus had a responsibility to bring the Bank to the people's attention "& have confidence that they will do their duty."[9]

Jackson wanted to replace the Bank with "*a national*, entirely *national* Bank of Deposit," one that would hold the federal government's money and exist solely under the Treasury Department's authority. Continuing Biddle's Bank after its charter expired in 1836, under any circumstances, never appeared for Jackson to be an acceptable option. Yet other issues took priority through his first term, and some in his administration sent mixed messages about the president's intentions. His new treasury secretary, Louis McLane, openly supported the Bank, and in deference to McLane's "frankness" and "open candour," the president's third annual message to Congress included a vague promise to leave rechartering the Bank "to the investigation of an enlightened

"Providence . . . has chosen you as the guardians of freedom" 179

people and their representatives."[10] Bank supporters interpreted these signs as indications that Jackson would compromise, but with the 1832 presidential election approaching, Henry Clay—now the nominee of the National Republican Party—urged Biddle to ask Congress to renew the Bank's charter immediately. The Bank currently had the votes it needed to pass a bill for its rechartering, Clay reasoned, and reapproving its charter before the election would present Jackson with a political dilemma. If Jackson vetoed a congressional act rechartering the Bank, the public backlash over his attack on the popular institution would damage his prospects for re-election. Conversely, if he signed the rechartering act into law, the president would likely win the election, but the Bank would then be safe until long after Jackson left office. Biddle had some reservations about the strategy, but ultimately, he agreed to Clay's plan. Thus, Congress in July 1832 approved an act to extend the Bank's charter, with a few minor changes, for an additional fifteen years.[11]

Jackson never considered signing the recharter bill. Instead, he accompanied his veto with an 8,000-word message—written primarily by Amos Kendall—designed to appeal directly to voters. The message explicitly rejected Congress's authority to charter a bank: despite the Supreme Court's ruling, Jackson asserted, each branch of the federal government had to decide constitutional issues for itself. Yet Jackson mainly argued that the Bank existed as a "monopoly" with "exclusive privileges . . . granted at the expense of the public" that benefited only its stockholders, making it "subversive to the rights of the States, and dangerous to the liberties of the people." Foreign investors owned almost one-third of the Bank's stock, and as president, Jackson could appoint only five of the institution's twenty-five directors. Nicholas Biddle meanwhile acknowledged openly that state banks existed only through his "forbearance," and while the Bank's exemption from state taxation "attacked and annihilated" state authority, throughout the Union its officers too often interfered in "the purity of our elections" and threatened to "control the affairs of the nation." "It is to be regretted that the rich and powerful too often bend the acts of government to their selfish purposes," the veto message lamented. When the laws acted "to make the rich richer and the potent more powerful," Jackson insisted in its stirring conclusion, "the humble members of society, . . .

180 *Andrew Jackson: Old Hickory in Christian America*

the farmers, mechanics, and laborers, . . . have a right to complain of the injustices of their Government."[12]

Jackson's foes never recognized the veto's popular appeal. Nicholas Biddle denounced the message as "a manifesto of anarchy," and as the 1832 election approached, he distributed 30,000 copies to provide voters with evidence of Jackson's supposed incompetence and demagoguery. Other National Republicans likewise rallied behind Clay and claimed that Jackson's message incited class warfare. In the Northeast, Anti-Masons assumed the mantle of Reverend Ely's "Christian Party in Politics" and nominated their own candidate in William Wirt, the former attorney general who had represented the Cherokee nation before the Supreme Court. Together, the two opposition parties labeled Jackson "King Andrew I" and denounced him as a despot, a tyrant who disregarded the Constitution so he could impose his own will on the nation. Kendall meanwhile directed Jackson's re-election campaign, which now portrayed the incumbent less as the Hero of New Orleans and more as the "champion of the people" against aristocracy and privilege, while Blair's editorials in the *Globe* set the campaign's tone, savagely attacking Clay and the Bank as entrenched selfish interests and denouncing the Anti-Masons for their "religious bigotry."[13]

As in his previous presidential campaigns, Jackson himself oversaw his proponents' efforts, monitoring voter trends and occasionally encouraging Blair to rebut a specific accusation against him. This time, he appeared less concerned about the results. Family matters and the political affairs confronting his administration—particularly the preparations for a response for when South Carolina would attempt to nullify tariff laws—preoccupied most of his attention. Yet he was also confident that he would win, sure that the public strongly approved his veto of the bill rechartering the Bank. "[I]nstead of crushing me as was expected & intended," he crowed, "it will crush the Bank." His only apprehension involved whether his supporters would fall in line to elect Van Buren as his vice president. Still, his friend's prospects seemed secure enough for Jackson to leave Washington for a late summer visit to the Hermitage. The results fulfilled his expectations, as he and Van Buren both won lopsided victories in the Electoral College. The Bank Veto and his aggressive pursuit of Indian Removal, though, may have hurt more than helped his candidacy. He won 63,000 more votes than

"Providence . . . has chosen you as the guardians of freedom" 181

he had in 1828, but his 54 percent of the total reflected a slight decline from the proportion he had won four years earlier. And, although his supporters increased their majority in the House of Representatives, his opponents gained control of the Senate.[14]

Many who voted for Jackson in 1832 expected Congress to modify the Bank's charter to meet the president's objections. Jackson, though, had now determined that the "hydra of corruption" had to be eliminated. Biddle, he knew, could bribe enough representatives to secure the two-thirds majority needed to override his veto, and once rechartered, the Bank's "corrupting influence" would "destroy the liberty of our country."[15] At first, he considered amassing evidence of mismanagement to get a court order to close the Bank immediately, but after consulting with Kendall, Blair, and Roger B. Taney—his avidly anti-Bank attorney general—Jackson instead determined that he could best deal the Bank a fatal blow by withdrawing federal money deposited in its vaults. The government's accounts made up about half the money deposited in the Bank, and removing these funds would severely impair the Bank's ability either to conduct business or to act corruptly. Withdrawing the deposits would also help Jackson move toward a goal he would make more explicit in the coming year: the promotion of a "hard money" currency consisting primarily of gold and silver coins, "the only currency," he concluded, "known to the constitution of the United States." "[T]he *paper system*, . . ." he explained, "has introduced a thousand ways of robbing honest labour of its earnings to make knaves rich, powerful and dangerous," and he assured Blair that, "as soon as the Gold circulates freely amongst the people all Banks will become unpopular with them, & the Banking business will be confined, where it ought, to the commercial world."[16]

Withdrawing the government's deposits faced several obstacles. Most of Jackson's allies, including William Lewis and Martin Van Buren, opposed the move, fearing it would produce a politically lethal economic crisis. Also, the secretary of the treasury would actually have to order the funds' withdrawal, and Jackson knew that Louis McLane would resist. The question remained, too, of what to do with the money once taken out of the Bank. Despite the hurdles, Jackson moved forward. In early 1833, he again reshuffled his cabinet, moving McLane to the State Department and bringing in anti-Bank Pennsylvanian William J. Duane as his new treasury secretary. Although a House

182 *Andrew Jackson: Old Hickory in Christian America*

investigating committee concluded that the deposits were safe in the Bank, Jackson seized on the committee's minority report to claim that the institution bordered on insolvency. Meanwhile, he decided to experiment with a system that kept federal money in state banks. He thus dispatched Kendall to visit the major northeastern cities, where Kendall found seven banks—soon labeled "pet banks"—that were willing to accept federal deposits and face Biddle's potential wrath. With the preparations complete, Jackson announced his decision to his Cabinet on September 18, 1833. To his surprise, Duane refused to cooperate; the Pennsylvanian opposed the funds' movement to state banks and insisted that the treasury secretary, rather than the president, had the legal authority to determine where to store federal funds. Jackson spent a week trying to convince Duane either to follow orders or to resign, but finally he dismissed Duane and replaced him with Taney, who on October 1 presented to the pet banks the drafts they needed to withdraw the federal government's money out of Biddle's Bank.[17]

As expected, Biddle responded by severely contracting the Bank's credit. Claiming that the sudden loss of funds forced the Bank to reduce its liabilities, he cut back the institution's loans, demanded repayment on advances it had already made, and presented notes to state banks for immediate redemption in gold and silver. The drastic reduction in available money sent the economy into a recession, and the national unity that had backed Jackson's repudiation of Nullification quickly disappeared. Leading merchants and bankers called on Jackson to return the federal deposits to the Bank. National Republicans and Antimasons meanwhile joined together as "Whigs"—a term from the American Revolution that proclaimed resistance to monarchy and tyranny—to condemn Jackson's "Executive usurpation." The Whig majority in the Senate led the assault. Henry Clay, whom Jackson described as "reckless & as full of fury as a drunken man in a brothel," called for investigations into the decision for removing the deposits and warned the nation that "a revolution, hitherto bloodless" threatened "the pure republican character of the Government" by producing "the concentration of power in the hands of one man." At Clay's instigation, the Senate demanded that Jackson hand over the paper that he had presented at the September 18 Cabinet meeting. After Jackson refused to comply, citing what later would be referred to as executive

"Providence . . . has chosen you as the guardians of freedom" 183

privilege, the Senate formally censured the president. In ordering the withdrawals, the censure resolution declared, Jackson had assumed for himself "authority and power not conferred by the Constitution and laws, but in derogation of both," while the president's reasons for dismissing Duane and removing the deposits, it concluded, were "unsatisfactory and insufficient."[18]

Yet Jackson remained firm. "This mamoth of power & corruption must die, . . ." he told his son; "the *monster must perish.*" Brushing off the attacks, he contended that Biddle had caused the recession and that the crisis confirmed the dangers of the Bank's powers. "Go to Nicholas Biddle," he reportedly told one delegation from New York. "We have no money here, gentlemen. Biddle has all the money. He has millions of specie in his vaults, at this moment, lying idle." Despite receiving death threats, Jackson assured followers that "no real general distress" existed because the panic affected only "those who live by borrowing, trade on loans, and the gamblers in stocks." The Senate's censure especially offended him, and he responded by sending to Congress a lengthy formal protest charging the upper chamber with unconstitutionally assuming for itself the power of impeachment; as president, he claimed, he stood as the people's direct representative in the federal government, and in removing the deposits he had carried out the popular will. "I think my protest will shew, that it is not I, but the Senate who have usurped power & violated the constitution," the president told his son, "and I am sure the people will recollect, that it was a corrupt & venal senate that overturned the liberty of Rome before ever Cezar reached her gates." Jackson's supporters meanwhile rallied behind him, with those who had questioned the "Bank War's" wisdom—like Van Buren and Lewis—suppressing their misgivings, aware that accepting the Bank's demise had become Jackson's ultimate test of loyalty.[19]

More than any other conflict in his political or military career, Jackson described his war against the Bank as a holy cause. "I trust my god & I fear not what man can do unto me," he told Van Buren. Comparing those who doubted his course with the people of Israel's faithlessness described in Exodus 32, he assured his vice president that, "were all the worshippers of the golden calf to memorialise me & request a restoration of the Deposits, I would cut my right hand from my body before I would do such an act. The golden calf may be

184   *Andrew Jackson: Old Hickory in Christian America*

worshipped by others but as for myself I will serve the Lord." Similarly, he likened the Bank to the Great Beast of Revelation 17 when he encouraged an associate to "Be not afraid of this whore of Babylon; its power is shorn, its days are numbered."[20] And, as he had foreseen, public blame for the recession gradually shifted. A week after the Senate censured Jackson, the House passed its own resolutions opposing the Bank's recharter, upholding the president's order to withdraw the deposits, and appointing a committee to investigate the Bank's role in bringing on the panic. Biddle's arrogant refusal to cooperate with the inquiry brought him a citation for contempt of Congress and severely damaged his public image, especially as economic conditions began to improve. Recovery continued as elections through the summer and fall of 1834 returned majorities of Jackson men to both the House and the Senate. With the public turning against him, Biddle finally gave up. In September, he eased his restrictions on credit and prepared to wind up the Bank's operations as a central bank. "Providence has smiled upon our endeavors," Jackson concluded, "and a grateful people sustain us."[21]

The Bank's defeat marked the culmination of Jackson's crusade for reform. Yet Jackson saw the "monied aristocracy" as a perpetual threat to self-government. The key to protecting liberty, he concluded, lay in forming a well-organized political party, led by trustworthy men and committed to upholding republican principles. Jackson had long held the traditional republican view that parties represented "factions" of self-serving politicians like the various cliques that opposed his administration, "each headed by an ambitious demagogue . . . without virtue or principle."[22] The opposition's strength and his supporters' frequent wavering now convinced him that pure Republicans would have to cooperate to ensure that the people and the founders' ideals directed the government. Throughout the Bank War, Jackson increasingly acted as a party leader. As his followers identified themselves as "Democrats," he helped his advisors develop a coherent message and consulted with congressional leaders about strategy while meeting with individual representatives to ensure their support. Loyalty to Democratic principles became a requirement for his appointees, and he encouraged public meetings and state legislatures to instruct congressmen and senators on how to vote on specific measures. Never did he see these actions as interfering with legislation or local affairs. Instead, he now

"Providence . . . has chosen you as the guardians of freedom" 185

claimed that he had "long believed, that it was only by preserving the identity of the Republican party as embodied and characterized by the principles introduced by Mr. Jefferson that the original rights of the States and the people could be maintained," and he justified his actions as necessary "to reconstruct" Jefferson's Party "and bring the popular power to bear with full influence upon the Government, by securing its permanent ascendancy."[23]

With the Bank vanquished, Jackson's main objective for his Democratic Party became securing Martin Van Buren's election as his successor. Though constitutionally eligible for re-election, Jackson's respect for the already widely accepted two-term tradition, along with his precarious health, prevented him from considering a third term. Despite Van Buren's initial reluctance to take on the Bank, Jackson still thought his vice president the man best suited to serve as chief executive. But Jackson knew that his friend would face a difficult campaign. Van Buren lacked Jackson's personal popularity, and recent antislavery activities in northern states discouraged many Southerners from trusting a candidate from New York. While visiting Tennessee in 1834, Jackson learned about a movement to nominate his one-time ally, Senator Hugh L. White, on the claim that White, rather than Van Buren, would best uphold the principles upon which Southerners had supported Jackson in 1828. Ultimately, Jackson expected the Whig opposition to unite behind Clay, but the Massachusetts legislature nominated Daniel Webster while William H. Harrison—a War of 1812 hero whom Jackson had dismissed as an American diplomat in Colombia—proved a surprisingly popular aspirant in the West. The appearance of multiple candidates convinced Jackson that Whigs intended "*to distract and divide the republican ranks.*" None of the candidates could win a national election, but each threatened to carry enough states to prevent Van Buren from winning an Electoral College majority and throw the election into the House of Representatives where, "by the power of the Bank, a concentration of all parties, and dregs of party, & corruption," would "deprive the people of their choice."[24]

At Jackson's urging, the Democratic National Convention met and nominated Van Buren early, in May 1835, so that "the minds of the people may be drawn" to him. Though Jackson repeatedly insisted that he would not interfere with the people's choice, his well-known preference and supportive public statements led to charges that he was

186   *Andrew Jackson: Old Hickory in Christian America*

attempting to "dictate" his will to the voters. Concern for the campaign likewise influenced several decisions late in his administration. Jackson's determination to silence Abolitionism stemmed partly from the need to reassure Southerners that they could rely on a Northern Democrat like Van Buren to defend slavery. With a surplus of funds amassing in the federal treasury, he reluctantly signed a law, popular among Democrats, that distributed the surplus to the states and expanded to ninety the number of "pet banks" holding federal funds. Jackson feared that the banks would use the sudden windfall to increase their issuances of paper money, delaying the nation's move toward a hard-money currency. The act did prohibit the banks from issuing notes worth less than five dollars, but to counter the banks—and to appease his fellow hard-money Democrats—Jackson issued a "Specie Circular" directing the treasury to accept only gold or silver for purchases of public lands.[25] These moves, along with a now-booming economy, Jackson's popularity, and Democratic reassurances to the South, helped Van Buren win a close but clear victory. To Jackson's dismay, Tennessee cast its electoral votes for White, but with his chosen successor elected and Democrats holding majorities in Congress, he prepared to leave public life confident that the Union would remain in reliable hands.

No one during Jackson's lifetime, or ever since, referred to the Democratic Party as the nation's "Christian Party." That label often would be applied to the Whigs. Jackson's opponents absorbed most of the voters who had supported the Anti-Masonic Party—which approached politics like a religious crusade—and won the backing of Northeastern Presbyterians and Congregationalists who, like Ezra Stiles Ely, expected devout Christians to hold political offices and enact policies that actively promoted their version of the faith. Many in the region had inherited from their New England ancestors a puritanical ethic that expected the church to guide the state, and with their spirits rekindled by the Second Great Awakening, they now awaited the nation's repentance so that Christ could return and establish His millennial kingdom on earth. A large number of these believers initially supported Jackson because he was a church-going Presbyterian, but his aggressive pursuit of Indian Removal and refusal to lead a "Christian Party in Politics" drove them into the opposition. The Whigs' confidence that government activity could ensure the Union's

"Providence . . . has chosen you as the guardians of freedom" 187

material prosperity meanwhile reassured them that Jackson's rivals would promote Americans' moral improvement as well. Theodore Frelinghuysen, the "Christian Statesman" and leader of several religiously influenced reform organizations, emerged as the most visible Christian Whig as revivalists became an important wing of the party that denounced Jackson as a lawless and sinful tyrant.[26]

Jackson's followers instead kept the Democratic Party committed to religious freedom. Democrats rejected calls for state-sponsored Christian activities and moral laws because they too closely resembled an established religion, and their stance won most of the votes of the era's skeptics, deists, and "free thinkers." Meanwhile, the party's populist appeal gained Democrats a strong following among the unchurched, leading one scholar years ago to suggest that the party found its greatest support among men "who bragged about their fondness for hard liquor, fast women and horses, and strong, racy language."[27] Actually, many Democrats continued to practice an orthodox faith—including Jackson, who declared that as president he would "do what my Judgment tells me is right . . . trusting to my god to guide & direct me in all things." His determination to attend church intensified through his presidency, and he insisted on holding the christening of Andrew and Emily Donelson's second child in the president's mansion, never considering a private religious ceremony in the president's official residence a possible breach in the wall separating church and state. Still, he avoided acting in ways that might appear to favor a particular branch of the faith, and he imposed no religious test on presidential appointees, rejecting at least one applicant despite a reference's glowing praise of the aspirant's service as a Presbyterian elder. The Democratic convention in 1835 made no reference to God when declaring the party's principles, just as the party's future platforms would omit any statement that might be construed as an endorsement of religion.[28]

But Jackson also knew that he led a Christian people, understood as a population widely holding a belief in the Judeo-Christian God's existence. Skepticism persisted, large numbers acted indifferently or impiously, and various sects interpreted the Bible in widely different ways. Still, outright atheism was extremely rare, and traditional Christian orthodoxy remained the dominant faith.[29] Many in the most popular Protestant denominations, as well as Catholics and members of

188   *Andrew Jackson: Old Hickory in Christian America*

smaller sects, agreed with Democrats on the need to keep church and state separate, and they resisted Whig calls to impose what dissenters feared would become a theocracy. Still, for Jackson, and for the vast majority of white Americans, their Christian faith made them a civilized people, and God required their adherence to a set of fundamental beliefs that transcended their denominational differences. "A poor ignorant woman" summarized these tenets when she wrote the president anonymously to encourage him to promote "a pure gospel Church upon earth." The gospel, she explained, was founded upon "faith in christ," "complying with his commands . . . to love god and man," "Baptism by immersion as soon as you beleave with all your heart that Jesus is the christ"—rather than "by throwing a few drops of watter on an infants face and profane the scriptures of truth by calling it Babtism"—and "receiving of the Lords Supper in commemoration of his death till he come again." Jackson noted on her letter that "he feels grateful to the writer of the within scriptural efusion," adding that, while "he differs with her with regard to babtism," he "fully accords with all the rest of her doctrine. This is worthy to be preserved and read by every christian."[30]

To Jackson, these doctrines promoted the virtuous behavior that he and others considered necessary in a republic. "[N]o people can flourish without true, genuine religion," he told an associate while serving as president, for religion "expels hypocrisy and deceit from their walks, purifies society, and calls down blessings upon a nation from above."[31] Jackson's public statements frequently petitioned the Almighty for these blessings. Most of his major state documents, like his first message to Congress, concluded with either a prayer-like affirmation of God's oversight or an appeal for divine approval of his actions. The Proclamation on Nullification, for instance, appealed to "the Great Ruler of Nations" to "bring those who have produced this crisis to see the folly, . . ." asserting that God had "chosen" the Union "as the only means of attaining the high destinies to which we may reasonably aspire." The Bank Veto message concluded with an admonition to "firmly rely on that kind Providence which I am sure watches with peculiar care over the destinies of our Republic." And in his Farewell Address—his last public statement—Jackson reminded his fellow citizens that "Providence . . . has chosen you as the guardians of freedom, to preserve it for the benefit of the human race."[32]

"Providence . . . has chosen you as the guardians of freedom" 189

Americans today might dismiss these flourishes as the window dressing that politicians often use to sanctify their messages. Jackson's personal faith and practices strongly suggest that he sincerely believed these appeals would bring God's approval to his nation. His religious invocations likewise resonated with scores of followers who practiced their faith while believing that he had delivered them from an aristocratic alliance of corrupt politicians and a monied elite. For many, trust in the leadership of a religious man sacralized Jacksonian politics. Most, more likely, saw his presidency as a secular venture but still took comfort in a recognition that God had blessed his efforts. While Jackson himself never expected Jesus to establish a millennial kingdom on earth, he nevertheless confidently believed "that a kind providence, will protect our happy Union, . . ." and that he was "(although a feble one) an instrument in the hand of providence for good and not evil."[33] The Democratic Party may not have been the nation's "Christian Party," but to Jackson it was a party of Christians who considered the Union a blessed country with a mission to demonstrate to the world that the people could govern themselves.

With his strong sense of morality and honor, Jackson also rejected the notion that the Whigs presented a legitimate "loyal" opposition. As president, too, he staked no claim to standing as the nation's religious leader. Still, his religious statements further promoted the early stages of an American civil religion by endorsing the notion that the nation had a divine purpose, one unaffiliated with a church but able to unite citizens across party and class divisions. The religious version of nationalism that Jackson promoted excluded nonwhites and allowed his fellow Southerners to deepen their commitment to slavery. His Democratic Party would likewise promote traditional and subordinate roles for women in a republic dominated by white men. Nevertheless, Jackson's public statements as president further advanced the presumption that his nation had a purpose and was guided by God's providential care, and he left office confident that his reforms and the defeat of the Union's foes were, at some level, part of a divine plan.

Notes

1. Andrew Jackson to Hardy Murfree Cryer, April 25, 1831, *PAJ*, 9:214; Jackson to Mary Ann Eastin Polk, January 2, 1833, *PAJ*, 11:3; Jackson

190 *Andrew Jackson: Old Hickory in Christian America*

to John Coffee, May 30, 1829, *PAJ*, 7:249; *Register of Debates*, Senate, 22nd Congress, 1st session (January 25, 1832) (1831–33), 1325; Jackson, "First Message to Congress," December 8, 1829, Richardson, *Messages and Papers*, 2:448–49; "Memorandum Book," [April 1829], *PAJ*, 7:193, [March 1830], *PAJ*, 8:167; Cole, *Presidency of Andrew Jackson*, 39–49; Meacham, *American Lion*, 81–84.

2. Remini, *Course of American Democracy*, 96; Cole, *Presidency of Andrew Jackson*, 47–49.

3. Latner, *Presidency of Andrew Jackson*, 17–19, 49–57, 76–79; Cole, *Presidency of Andrew Jackson*, 88–93.

4. Andrew Jackson, "First Message to Congress," December 8, 1829, *Messages and Papers*, 2:443, 448, 452, 462.

5. Andrew Jackson, "Veto Message," May 27, 1830, *Messages and Papers*, 2:483, 487, 492; Latner, *Presidency of Andrew Jackson*, 98–107; Cole, *Presidency of Andrew Jackson*, 63–67; Andrew Jackson to John Overton, May 13, 1830, *PAJ*, 8:261.

6. Robert V. Remini, *Andrew Jackson and the Bank War* (New York: W.W. Norton & Co., 1967), 23–39, hereafter cited Remini, *Bank War*; Bray Hammond, *Banks and Politics in America from the Revolution to the Civil War* (Princeton: Princeton University Press, 1957).

7. Jackson, "First Message to Congress," *Messages and Papers*, 2:462; Cole, *Presidency of Andrew Jackson*, 56–59.

8. Andrew Jackson to Thomas H. Benton, [June 1832], *Correspondence*, 4:445; Remini, *Bank War*, 17–19, 30–31; Opal, *Avenging the People*, 181–89; Remini, *Course of American Democracy*, 43–48; Parton, *Life of Andrew Jackson*, 3:258–69.

9. Andrew Jackson to James A. Hamilton, December 19, 1829, *PAJ*, 7:642.

10. Andrew Jackson to James A. Hamilton, June 3, 1830, *PAJ*, 8:343; Jackson to Martin Van Buren, December 6, 1831, *PAJ*, 9:731; Remini, *Bank War*, 67–75; Cole, *Presidency of Andrew Jackson*, 96–99.

11. Remini, *Bank War*, 75–80; Cole, *Presidency of Andrew Jackson*, 100–103; Latner, *Presidency of Andrew Jackson*, 107–17.

12. Andrew Jackson, "Veto Message," July 10, 1832, Messages and Papers, 2:576, 577, 581, 588, 590.

13. Parton, *Life of Andrew Jackson*, 3:411–13, 416; Cole, *Presidency of Andrew Jackson*, 105–106, 145; Lee Benson, *The Concept of Jacksonian Democracy: New York as a Test Case* (Princeton: Princeton University Press, 1961), 193–96; Michael F. Holt, *The Rise and Fall of the American Whig Party: Jacksonian Politics and the Onset of the Civil War* (New York: Oxford University Press, 1999), 15–18.

14. Andrew Jackson to Andrew J. Donelson, August 9, 1832, *Papers of Andrew Jackson*, 10:449; Cole, *Presidency of Andrew Jackson*, 145–50; Latner, *Presidency of Andrew Jackson*, 138–39; Howe, *What Hath God Wrought?*, 381–86.

15. Andrew Jackson to James K. Polk, December 16, 1832, *PAJ*, 10:729; Jackson to Hardy Murfree Cryer, April 7, 1833, *PAJ*, 11:231.

16. "Memorandum on the Bank of the United States," March 1833, *PAJ*, 11:219–20; Andrew Jackson to William Duane, June 26, 1833, *PAJ*, 11:437; Jackson to Roger B. Taney, October 13, 1836, *PAJ*, 5:430; Jackson to Francis P. Blair, August 30,

"Providence . . . has chosen you as the guardians of freedom" 191

1834, *PAJ*, 12:470–71; Remini, *Bank War*, 109–12; Cole, *Presidency of Andrew Jackson*, 197–98.

17. Remini, *Bank War*, 112–26; Meacham, *American Lion*, 255–59, 263–68; Cole, *Presidency of Andrew Jackson*, 193–98; Latner, *Presidency of Andrew Jackson*, 170–82; Howe, *What Hath God Wrought?*, 386–89.

18. Remini, *Bank War*, 126–42; Holt, *Rise and Fall of the American Whig Party*, 23–30; Cole, *Presidency of Andrew Jackson*, 197–98; Andrew Jackson to Andrew Jackson, Jr., February 16, 1834, *PAJ*, 12:84.

19. Andrew Jackson to Andrew Jackson, Jr., February 16, 1834, *PAJ*, 12:84; Andrew Jackson to Andrew Jackson, Jr., April 15, 1834, *PAJ*, 12:215; Jackson to James A. Hamilton, February 2, 1834, *PAJ*, 12:57–58; Parton, *Life of Andrew Jackson*, 3:539, 549–50, 558; Cole, *Presidency of Andrew Jackson*, 204–206, 208–209, 211–15; Meacham, *American Lion*, 268–79; Howe, *What Hath God Wrought?*, 389–91.

20. Andrew Jackson to Sarah Yorke Jackson, February 18, 1834, *PAJ*, 12:107; Jackson to Martin Van Buren, January 3, 1834, *PAJ*, 12:6; Jackson to Robert M. Burton, April 27, 1834, *PAJ*, 12:241.

21. Andrew Jackson to Amos Kendall, August 8, 1834, *PAJ*, 12:402; Remini, *Bank War*, 160–68, 173–75; Cole, *Presidency of Andrew Jackson*, 206–208, 210–11, 215.

22. Andrew Jackson to Sarah Yorke Jackson, May 6, 1832, *PAJ*, 10:265.

23. Remini, *Bank War*, 154–63; Latner, *Presidency of Andrew Jackson*, 124–36; Cole, *Presidency of Andrew Jackson*, 141–45, 201 204, 208–15, 245–53; Andrew Jackson to Joseph C. Guild, April 24, 1835, *Correspondence*, 5:339.

24. Andrew Jackson to Martin Van Buren, October 5, 1834, *PAJ*, 12:506; Andrew Jackson and James K. Polk, August 3, 1835, *Correspondence*, 5:358; Richard P. McCormick, "Was There a 'Whig Strategy' in 1836?" *Journal of the Early Republic* 4 (Spring 1984):47–70.

25. Andrew Jackson to Martin Van Buren, October 4, 1834, *PAJ*, 12:506; Remini, *Bank War*, 168–73; Latner, *Presidency of Andrew Jackson*, 184–92; Cole, *Presidency of Andrew Jackson*, 229–36, 266.

26. Carwardine, *Evangelicals and Politics in Antebellum America*, 97–132; Benson, *Concept of Jacksonian Democracy*, 192–207; Haselby, *Origins of American Religious Nationalism*, 282–315; Holt, *Rise and Fall of the Whig Party*, 30–32, 117; Paul E. Johnson, *A Shopkeeper's Millennium: Society and Revivals in Rochester, New York, 1815-1837* (New York: Hill & Wang, 1978), 128–35.

27. Benson, *Concept of Jacksonian Democracy*, 201.

28. Andrew Jackson to Ralph E. W. Earl, March 16, 1829, *PAJ*, 7:98; John Rowan to Jackson, March 11, 1829, *PAJ*, 7:92–94; Meacham, *American Lion*, 118.

29. James C. Turner, *Without God, Without Creed: The Origins of Unbelief in America* (Baltimore: Johns Hopkins University Press, 1986), 73–113; Noll, *A History of Christianity in the United States and Canada*, 165–244; Kidd, *America's Religious History*, 70–91.

30. "Unknown" to Andrew Jackson, October 10, 1833, *PAJ*, 11:728–30.

31. Jackson to Robert M. Burton, November 1831, *PAJ*, 9:706.

32. Andrew Jackson, "Proclamation Regarding Nullification," December 10, 1832, *Messages and Papers*, 2:656; Jackson, "Veto Message," July 10, 1832, 2:591; Jackson, "Farewell Address," March 4, 1837, *Messages and Papers*, 3:308.

33. Andrew Jackson to Andrew J. Donelson, August 30, 1832, *PAJ*, 10:480; Jackson to Sarah Yorke Jackson, March 25, 1834, *PAJ*, 12:167–68.

12

"I await with resignation the call of my god"

In his last official duty as president, Andrew Jackson attended Martin Van Buren's inauguration on March 4, 1837. The occasion, as Thomas Hart Benton observed, proved a rare instance in which "the rising was eclipsed by the setting sun." The cheering crowds showed that Jackson remained personally popular, at least among his fellow Democrats. The retiring president himself no doubt felt a sense of satisfaction. God had spared him to succeed in "restoring the constitution to its original reading in practice, and lay a lasting foundation for the perpetuation of our happy government." Almost certainly, too, he felt a sense of vindication. Seven weeks earlier, the Senate voted to "expunge" its censure of Jackson during the Bank War. As instructed, the Senate's secretary drew a box around the censure resolution in its official journal and wrote across it, "Expunged by order of the Senate this Sixteen day of January in the year of our Lord, 1837." Senator Benton then acquired the secretary's pen and sent it to Jackson as a memento.[1]

Jackson's presidency had profoundly affected his nation. Aside from expelling Native Americans, thwarting nullification, and destroying the "Monster Bank," his administration successfully paid off the national debt and completed an agreement to reopen trade with Great Britain's West Indian colonies, an important market that had been largely closed to American merchants since 1783. Skillful diplomacy had secured a number of commercial treaties, and by backing sensitive negotiations with a threat of force, Jackson compelled France to honor its agreement to pay damages for American ships plundered during the Napoleonic Wars. In his last years in office, Jackson oversaw several reforms designed to improve the government's efficiency. John

Andrew Jackson. Jonathan M. Atkins, Oxford University Press. © Jonathan M. Atkins 2025.
DOI: 10.1093/9780191886812.003.0012

194   *Andrew Jackson: Old Hickory in Christian America*

Marshall's death in the summer of 1835 allowed him to reward Roger Taney with his appointment as Chief Justice, and Jackson's selection of four other justices ensured that Democrats would guide the Supreme Court through the next generation.[2]

Eight years in office had taken their toll. Twice, Jackson faced physical assaults. In 1833, a naval officer dismissed for theft accosted him and twisted his nose hard enough to draw blood—an act of disrespect in Jackson's honor-based world—after the president rejected the dismissed officer's appeal. Two years later, a mentally deranged house painter, with pistols in both hands, managed to get within eight feet of Jackson. The assailant attempted to shoot him, but neither weapon fired, sparing Jackson the distinction of becoming the first assassinated president.[3] Yet while surviving, the demands of his duties drained his health. Often, he enjoyed long spells in good condition, and a Philadelphia surgeon eased some of his discomfort in January 1830 by removing from his left shoulder the ball that Jesse Benton had lodged there seventeen years earlier. But Charles Dickenson's bullet still lay embedded near his heart, causing frequent infections that made him cough up blood. At the same time, the aches and pains of aging— he would turn seventy years old eleven days after leaving office— became more pronounced. He frequently suffered headaches and attacks of diarrhea, both aggravated by his continued self-treatment with bleedings and doses of mercury and lead. While in office, annual excursions either to Tennessee or to the Rip Raps, an island off the Virginia coast that became a favorite retreat, provided some rest, but in the early summer of 1833, exhaustion forced him to cut short a tour of New England. Another major hemorrhaging struck him in November 1836, and though he improved in time to attend Van Buren's inauguration, in his last months in office he left his room only four times.

Jackson would actually survive another eight years after his presidency, but the lingering ailments constantly reminded him of his mortality. The passing of several friends and associates kept his eventual demise on his mind. John Overton, his first friend in Tennessee, died in April 1833. Three months later, John Coffee, perhaps his closest comrade, also passed away. Jackson stoically accepted but deeply grieved their loss. "[I]t is useless to mourn," he noted after learning of Coffee's death; "he is gone the way of all the earth, & I will soon follow him—peace to his manes." The presence in the executive mansion of

"I await with resignation the call of my god" 195

Andrew and Emily Donelson's children, and eventually of his own grandchildren, offered a cheerful distraction, but Emily's shocking death from tuberculosis when she was only twenty-eight dealt him a particularly hard blow. Very likely he had Rachel's young niece and his other friends in mind when he acknowledged in his Farewell Address to the nation that "before long I must pass beyond the reach of human events."[4]

Personal finances also weighed heavily on Jackson's mind. Much of his presidential salary he had spent on dinners and social affairs to entertain guests at the level expected of a chief executive. Bad luck and his overseers' poor management meanwhile contributed to limiting the income from his plantation. Shortly after his second inauguration, an accident caused $1,000 in damages to a carriage that he had recently purchased. In 1832, he spent $2,600 remodeling the house at the Hermitage, but two years later, a fire destroyed its second floor. Slaves managed to save Jackson's personal papers, military mementos, and other personal items, but the damage left the home uninhabitable. Jackson accepted the loss with resignation. "[A]s it appears one of those accidental occurrences where there is no blame to attach to any, . . . I do meet it, as an act of providence, . . ." he consoled his son, "and [am] prepared to say at all times & under all circumstances, 'the Lords will be done.'" The foundation and walls remained intact, and because Rachel had selected the location, Jackson was determined to rebuild the home on the same site. Workers completed construction in time for Jackson to move in after he left Washington, but expanding the mansion's size, refurnishing the entire house, and cost overruns more than doubled the original estimates. "The burning of my house and furniture has left me poor," he noted after departing from Washington, claiming that he left the presidency "with barely $90 in our pockets."[5]

Family matters also concerned the retiring president. Most of his wards had reached adulthood, though one, Andrew J. Hutchings, persistently troubled him. Several schools expelled Hutchings for misbehavior before Jackson could set him up on the Hutchings family plantation in Alabama when he turned twenty-one in 1833. Another charge, Rachel's grandniece Mary Ann Eastin, lived as part of Jackson's official family in Washington before her marriage at the executive mansion in April 1832.[6] By then, Jackson's adopted son had also found a bride. Perhaps to assert his independence, Andrew Jr. appeared

196 *Andrew Jackson: Old Hickory in Christian America*

determined to marry as soon as he reached adulthood. The youth caused his father some embarrassment when he attempted to court a Philadelphia debutante without first gaining her father's permission. The young lady turned down Andrew Jr.'s proposal, as did a Tennessee planter's daughter whom the president observed had "give[n] herself up to coquetry." The matchmaker in President Jackson hinted that Andrew Jr. should consider William Lewis's daughter, as he reminded his son that Mary Anne Lewis was always "a great favorite of mine, and . . . also of your deer deceased mother." Instead, Andrew Jr. became engaged to Sarah Yorke, the orphaned daughter of a Philadelphia merchant. The couple's brief courtship worried Jackson. Sarah was four years older than Andrew Jr., and Jackson likely wondered whether she agreed to the marriage less for love than for security. He admitted, too, that he "would have been better satisfied" if his son "had married in a family I knew." Nevertheless, while his responsibilities prevented him from attending their wedding in Philadelphia in November 1831, the president gave the union his blessing. The connection was "respectable," he concluded, and Andrew Jr. "appears to be happy."[7]

Despite Jackson's concerns, his new daughter-in-law quickly became one of his favorites. The newlyweds spent their honeymoon at the president's mansion, where Sarah impressed Jackson as "amiable accomplished, & pretty, and well educated."[8] After the couple left Washington so Andrew Jr. could take over management of the Hermitage, Jackson wrote regularly to both, often producing longer and more thoughtful letters to Sarah. Eventually, she bore him five grandchildren, with the first two aptly named Rachel and Andrew, though two boys born during his retirement, Thomas and Robert, died in infancy. After the fire at the Hermitage, Sarah returned to Washington to act as the president's hostess while her husband remained to oversee the rebuilding. Mutual worries about Andrew Jr. probably tightened Jackson's and Sarah's bond. Jackson always expressed love and affection for his adopted son, but he evidently recognized Andrew Jr.'s limitations at an early age. While he always hoped that Andrew J. Donelson would carry on his political legacy and one day become president, Jackson never expressed a desire for his son to play an active role in public life. Instead, Andrew Jr. was to take over at the Hermitage and succeed Jackson as the family patriarch. But as a plantation manager, Andrew Jr. proved a disaster. With a pampered

"I await with resignation the call of my god"   197

upbringing, a dominating father, and apparent intellectual limitations, the younger Jackson proved naïve in business, a spendthrift, and, his father worried, a heavy drinker.[9]

Andrew Jr.'s irresponsibility plagued Jackson's final years. By the time Jackson left office, his son had already faced several lawsuits for debt, with his father bailing him out each time, and the young man persistently ignored Jackson's warnings that "the world is not to be trusted. Many think you rich" and would, "if the[y] can, strip you of your last shilling, and afterwards laugh at your folly." Frequently, he reminded Andrew Jr. to "buy nothing on credit when you have the cash to pay for it," and to "buy nothing on credit that is not absolutely necessary for your comfort, or that of your family." Yet Andrew Jr.'s repeated missteps eventually led Jackson to plead in frustration, "My son, why will you not learn to transact your affairs like a man of business?"[10] Reluctantly, Jackson agreed to join his son in purchasing Halcyon, a plantation in Mississippi, but as he feared, the farm's cotton and timber sales never covered its costs. Over Andrew Jr.'s objections, Jackson in spring 1845 determined to sell Halcyon and twenty of its slaves, mainly because his son "wanted that energy to deal with designing, and dishonest men necessary for the welfare of a distant plantation." Jackson died before he could proceed with his plan, and within a decade of his death, Andrew Jr. not only had lost Halcyon but had accumulated $150,000 in debts. Tennessee's state government helped the family avoid disgrace by purchasing the Hermitage, without acknowledging Andrew Jr.'s mismanagement, and letting his family remain there for the remainder of their lives.[11]

Jackson himself never faced losing the Hermitage. His challenges mainly involved having sufficient cash available to meet his expenses. Though eventually he had to sell his race horses, Francis P. Blair and Jean B. Plauché, a Louisiana merchant who had fought with him at New Orleans, provided loans to help him get by, and in 1844 he gladly accepted the funds when, due to his prodding and after a rancorous debate, Congress reimbursed him, with interest, for the $1,000 fine he had paid for contempt of court after arresting Judge Dominick Hall in 1815. Still, Jackson kept his financial difficulties in perspective. When a wealthy Democratic activist in Boston offered help, Jackson assured him "that we are not broke, we still hold unencumbered by morgage, my home stead containing 980 acres, and on the Mississippi river one

198   *Andrew Jackson: Old Hickory in Christian America*

of the best tracts on it of 1180 [acres], with one hundred and fifty odd negroes." He thus spent most of his post-presidential years living the relatively comfortable life of a Southern planter. As his health permitted, he managed his estate, visited Rachel's grave, called on neighbors, provided information for a biography to be written by his friend Amos Kendall, and hosted the friends and guests who frequently came to the Hermitage to pay their respects. Much of his time he now devoted to prayer and reading his Bible, leading nightly devotionals with the family and the household servants.[12] And, more than a year after returning home from Washington, he finally kept his promise to Rachel and became a member of the Presbyterian church.

Notwithstanding his beliefs and his long-standing promise, Jackson hesitated to join the church. He told James Smith, a Nashville minister who preached regularly at the Hermitage church, that, because of his wife's and his mother's influence, he "felt more identified" with the Presbyterian church than with any other, "but he did not believe the doctrines of that Church," which membership would require him to endorse. One issue likely involved Jackson's disagreement with the denomination's understanding of predestination. As Calvinists, Presbyterians held that, before creation, God had elected certain individuals for salvation while consigning others to be damned, while Jackson believed, as he told a visitor to the Hermitage, that "every man has *a chance* for his own salvation." But Jackson also admitted to Smith that "he knew a Presbyterian elder who had sworn to a lie"—a possible reference to Reverend John Campbell's attacks on Margaret Eaton, though Smith presumed Jackson referred to someone who "belongs to the Church here." Likely, too, Jackson's persistent commitment to honor still made him wary of submitting to the church's discipline and direction. Smith, for his part, remained disturbed because Jackson apparently "knew nothing of regeneration," the belief that, at some identifiable point, God transformed a sinner into someone who desired forgiveness and dedicated himself to righteous living. Raised a Christian from his earliest days, Jackson had gradually grown more devout, but he never indicated he had undergone such a conversion experience. Without evidence of regeneration, the minister did not believe the former president should be eligible for church membership.[13]

While Smith expressed reservations, another minister apparently took advantage of a spiritual crisis in the Jackson family to get the

"I await with resignation the call of my god" 199

former president into the church. When Andrew Jr. and Sarah lived in Washington, Sarah's minister from Philadelphia baptized her first two children, but with the birth of her third child, Samuel, in 1837, she learned to her distress that ministers in Tennessee—adhering more closely to Presbyterian tradition—baptized only the children of church members. Sarah considered herself too sinful to join the church, but she feared that, if Samuel died unbaptized, he would be condemned. Reverend Smith resisted Sarah's pleas to baptize her son, and while Sarah and her father-in-law fretted over this prospect, another Presbyterian pastor, Reverend John Todd Edgar, preached at a service that the family attended at the Hermitage church. Dr. Edgar later claimed that his message that day drove Jackson into a night of agitation, prayer, and meditation; the next morning, "a great peace fell upon" the general that, Edgar concluded, signified Jackson's conversion. Reverend Smith observed that Jackson actually "objected . . . *strenuously*" to Edgar's sermon, but by then, Smith had resolved to put aside his misgivings and baptize Samuel. However, Smith fell ill before he could go to the Hermitage, so Edgar went to the plantation in Smith's place. Edgar insisted that the child's baptism required Sarah's church membership, and his inflexibility compelled the family to make a decision. Andrew Jr. apparently stayed away, and neither minister referred to Sarah's having experienced conversion. Nevertheless, on July 15, 1838, Jackson stood before the Hermitage church congregation, declared his and Sarah's belief in Presbyterian doctrine, and the two formally became members of the church.[14]

Reverend Smith acknowledged that "it was an affecting scene to see the old man at the Lords table," and he recognized that the Hero had been "much exercised on the subject of religion." Still, because he doubted whether Jackson had experienced regeneration, the minister confided that he "would not have received General Jackson into our church." "I fear Edgar has [t]hat to answer for," Smith told his uncle, implying that his colleague had manipulated Jackson into membership.[15] Jackson himself never referred to anything resembling a conversion. Instead, he reiterated six weeks after his first communion that he

would long since have made this *public* declaration to the almighty God, but knowing the wickedness of this world and how prone many are to

200 *Andrew Jackson: Old Hickory in Christian America*

evil, that the scoffer of religion would have cryed out hypocracy—*he has joined the church for political effect*[.] I thought it best to postpone the public act, until my retirement to the shade of private life, when no false imputation could be made that might be injurious to religion.[16]

Jackson would soon afterward decline his appointment as one of the church's ruling elders, claiming that he was "too young in the church for such an office." Nevertheless, he quickly became a fixture in the congregation. His faith seems to have provided great comfort for him in his last years, especially as he mourned the passing of more friends and family members. Ralph Earl's death, two months after Jackson gave his testimony at the Hermitage church, particularly proved "a severe bereavement." The artist had returned to Tennessee with Jackson and often still accompanied the former president on his travels. "[M]y sincere friend and constant companion . . . is gone to happier climes than these 'Where the wicked cease to trouble and the weary are at rest,'" Jackson lamented, quoting Job 3:17. "I shall soon follow him," he added, "and, I trust, meet him in the realms of bliss, thro the mediation of a glorious redeemer."[17]

While preparing for the next world, Jackson also remained deeply engaged in this one. He continued to watch the nation's political affairs closely, corresponding regularly with Amos Kendall and Francis Blair while generously offering his advice to President Van Buren. A depression wracked the economy only a few weeks after Jackson left office. Whigs blamed the collapse on the "Bank War," but Jackson's hostility toward a central bank never wavered. Instead, he enthusiastically approved Van Buren's plan to create an "Independent Treasury," or "subtreasury," that would keep federal money in special Treasury Department offices and effectively "divorce" the government from all banks. Mustering his strength, Jackson made several campaign appearances in Tennessee to promote his friend's re-election in 1840, but despite Jackson's efforts, Whigs not only easily defeated Van Buren but also won control of both chambers of Congress. Jackson blamed the outcome on "the perjury, bribery, fraud, and imposition upon the people by the vilest system of slander, that ever before has existed, even in the most corrupt days of ancient Rome." When the new president, William H. Harrison, unexpectedly died one month into his term, Jackson expressed no sympathy; to the contrary, he assured Blair

"I await with resignation the call of my god" 201

that "a kind and overruling providence has interfered to prolong our glorious Union." And while he anticipated and appreciated the decision of Harrison's successor, John Tyler, to veto Whig laws to create a third Bank of the United States, Jackson counseled Democrats to reject Tyler's overtures for their support. The party needed to renominate Van Buren in 1844, Jackson contended, for his friend's re-election offered the only way to refute "the corruption and frauds by which he lost his election in 1840."[18]

As the 1844 presidential election approached, Jackson became obsessed with a concern left unresolved from his own administration. While in office, Jackson had attempted to buy the state of Texas from Mexico. Mexican officials rejected his offers, but in Spring 1836, Texas' settlers—mostly Americans from the Southern states—rebelled and ousted Mexican authority. By then, abolitionist activism had stoked Jackson's fear that the admission of a new slave state might enhance sectional tensions and threaten Van Buren's election. Rejecting the Texans' appeals, Jackson instead formally recognized Texas' independence and counseled the "Lone Star Republic's" leaders to wait until conditions for joining the Union appeared more favorable. Later, during Tyler's administration, reports filtered into American newspapers claiming that Great Britain also intended to recognize Texas' independence in exchange for the state's abolition of slavery. These rumors convinced Jackson that the nation's long-standing enemy now intended to dominate Texas and at the same time assert control over the Oregon Territory in the Pacific Northwest, which the United States had jointly occupied with Britain since 1818. Surrounded by its hostile former mother country, the Union would again find its independence threatened and likely face war. "What mischief and havock would be inflicted upon us before we could organize an army to repel this egression," he worried. "We must regain Texas, *peaceably if we can, forcibly if we must.*" When Tyler announced in April 1844 that his administration had negotiated a treaty for Texas' annexation to the United States, Jackson hoped the Senate would quickly ratify the agreement, and he gloated when Henry Clay, now the Whigs's presidential nominee, announced his opposition to the treaty.[19]

But then, to Jackson's dismay, Van Buren announced that he also opposed the treaty, fearing Texas' annexation would lead to a war with Mexico. Van Buren's announcement devastated Jackson. "I am quite

202   *Andrew Jackson: Old Hickory in Christian America*

sick really," he lamented to Blair, concluding that Van Buren's statement was "a fatal letter to our hopes politically." Publicly, he continued to support his old friend, arguing that Van Buren had based his position on "knowledge only of circumstances bearing on the subject as they existed at the close of his administration without a view of the disclosures since made, and which manifest the p[r]obability of a dangerous interference with the affairs of Texas by a foreign power." He realized, though, that Van Buren's stance gave him little chance to win, and when the Democratic Convention nominated fellow Tennessean James K. Polk on a platform promising the annexation of Texas and American occupation of Oregon, Jackson acknowledged the candidate to be "the strongest the Democracy could have selected." Though now too old and infirm to make public appearances, Jackson aided Polk's campaign where he could. Mainly, he wrote several letters to encourage wavering Democrats to unite behind the nominee. He declined when Polk asked him to encourage John Tyler to withdraw from the race; an attempt to influence Tyler, Jackson protested, "would be seized upon as bargain and intrigue for the Presidency." Still, he allowed William B. Lewis to share with Tyler a letter explaining why Jackson thought the incumbent's candidacy would lead to Clay's election. The letter contributed to Tyler's decision to drop out of the contest, and Jackson—picking up on Tyler's hint—prompted Blair to "desist from the abuse of Tyler or his supporters" in the *Globe*.[20]

Jackson's efforts undoubtedly contributed to Polk's victory in the closest presidential election to date, and the former president rejoiced when Tyler interpreted Polk's election as a mandate and secured Texas' annexation through a joint resolution of Congress. Once Polk took office, some of the new president's early decisions disturbed Jackson. Determined to be "myself President of the U.S.," Polk disregarded Jackson's advice and dismissed William B. Lewis—without first informing Lewis—from the government office he had held for the past sixteen years. More disturbingly, Polk forced Francis Blair out of his position as the Washington *Globe*'s editor; renaming the paper the Washington *Union*, Polk explained to Jackson that Blair remained too closely attached to Van Buren, and he wanted his administration's organ to "look to the success or glory of my administration for its own sake." Jackson consoled his old friend that Polk's "foolish" decision "troubled" him, as it seemed "calculated to divide instead of uniting

"I await with resignation the call of my god" 203

the democracy."[21] Nevertheless, the Democratic Party's control of the government left Jackson content. "Providence presided over the councils of the convention, Polk was selected, and elected, and I believe it a providential result," he told Blair, echoing an earlier comment he made comparing himself to the prophet who had held the baby Jesus in Luke 2:29: "now I can say as Simeon of old," he had told Kendall, " 'Lord, let thy servant depart in peace.' "[22]

By then, Jackson knew he had little time left. Through the first several years of his retirement, headaches, insomnia, coughing up blood, and his bowel disorder continued to plague him. He managed to get out occasionally, making his last extended excursion when he traveled to New Orleans in 1840 to attend a ceremony commemorating the twenty-fifth anniversary of his greatest victory—stopping at the Mississippi plantation on the way to pay off some of his son's debts. But soon after his return, his health declined rapidly. Often complaining of a pain in his left side, he suffered an apparent heart attack in July 1841. Though he recovered, increased difficulty breathing and frequent bouts with "dropsy"—an intense swelling in his hands and feet—now accompanied his usual maladies. While his mind remained sharp and he still wrote with a steady hand, his letters frequently commented on his feeble condition or noted that he found it difficult to write. By early 1844, he lamented that he could only leave his room to walk to the Hermitage's colonnade "to breath for a short time a little fresh air," and while promoting Texas annexation and Polk's election, he spent most of his time in a chair in his room, struggling to write letters, to greet the stream of guests who still came to get a last glimpse of the Hero, and to read Rachel's Bible and hymn book. Confident that he would soon join Rachel in heaven, he assured his nephew shortly after Polk's election that "I await with resignation the call of my god."[23]

The following summer, the call finally came. On June 1, 1845, his swelling and his breathing difficulties seriously worsened. Three doctors rushed to the Hermitage, but they agreed they could do little beyond keeping him comfortable. Through the following week, he received visits from friends who came to say goodbye, and he mustered the strength to dictate a final letter to warn President Polk about possible corruption in the Treasury Department. Otherwise, he spent most of his last moments in prayer, reassuring family members that he welcomed his passing. Witnesses later described an emotional

204   *Andrew Jackson: Old Hickory in Christian America*

deathbed scene, with Jackson bestowing final blessings to his kin and admonishing the grandchildren to "keep holy the Sabboth day and read the New Testament." Hannah, who with the manservant George refused to leave when a doctor ordered slaves out of the room, recalled Jackson proclaiming as he expired that he had "a right to the Tree of Life" described in Revelation 22. Andrew Jr. claimed that his father's last words promised "to meet you all in heaven, both white and black." One of the doctors recalled Jackson repeating "both white and black," while James Parton—relating William Lewis's account—noted that his final statement admonished all to "be good children, and we will all meet in heaven."[24] Whatever his last words, Jackson spoke them shortly before he died, at around six p.m., on Sunday, June 8.

As Jackson had directed, his body was interred next to Rachel's in the tomb he had built in the Hermitage's garden. An estimated 3,000 mourners attended his funeral, held two days after he died. John Todd Edgar preached to the crowd from the mansion's front porch, using as his text Revelation 7:13–14, a passage on the delivery from "the great tribulation" of the persecuted who had "washed their robes, and made them white in the blood of the Lamb." During his sermon, Dr. Edgar held Jackson's Bible up before the crowd, related his account of Jackson's profession of faith at the nearby church, and "dwelt upon his private character & upon his christian conduct." The crowd and the bustle of the day's activities intimidated "Poor Poll," a parrot that Jackson had bought for Rachel as a pet eighteen years earlier. The "wicked parrot, . . ." one attendee recalled years later, "got excited and commenced swearing so *loud* and *long* as to disturb the people and had to be carried from the house."[25]

Across the Union, the public joined in commemorating Jackson. President Polk closed all government offices for a day, directed a memorial service to be held in the capital, and ordered civilian and military officers to wear badges of mourning for six months. Numerous local communities held services to honor the man whom many considered the greatest American since George Washington. Eulogists celebrated Jackson's accomplishments and devotion to his country, with most stressing his rise from poverty and his suffering in the American Revolution. Nearly all praised his stand against Nullification. With voters now bitterly divided between Democrats and Whigs, most avoided mentioning other major developments in his presidency.

"I await with resignation the call of my god" 205

Some tributes portrayed Jackson as the instrument of providence, while many at least mentioned his Christian faith. His delay in joining a church and Andrew Jr.'s widely published account of his father's final moments led many orators to claim that Jackson "could not render that devotion to his God" until his final years. One minister regretted "that he had not thus consecrated himself in early life." Those who knew him better echoed Nashville editor Jeremiah G. Harris, who declared that Jackson "from his childhood . . . had revered Christianity," and that, throughout his exploits, "the purest religious feelings animated his heart and shaped his inclinations."[26]

Jackson had, in fact, identified with Christianity throughout his life. "[M]y god knows whether I have or not always acknowledged, a Saviour with a firm belief in the Scriptures," he noted shortly before his death; "therefore I care not what men think on this important subject."[27] Religion may not have always animated or shaped him, but it explained the world to him and provided him with a basis for understanding right and wrong. Christian principles often failed to override his demand for vindication. Nevertheless, he merged his faith with his era's ethic of honor, convincing himself that an honorable man would also be a good Christian while—like many before and since—adapting Christian teachings to serve his needs. His faith differed from the fervor of the revivals that flourished through his lifetime. Rachel apparently experienced a rekindling of her spirit, but despite Dr. Edgar's account, claims of Jackson himself having a life-altering moment of conversion remain suspicious, as he left no evidence that he thought he either needed or went through such a regeneration. He likewise never looked forward to a coming millennium and refused to use his authority to enforce church decrees. Religious liberty, rather than the establishment of a Kingdom of God on earth, stood for him as a core tenet of a democratic republic, even though he thought citizens should adhere to the Christian religion so they could practice the virtue they needed to govern themselves.

Ultimately, Jackson's religion reflected the strong influence of Christianity on his era. Thomas Hart Benton observed that if Jackson had lived "in the time of Cromwell he would have been a Puritan."[28] In Jackson's own time, he reflected a strain of Christianity widespread among his countrymen: traditionally orthodox, broadly ecumenical, separate from politics, but part of the nation's identity. Most of his

206   *Andrew Jackson: Old Hickory in Christian America*

fellow countrymen avoided zealotry, but many, like Jackson, acknowledged, accepted, and practiced this version of the faith. Their religion, they believed, made them a civilized and free people living in, as Jackson himself put it, "the best country" with "the best institutions in the world."[29] The white, slaveholding, violent, and expansive republic of the Age of Jackson often contradicted what many Christians, before and afterward, consider core tenets of their faith. Nevertheless, Old Hickory's America was a Christian nation, a world far different from the America of later generations.

Notes

1. Benton, *Thirty Years View*, 1:735; Andrew Jackson to Sarah Yorke Jackson, March 25, 1834, *PAJ*, 12:167–68; Cole, *Presidency of Andrew Jackson*, 264–66.
2. Parton, *Life of Andrew Jackson*, 3:561–82; Cole, *Presidency of Andrew Jackson*, 237–44; John M. Belohlavek, *"Let the Eagle Soar!" The Foreign Policy of Andrew Jackson* (Lincoln: University of Nebraska Press, 1985), 90–126.
3. Remini, *Course of American Democracy*, 60–62, 228–30; Parton, *Life of Andrew Jackson*, 3:486–88, 582–84; Kenneth S. Greenberg, *Honor & Slavery: Lies, Duels, Noses, Masks, Dressing as a Woman, Gifts, Strangers, Humanitarianism, Death, Slave Rebellions, The Proslavery Argument, Baseball, Hunting, Gambling in the Old South* (Princeton: Princeton University Press, 1996), 16–23.
4. Andrew Jackson to Martin Van Buren, July 24, 1833, *PAJ*, 11:498; Andrew Jackson, "Farewell Address," March 4, 1837, *Messages and Papers*, 3:308.
5. Andrew Jackson to Andrew Jackson, Jr., October 23, 1834, *PAJ*, 12:560–61; A. D. Campbell to Andrew Jackson, March 15, 1837, *Correspondence*, 5:465.
6. Meredith, "'There Was Somebody Always Dying and Leaving Jackson as Guardian,'" 61–68.
7. Andrew Jackson to Andrew Jackson Jr., September 21, 1829, *PAJ*, 7:446–47; Jackson to Francis Smith, May 19, 1830, *PAJ*, 8:268–69; Jackson to John Coffee, November 20, 1831, *PAJ*, 9:700; Jackson to Andrew Jackson Jr., September 16, 1831, *PAJ*, 9:577.
8. Andrew Jackson to Martin Van Buren, December 6, 1831, *PAJ*, 9:732.
9. Cheatham, *Andrew Jackson, Southerner*, 146–47, 150–51.
10. Andrew Jackson to Andrew Jackson, Jr., November 16, 1833, *PAJ*, 11:767; Jackson to Andrew Jackson, Jr., December 22, 1833, *PAJ*, 11:826; Jackson to Andrew Jackson, Jr., June 2, 1834, *PAJ*, 12:280.
11. Andrew Jackson to Francis P. Blair, March 3, 1845, *Correspondence*, 6:376; Cheatham, *Andrew Jackson, Southerner*, 182–85; Parton, *Life of Andrew Jackson*, 3:630–31, 684.
12. Andrew Jackson to William B. Lewis, August 19, 1841, *Correspondence*, 6:119–120; Warshauer, *Andrew Jackson and the Politics of Martial Law*, 81–100, 161–75.

"I await with resignation the call of my god" 207

13. James Smith to Finis Ewing, 1838, Finis Ewing Papers, Tennessee Historical Society, Nashville; Parton, *Life of Andrew* Jackson, 3:633.
14. James Smith to Finis Ewing, 1838, Finis Ewing Papers; Parton, *Life of Andrew* Jackson, 3:644–48; Remini, *Course of American Democracy*, 444–47.
15. James Smith to Finis Ewing, 1838, Finis Ewing Papers.
16. Andrew Jackson to William P. Lawrence, August 24, 1838, *Correspondence*, 5:565.
17. Andrew Jackson to Nicholas P. Trist, September 19, 1838, *Correspondence*, 5:565–66; Parton, *Life of Andrew Jackson*, 3:648.
18. Andrew Jackson to Martin Van Buren, November 24, 1840, *Correspondence*, 6:83–84; Jackson to Francis P. Blair, April 19, 1841, *Correspondence*, 6:105; Jackson to Blair, August 11, 1843, *Correspondence*, 6:226; Howe, *What Hath God Wrought?*, 503–508, 571–88.
19. Andrew Jackson to Aaron V. Brown, February 9, 1843, *Correspondence*, 6:202; Jackson to William B. Lewis, September 18, 1843, *Correspondence*, 6:230; David M. Pletcher, *The Diplomacy of Annexation: Texas, Oregon, and the Mexican War* (Columbia: University of Missouri Press, 1973), 9–110; Cole, *Presidency of Andrew* Jackson, 130–34; Belohlavek, *"Let the Eagle Soar!,"* 215–38.
20. Andrew Jackson to Francis P. Blair, May 11, 1844, *Correspondence*, 6:285, 287; Jackson to Blair, June 7, 1844, *Correspondence*, 6:297; Andrew Jackson to James K. Polk, July 26, 1844, *Correspondence*, 6:303; Jackson to William B. Lewis, August 1, 1844, *Correspondence*, 6:315; John Tyler to Jackson, August 1844, *Correspondence*, 6:315; Jackson to Blair, August 29, 1844, *Correspondence*, 6:317; Pletcher, *Diplomacy of Annexation*, 113–49, 172–207.
21. James K. Polk to Cave Johnson, December 21, 1844, *Correspondence of James K. Polk*, 14 vols., ed. Herbert Weaver, Wayne Cutler, and Michael David Cohen (Knoxville: University of Tennessee Press, 1969–2021), 8:456; Polk to Andrew Jackson, March 17, 1845, *Correspondence*, 6:382; Jackson to Francis P. Blair, April 9, 1845, *Correspondence*, 6:395–96.
22. Andrew Jackson to Francis P. Blair, March 10, 1845, *Correspondence*, 6:379; Jackson to Amos Kendall, November 23, 1844, Jackson Papers, Library of Congress, Washington, D.C.
23. Andrew Jackson to Francis P. Blair, January 19, 1844, *Correspondence*, 6:257; Jackson to Andrew J. Donelson, November 18, 1844, *Correspondence*, 6:330.
24. "'Old Hannah's' Narration of Jackson's Last Days," *Correspondence*, 6:415; Remini, *Course of American Democracy*, 521, 523, 524; Parton, *Life of Andrew Jackson*, 3:677–78.
25. Remini, *Course of American Democracy*, 525–27; Parton, *Life of Andrew Jackson*, 3:679; Samuel G. Heiskell, *Andrew Jackson and Early Tennessee History*, 3 vols. (Nashville: Ambrose Printing Company, 1921), 3:54.
26. B. M. Dusenbery, compiler, *Monument to the Memory of General Andrew Jackson, Containing Twenty-five Eulogies and Sermons, Delivered on Occasion of His Death* (Philadelphia: Walker & Gillis, 1846), 314, 328–29, 367.
27. "Characteristic Indorsements," *Correspondence*, 6:416.
28. Benton, *Thirty Years' View*, 1:737.
29. Parton, *Life of Andrew Jackson*, 3:490.

Selected Bibliography

Primary

Manuscript and Document Collections

Andrew Jackson Papers, Library of Congress, Washington, D.C.

Annals of Congress, https://memory.loc.gov/ammem/amlaw/lwac.html.

Broadsides, Leaflets, and Pamphlets from America and Europe, Library of Congress, Washington, D.C.

Finis Ewing Papers, Tennessee Historical Society, Nashville.

Miller Center, University of Virginia, https://millercenter.org.

Westminster Shorter Catechism. The Westminster Presbyterian, A Ministry of the Presbytery of the United States, in the Free Church of Scotland. http://www.westminsterconfession.org/confessional-standards/the-westminster-shorter-catechism.php.

Printed Primary Sources

Bassett, John Spencer, ed., *Correspondence of Andrew Jackson*, 7 vols. Washington: Carnegie Institution, 1926–1935.

Benton, Thomas Hart. *Thirty Years View; or A History of the Working of the American Government for Thirty Years, from 1820 to 1850*, 2 vols. New York: D. Appleton and Company, 1883.

Brinkerhoff, Roeliff. *Recollections of a Lifetime*. Cincinnati: The Robert Clark Company, 1900.

Calhoun, John C. *Exposition and Protest, Reported by the Special Committee of the House of Representatives, on the Tariff*. Charleston: D.W. Sims, 1829.

Cartwright, Peter. *Autobiography of Peter Cartwright*. New York: Nelson and Phillips, 1856.

Craighead, Rev. James Geddes. *The Craighead Family: A Genealogical Memoir of the Descendants of Rev. Thomas and Margaret Craighead, 1658–1876*. Philadelphia: Sherman & Co., Printers, 1876.

Davis, Charles S. "The Journal of William Moultrie While a Commissioner on the North and South Carolina Boundary Survey, 1772." *Journal of Southern History* 8 (November 1942): 549–55.

Denson, Jesse. *The Chronicles of Andrew; Containing an accurate and brief account of General Jackson's victories in the south, over the Creeks, also His Victories over the British at Orleans, with a biographical sketch of his life*. Lexington, KY: Printed for the author, 1815.

210   *Selected Bibliography*

Dusenbery, B. M., compiler. *Monument to the Memory of General Andrew Jackson, Containing Twenty-five Eulogies and Sermons, Delivered on Occasion of His Death.* Philadelphia: Walker & Gillis, 1846.

Eaton, John H. *The Letters of Wyoming, to the People of the United States, on the Presidential Election, and in Favour of Andrew Jackson.* Philadelphia: S. Simpson & J. Conrad, 1824.

Ely, Ezra Stiles. *The Duty of Christian Freemen to Elect Christian Rulers.* Philadelphia: William F. Geddes, 1828.

Everts, Jeremiah. *Essays on the Present Crisis in the Condition of the American Indians; First Published in The National Intelligencer, under the Signature of William Penn.* Philadelphia: Thomas Kite, 1830.

Heiskell, Samuel G. *Andrew Jackson and Early Tennessee History,* 3 vols. Nashville: Ambrose Printing Company, 1921.

Hooker, Richard J., ed. *The Carolina Backcountry on the Eve of the Revolution: The Journal and Other Writings of Charles Woodmason, Anglican Itinerant.* Chapel Hill: University of North Carolina Press, 1953.

McCoy, Isaac. *Remarks on the Practicability of Indian Reform, Embracing Their Colonization.* Boston, Lincoln & Edmands, 1827.

Reid, John, and John Henry Eaton. *The Life of Andrew Jackson, Major General, in the Service of the United States.* Philadelphia: M. Carey and Son, 1817.

Richardson, James D., ed., *A Compilation of the Messages and Papers of the Presidents,* 10 vols. Washington: Government Printing Office, 1899.

Smith, Sam B., Harriet Chappell Owsley, Harold D. Moser, Daniel Feller et al., eds., *The Papers of Andrew Jackson,* 12 vols. to date. Knoxville: University of Tennessee Press, 1980–present.

Tocqueville, Alexis de. *Democracy in America,* tr. Henry Reeve. New York: Alfred A. Knopf, 1945; orig. pub. 1835.

Van Buren, Martin. "Autobiography of Martin Van Buren," in *Annual Report of the American Historical Association for the Year 1918,* vol. 2. Washington: Government Printing Office, 1920.

Weaver, Herbert, Wayne Cutler, Tom Chaffin, and Michael David Cohen, eds. *Correspondence of James K. Polk.* Knoxville: University of Tennessee Press, 1969–2021.

Wise, Henry A. *Seven Decades of the Union.* Philadelphia: J.B. Lippincott & Co., 1881.

Secondary

Abernethy, Thomas Perkins. *From Frontier to Plantation in Tennessee: A Study in Frontier Democracy.* Chapel Hill: University of North Carolina Press, 1932.

Allgor, Catherine E. *Parlor Politics: In Which the Ladies of Washington Help Build a City and a Government.* Charlottesville: University Press of Virginia, 2000.

Arnold, James E. "The Hermitage Church." *Tennessee Historical Quarterly* 28 (Summer 1969): 113–25.

Selected Bibliography 211

Bankhurst, Benjamin. *Ulster Presbyterians and the Scots Irish Diaspora, 1750–1764.* New York: Palgrave Macmillan, 2013.

Banner, Stuart. *How the Indians Lost Their Land: Law and Power on the Frontier.* Cambridge, MA: The Belknap Press of Harvard University Press, 2005.

Belohlavek, John M. *"Let the Eagle Soar!" The Foreign Policy of Andrew Jackson.* Lincoln: University of Nebraska Press, 1985.

Benson, Lee. *The Concept of Jacksonian Democracy: New York as a Test Case.* Princeton: Princeton University Press, 1961.

Boles, John B. *The Great Revival 1787–1805.* Lexington: University Press of Kentucky, 1972.

Booraem, Hendrik. *Young Hickory: The Making of Andrew Jackson.* Dallas: Taylor Trade Publishing, 2001.

Brooke, Peter. *Ulster Presbyterianism: The Historical Perspective 1610–1970.* New York: St. Martin's Press, 1987.

Brown, Richard Maxwell. *The South Carolina Regulators.* Cambridge, MA: The Belknap Press of Harvard University Press, 1963.

Buchanan, John. *Jackson's Way: Andrew Jackson and the People of the Western Waters.* New York: John Wiley & Sons, 2001.

Bullock, Steven C. "A Pure and Sublime System: The Appeal of Post-Revolutionary Freemasonry." *Journal of the Early Republic* 9 (Autumn 1989): 359–73.

Bullock, Steven C. *Revolutionary Brotherhood: Freemasonry and the Transformation of the American Social Order, 1730–1840.* Chapel Hill: University of North Carolina Press, 1996.

Burstein, Andrew. *The Passions of Andrew Jackson.* New York: Alfred A. Knopf, 2003.

Bynum, William B. " 'The Genuine Presbyterian Whine': Presbyterian Worship in the Eighteenth Century." *American Presbyterians* 74 (Fall 1996): 157–70.

Carwardine, Richard J. *Evangelicals and Politics in Antebellum America.* New Haven: Yale University Press, 1993.

Cheathem, Mark R. "Andrew Jackson, Slavery, and Historians." *History Compass* 9 (2011): 326–38.

Cheathem, Mark R. *Andrew Jackson, Southerner.* Baton Rouge: Louisiana State University Press, 2013.

Cheathem, Mark R. "Hannah, Andrew Jackson's Slave." *Humanities* 35 (March/April 2014): https://www.neh.gov/humanities/2014/marchapril/feature/han nah-andrew-jacksons-slave.

Cheathem, Mark R. *Old Hickory's Nephew: The Political and Private Struggles of Andrew Jackson Donelson.* Baton Rouge: Louisiana State University Press, 2007.

Cole, Donald B. *The Presidency of Andrew Jackson.* Lawrence: University Press of Kansas, 1993.

Cole, Donald B. *Vindicating Andrew Jackson: The 1828 Election and the Rise of the Two-Party System.* Lawrence: University Press of Kansas, 2009.

Conkin, Paul K. "Evangelicals, Fugitives, and Hillbillies: Tennessee's Impact on American National Culture." *Tennessee Historical Quarterly* 54 (Fall 1995): 246–71.

Cumfer, Cynthia. *Separate Peoples, One Land: The Minds of Cherokees, Blacks, and Whites on the Tennessee Frontier.* Chapel Hill: University of North Carolina Press, 2007.

212 Selected Bibliography

Ely, James W. Jr. "The Legal Practice of Andrew Jackson." *Tennessee Historical Quarterly* 38 (Winter 1979): 421–35.

Feller, Daniel. "The Seminole Controversy Revisited: A New Look at Andrew Jackson's 1818 Florida Campaign." *Florida Historical Quarterly* 88 (Winter 2010): 309–25.

Finger, John R. *Tennessee Frontiers: Three Regions in Transition.* Bloomington: Indiana University Press, 2001.

Freehling, William W. *Prelude to Civil War: The Nullification Controversy in South Carolina, 1816–1836.* New York: Oxford University Press, 1965.

Freeman, Joanne B. *Affairs of Honor: National Politics in the New Republic.* New Haven: Yale University Press, 2001.

Gismondi, Melissa Jean. "Rachel Jackson and the Search for Zion, 1760s–1830s." Ph.D. dissertation, University of Virginia, 2017.

Goodstein, Anita Shafer. *Nashville 1780–1860: From Frontier to City.* Gainesville: University of Florida Press, 1989.

Gorn, Elliott J. "'Gouge and Bite, Pull Hair and Scratch': The Social Significance of Fighting in the Southern Backcountry." *American Historical Review* 90 (February 1985): 18–43.

Greenberg, Kenneth S. *Honor & Slavery: Lies, Duels, Noses, Masks, Dressing as a Woman, Gifts, Strangers, Humanitarianism, Death, Slave Rebellions, The Proslavery Argument, Baseball, Hunting, Gambling in the Old South.* Princeton: Princeton University Press, 1996.

Griffin, Patrick. *The People with No Name: Ireland's Ulster Scots, America's Scots-Irish, and the Creation of a British Atlantic World, 1689–1764.* Princeton: Princeton University Press, 2001.

Gullotta, Daniel Nicholas. "To Make a Christian of Andrew Jackson." Ph.D. dissertation, Stanford University, 2023.

Guyatt, Nicholas. *Providence and the Invention of the United States, 1607–1876.* Cambridge: Cambridge University Press, 2007.

Hammond, Bray. *Banks and Politics in America from the Revolution to the Civil War.* Princeton: Princeton University Press, 1957.

Harwell Wells, C. A. "The End of the Affair? Anti-Dueling Laws and Social Norms in Antebellum America." *Vanderbilt Law Review* 54 (May 2001): 1813–37.

Haselby, Sam. *The Origins of American Religious Nationalism.* New York: Oxford University Press, 2015.

Hatch, Nathan O. *The Democratization of American Christianity.* New Haven: Yale University Press, 1989.

Hay, Robert P. "The Case for Andrew Jackson in 1824: Eaton's 'Wyoming Letters.'" *Tennessee Historical Quarterly* 29 (Summer 1970): 139–51.

Heidler, David S., and Jeanne T. Heidler. "Not a Ragged Mob; The Inauguration of 1829." *White House History* 15 (1997): 134–43.

Heidler, David S., and Jeanne T. Heidler. *Old Hickory's War: Andrew Jackson and the Quest for Empire.* Mechanicsburg, PA: Stackpole Books, 2003.

Heidler, David S., and Jeanne T. Heidler. *Rise of Andrew Jackson: Myth, Manipulation, and the Making of Modern Politics.* New York: Basic Books, 2018.

Selected Bibliography

Heyrman, Christine Leigh. *Southern Cross: The Beginnings of the Bible Belt* (Chapel Hill: University of North Carolina Press, 1997.

Hickey, Donald R. *Glorious Victory: Andrew Jackson and the Battle of New Orleans.* Baltimore: Johns Hopkins University Press, 2015.

Hickey, Donald R. *The War of 1812: A Forgotten Conflict.* Urbana: University of Illinois Press, 2012.

Holmes, Andrew R. *The Shaping of Ulster Presbyterian Belief and Practice, 1770–1840.* New York: Oxford University Press, 2006.

Holt, Michael F. "The Antimasonic and Know Nothing Parties," in *Political Parties and American Political Development from the Age of Jackson to the Age of Lincoln.* Baton Rouge: Louisiana State University Press, 1992.

Holt, Michael F. *The Rise and Fall of the American Whig Party: Jacksonian Politics and the Onset of the Civil War.* New York: Oxford University Press, 1999. Hopkins, Callie. "The Enslaved Household of President Andrew Jackson." *White House Historical Association,* https://www.whitehousehistory.org/slavery-in-the-andrew-jack son-white-house.

Howe, Daniel Walker. *What Hath God Wrought? The Transformation of America, 1815–1848.* New York: Oxford University Press, 2007.

Johnson, Paul E. *A Shopkeeper's Millennium: Society and Revivals in Rochester, New York, 1815–1837.* New York: Hill & Wang, 1978.

Kanon, Tom. *Tennesseans at War, 1812–1815: Andrew Jackson, The Creek War, and the Battle of New Orleans.* Tuscaloosa: University of Alabama Press, 2014.

Kendall, Amos. *Life of Andrew Jackson, Private, Military, and Civil, with Illustrations.* New York: Harper & Brothers, 1843.

Kidd, Thomas. *America's Religious History: Faith, Politics, and the Shaping of a Nation.* Grand Rapids, MI: Zondervan, 2019.

Kidd, Thomas S. *God of Liberty: A Religious History of the American Revolution.* New York: Basic Books, 2010.

Kidd, Thomas S., and Barry Hankins. *Baptists in America: A History.* New York: Oxford University Press, 2015.

Klein, Rachel N. *Unification of a Slave State: The Rise of the Planter Class in the South Carolina Backcountry, 1760–1808.* Chapel Hill: University of North Carolina Press, 1990.

Kupfer, Barbara Stern. "A Presidential Patron of the Sport of Kings: Andrew Jackson." *Tennessee Historical Quarterly* 29 (Fall 1970): 243–55.

Latner, Richard B. *Presidency of Andrew Jackson: White House Politics, 1829–1837.* Athens: University of Georgia Press, 1979.

Lewis, Kenneth E. *The Carolina Backcountry Venture: Tradition, Capital, and Circumstance in the Development of Camden and the Wateree Valley, 1740–1810.* Columbia: University of South Carolina Press, 2017.

Leyburn, James G. *The Scotch-Irish: A Social History.* Chapel Hill: University of North Carolina Press, 1962.

Loveland, Anna C. *Southern Evangelicals and the Social Order 1800–1860.* Baton Rouge: Louisiana State University Press, 1980.

214 *Selected Bibliography*

Marszalek, John F. *The Petticoat Affair: Manners, Mutiny, and Sex in Andrew Jackson's White House.* New York: The Free Press, 1997.

Masterson, William H. *William Blount.* Baton Rouge: Louisiana State University Press, 1954.

Mathews, Donald G. *Religion in the Old South.* Chicago: University of Chicago Press, 1977.

McCormick, Richard P. "Was There a 'Whig Strategy' in 1836?" *Journal of the Early Republic* 4 (Spring 1984): 47–70.

McLoughlin, William G. *Cherokee Renascence in the New Republic.* Princeton: Princeton University Press, 1986.

Meacham, Jon. *American Lion: Andrew Jackson in the White House.* New York: Random House, 2008.

Meredith, Rachel. "'There Was Somebody Always Dying and Leaving Jackson as Guardian': The Wards of Andrew Jackson." M.A. Thesis, Middle Tennessee State University, 2013.

Merrill, James H. *The Indians' New World: Catawbas and Their Neighbors from European Contact through the Era of Removal.* Chapel Hill: University of North Carolina Press, 1989.

Middlekauf, Robert. *The Glorious Cause: The American Revolution, 1763–1789.* New York: Oxford University Press, 1982.

Mooney, Chase C. *William H. Crawford: 1772–1834.* Lexington: University Press of Kentucky, 1974.

Moore, Peter N. *World of Toil and Strife: Community Transformation in Backcountry South Carolina, 1750–1805.* Columbia: University of South Carolina Press, 2007.

Nadelhaft, Jerome J. *The Disorders of War: The Revolution in South Carolina.* Orono: University of Maine at Orono Press, 1981.

Niven, John. *John C. Calhoun and the Price of Union.* Baton Rouge: Louisiana State University Press, 1988.

Noll, Mark A. *A History of Christianity in the United States and Canada.* Grand Rapids: William B. Eerdmans Publishing Co., 1992.

Norton, Herman A. *Religion in Tennessee 1777–1945.* Knoxville: University of Tennessee Press, 1981.

Opal, J. M. *Avenging the People: Andrew Jackson, the Rule of Law, and the American Nation.* New York: Oxford University Press, 2017.

Owsley, Frank L. Jr. *Struggle for the Gulf Borderlands: The Creek War and the Battle of New Orleans, 1812–1815.* Tuscaloosa: University of Alabama Press, 2000.

Pancake, John S. *The Destructive War: The British Campaign in the Carolinas, 1780–1782.* Tuscaloosa: University of Alabama Press, 1985.

Parsons, Lynn Hudson. *The Birth of Modern Politics: Andrew Jackson, John Quincy Adams, and the Election of 1828.* New York: Oxford University Press, 2009.

Parton, James. *Life of Andrew Jackson,* 3 vols. Boston and New York: Houghton, Mifflin & Company, 1859–60.

Pletcher, David M. *The Diplomacy of Annexation: Texas, Oregon, and the Mexican War.* Columbia: University of Missouri Press, 1973.

Selected Bibliography 215

Prucha, Francis Paul. "Andrew Jackson's Indian Policy: A Reassessment." *Journal of American History* 56 (December 1969): 527–39.

Prucha, Francis Paul. *The Great Father: The United States Government and the American Indians*, 2 vols. Lincoln: University of Nebraska Press, 1984.

Putnam, A. Waldo. *History of Middle Tennessee; or, Life and Times of General James Robertson*. Nashville: Printed for the Offer, 1859.

Ramsey, J.G.M. *The Annals of Tennessee to the End of the Eighteenth Century*. Charleston: John Russell, 1853.

Ratcliffe, Donald. *The One-Party Presidential Contest: Adams, Jackson, and 1824's Five-Horse Race*. Lawrence: University Press of Kansas, 2015.

Ray, Kristofer. *Middle Tennessee 1775–1825: Progress and Popular Democracy on the Southwestern Frontier*. Knoxville: University of Tennessee Press, 2007.

Remini, Robert V. *Andrew Jackson and the Bank War*. New York: W.W. Norton & Co., 1967.

Remini, Robert V. "Andrew Jackson Takes an Oath of Allegiance to Spain." *Tennessee Historical Quarterly* 54 (Spring 1995): 2–15.

Remini, Robert V. *Andrew Jackson: The Course of American Democracy, 1833–1845*. New York: Harper & Row, 1984; rpt. Baltimore: Johns Hopkins University Press, 1998.

Remini, Robert V. *Andrew Jackson: The Course of American Empire, 1767–1821*. New York: Harper & Row, 1977; rpt. Baltimore: Johns Hopkins University Press, 1998.

Remini, Robert V. *Andrew Jackson: The Course of American Freedom, 1822–1832*. New York: Harper & Row, 1981; rpt. Baltimore: Johns Hopkins University Press, 1998.

Remini, Robert V. *Andrew Jackson and His Indian Wars*. New York: Penguin Books, 2001.

Remini, Robert V. *The Battle of New Orleans: Andrew Jackson and America's First Military Victory*. New York: Penguin Books, 1999.

Rogin, Michael Paul. *Fathers and Children: Andrew Jackson and the Subjugation of the American Indian*. New York: Alfred A. Knopf, 1975.

Satz, Ronald N. *American Indian Policy in the Jacksonian Era*. Norman: University of Oklahoma Press, 1974.

Sherwood, Henry Noble. "The Formation of the American Colonization Society." *Journal of Negro History* 2 (July 1917): 209–28.

Smith, Gary Scott. *Religion in the Oval Office: The Religious Lives of American Presidents*. New York: Oxford University Press, 2015.

Smith, Miles IV. "What Andrew Jackson Could Teach Donald Trump about Religion." The Gospel Coalition, July 21, 2017, https://www.thegospelcoalit ion.org/blogs/evangelical-history/what-andrew-jackson-could-teach-donald-trump-about-religion/.

Snay, Mitchell. *Gospel of Disunion: Religion and Separatism in the Antebellum South*. Cambridge: Cambridge University Press, 1993.

Thompson, Ernest Trice. *Presbyterians in the South*, 3 vols. Richmond, VA: John Knox Press, 1963–1973.

216　　　　　　　　*Selected Bibliography*

Toplovich, Ann. "Marriage, Mayhem, and Presidential Politics: The Robards-Jackson Backcountry Scandal." *Ohio Valley History* 5 (Winter 2005): 3–22.

Trinterud, Leonard J. *The Forming of an American Tradition: A Re-examination of Colonial Presbyterianism.* Philadelphia: The Westminster Press, 1949.

Turner, James C. *Without God, Without Creed: The Origins of Unbelief in America.* Baltimore: Johns Hopkins University Press, 1986.

Walker, Arda. "The Religious Views of Andrew Jackson." East Tennessee Historical Society's *Publications* 17 (1945): 61–70.

Wallace, Anthony F.C. *The Long, Bitter Trail: Andrew Jackson and the Indians.* New York: Hill & Wang, 1993.

Ward, John William. *Andrew Jackson: Symbol for an Age.* London: Oxford University Press, 1953.

Warshauer, Matthew. *Andrew Jackson and the Politics of Martial Law: Nationalism, Civil Liberties, and Partisanship.* Knoxville: University of Tennessee Press, 2006.

Warshauer, Matthew. "Andrew Jackson: Chivalric Slave Master." *Tennessee Historical Quarterly* 65 (Fall 2006): 203–29.

Wood, Kirsten E. "'One Woman So Dangerous to Public Morals': Gender and Power in the Eaton Affair." *Journal of the Early Republic* 17 (Summer 1997): 237–75.

Wyatt-Brown, Bertram. "Andrew Jackson's Honor." *Journal of the Early Republic* 17 (Spring 1997): 1–36.

Wyatt-Brown, Bertram. *Southern Honor: Ethics and Behavior in the Old South.* New York: Oxford University Press, 1982.

Index

For the benefit of digital users, indexed terms that span two pages (e.g., 52–53) may, on occasion, appear on only one of those pages.

abolition, abolitionists 166–69, 185–86
Adams, John 33–34, 42, 61
Adams, John Quincy 85–87, 88–91,
    93–94, 139–40, 143, 146–47, 173–
    74, 176–77
  presidential candidate 1824 98–99,
    103–4, 106–8
  presidential candidate 1828 108–10
Alfred 157–58, 160–61
Allison Loan 42–44, 178
Ambrister, Robert 87–88, 89–90, 136
American Bible Society 108–9
American Board of Commissioners for
    Foreign Missions 139–40, 142–
    43, 145–46
American Colonization Society 161–62
American Sunday School Union 119–20
Anglican Church 3–4, 5–6, 33–34
  see also Episcopal Church
Anti-Masonic Party 110, 176–77, 180,
    182–83, 186–87
Arbuthnot, Alexander 87–88, 89–
    90, 136
Augustus 167–68
Avery, Waightstill 21, 27, 44

Bank of the United States, Second 177–
    85, 193–94, 200–1
Bank Veto Message 179–80, 188
Baptists, Baptist Church 5, 35–37, 100,
    103, 110–11, 118–19, 139–40, 143
Barry, William T. 120, 125–26
Benton, Jesse 64, 81, 103, 194

Benton, Thomas Hart 8, 18–19, 22–23,
    59, 79–80, 105, 178, 193, 205–6
  brawl with Jackson 64, 81
Berrien, John M. 120, 125, 127–28, 142
Biddle, Nicholas 177–80, 181–84
Black Hawk War 146
Blackburn, Gideon 37, 66, 136–37, 157
Blair, Francis Preston 117, 145–46, 164–
    65, 174–76, 180–81, 197–98, 200–3
Blount, William 31–33, 41, 42–43, 44,
    46, 47, 79–80, 98
Blount, Willie 63, 65–67, 78–79
Board for the Emigration, Preservation,
    and Improvement of the Aborigines
    in America 143
Branch, John 120, 124, 125, 127–28
Brinkerhoff, Roeliff 161
Bronaugh, James 101–2
Burr, Aaron 49, 52–54

Calhoun, John C. 78, 84–85, 86, 87, 88,
    89, 98–99, 105–6, 108–9, 120, 128–
    29, 145–46, 161–62, 174–75
  break with Jackson 125–27, 164–65
  and Nullification 163–66
Call, Richard K. 81, 115–16, 122–23
Callava, José María 92–94
Calvinists, Calvinism 6–7, 10–11, 28–29,
    37, 198
Campbell, George W. 53–54
Campbell, John N. 123–25, 129–30, 198
Carroll, William 64, 66, 97, 98, 142
Cartwright, Peter 77–78, 81–82, 161–62

218 *Index*

Cass, Lewis 145–46

Catawbas 3, 133–34

Catholicism, Catholic Church 4–5, 73–74, 93, 103, 110–11, 187–88

Cherokees 3, 13, 32, 42, 47–48, 58, 67–68, 83–84, 133–35, 136–37, 138–39, 144–45, 180
 conflict with Georgia 140, 142, 146, 164

Chesapeake Affair 61–62

Chickamaugas 32, 58, 133–34

Chickasaws 84, 133, 144–45, 146

Choctaws 84, 91, 133, 144–45, 155

civil religion ix–x, 189

Claiborne, William C.C. 48–49, 52–53, 77–78, 80

Clay, Henry 89–91, 105, 107–10, 125, 145–46, 166, 176, 185
 National Republican/Whig party leader 176–77, 178–79, 180, 182–83
 presidential candidate 98, 106–7, 110, 146–47, 178–79, 180, 201–2

Cocke, John 48–49, 66–67

Cocke, William 42, 46, 48–49, 134–35

Coffee, John 84, 100–1, 105, 107, 108, 116–17, 144–45, 194–95
 as business partner 43, 49–50
 as military commander 65, 70–71

Congregational Church 110–11, 139–40, 142–43, 186–87

Cornwallis, Charles 15, 19

"corrupt bargain" 107–11

Craighead, Thomas 35–36, 37, 44–45, 54–55, 64–65

Crawford, Elizabeth 16–17

Crawford, James 1–2, 3, 6, 7–8, 9, 14–16, 153

Crawford, Jane 1–2

Crawford, Robert 1–2, 3, 8, 13, 14–15, 19, 21, 58, 153

Crawford, Thomas 16

Crawford, Will 8, 20–22

Crawford, William H. 83–87, 88, 90–91, 93, 108–9, 126

presidential candidate 1824 98–99, 103–4, 105–7, 110

Creeks 62–63, 69–70, 83–84, 89–90, 133, 134–35, 140, 142, 144–45, 146
 Creek War 64–68, 70–71, 73, 78–79, 109–10, 135–36, 155

Davie, William Richardson 13–15, 20–21, 58

Davies, Samuel 4, 5–6

Democratic Party 164–65, 184–88, 189, 193–94, 200–3, 204–5

Denson, Jesse 73–74

Dickinson, Charles 49–53, 54, 57, 61–62, 64, 81, 106, 194

Dinsmore, Silas 155

Donelson, Alexander "Sandy" 68, 69

Donelson, Andrew Jackson 57–59, 80, 108, 117, 124–25, 127, 128–29, 159–60, 187, 194–95, 196–97

Donelson, Emily 117, 121, 122, 124, 127, 128–29, 187, 194–95

Donelson, John 27–29

Donelson, Rachel Stockley 27–30

Donelson, Samuel 42–43, 57–58

Donelson Severn 57–58

Donelson, Stockly 160–61

Drayton, William 85–86, 106

Duane, William J. 181–83

Dubourg, Guillaume 73–74

Earl, Ralph E. W. 79–80, 200

Eastin, Mary Ann 195–96

"Eaton Affair" 120–26, 127–30, 133

Eaton, John H. 83, 103–4, 106, 108, 117, 142, 144–46, 156–57
 in Eaton Affair 120–26, 127–30

Eaton, Margaret O'Neal Timberlake 120–26, 127–30, 164–65, 198

Edgar, John Todd 198–99, 204, 205

Ely, Ezra Stiles 102, 110, 116–17, 124–25, 180, 186–87
 in Eaton Affair 122, 123–25, 129–30

Emuckfau 66–67, 68

Index   219

Enitachopko 66–67
Episcopal Church 22, 103, 118, 143
  see also Anglican Church
Erwin, Andrew 84–85
Erwin, Joseph 49–50
Evarts, Jeremiah 142–43, 146–47

Federalists, Federalist Party 41–42,
  85–86, 106
Florida Invasion 126
  War of 1812 69–70
  In 1818 86–91
Forsythe, John 126, 144
Fort Jackson 67–68, 69
  Treaty of 69–70, 83–84, 89–90
Fort Mims 64–65, 134–35, 186–87
Fort Strother 65–66
Frelinghuysen, Theodore 144, 186–87

Gaines, Edmund P. 86, 87
George 153–54, 157–58, 160–61, 203–4
Ghent, Treaty of 69, 73, 78
Gilbert, 159
Gracey 157–58, 161
Graham, George 84–85
Green, Duff 125, 164–65
Grundy, Felix 128–29

Halcyon 153, 197, 203
Hall, Dominick A. 77–78, 83, 197–98
Hannah 153–54, 157–59, 161, 168–
  69, 203–4
Harris, Jeremiah G. 204–5
Harrison, William H. 185, 200–1
Hermitage, The 44, 49, 52–53, 57, 58–
  59, 62–63, 68, 74, 78–80, 82, 83, 89,
  92, 94, 97–98, 108, 115, 116, 117,
  135–36, 147–48, 153–54, 155–61,
  180–81, 195, 196–99, 203–4
Hermitage Church 100–1, 116, 198–
  99, 200
honor 9–11, 18–19, 20, 36–37, 44–46,
  52, 100–1, 157, 189, 194, 198, 205
Horseshoe Bend 67–68, 133–34
Houston, Samuel 51, 136–37

Humphreys, William 8, 13
Hunter's Hill 31–32, 43–44
Hutchings, Andrew J. 195–96
Hutchings, John 43, 49–50

Ingham, Samuel D. 120, 124,
  125, 127–28
internal improvements 106–7, 176
  see also Maysville Turnpike
  Veto

Jackson, Andrew 1, 2–3, 19–20, 21–25,
  27, 35, 44, 46, 54–55, 57, 77, 117,
  120, 126
  in American Revolution 13–17, 58,
    61, 74, 133–34, 204–5
  assassination attempt 194
  and "Bank War" 177–85, 193–94
  and battle of New Orleans 59–60, 70–
    73, 74, 77, 97–98, 154–55, 197–98
  boyhood 3, 6–9
  brawl with Bentons 7–8, 64, 106, 107
  and Burr Conspiracy 49, 52–
    54, 61–62
  as businessman/storekeeper 42–44
  censure by Senate 182–83, 193
  characteristics x, 8–9, 18, 20–21, 22–
    23, 104, 105
  and Charles Dickinson 49–52, 54, 64
  and Christianity ix–x, 6–7, 10–11,
    18–19, 24–25, 34–35, 37–38,
    44–45, 80, 81–83, 101–3, 110, 118,
    129–30, 133–34, 148–49, 157–58,
    187–89, 204–6
  and church membership 37, 81–82,
    100–1, 198–200
  commander of Seventh District 69–
    70, 79–80, 83–91
  on "corrupt bargain" 107–9
  in Creek War 64–68, 78–79
  death of 203–5
  and Democratic Party 185–86, 187,
    189, 193–94, 200–3
  and dueling 20, 27, 45, 47–48, 50–52,
    64, 84–85

220 *Index*

Jackson, Andrew (*cont.*)
  and Eaton Affair 120–21, 122–26,
    127–30, 174–75
  education of 7–8
  "Farewell Address" 146–47,
    188, 194–95
  financial affairs 42–44, 62–63, 78–79,
    91, 160–61, 178, 195, 197–98
  Florida Invasion controversy 86–91,
    92, 97–98, 126
  foreign relations while president 193–
    94, 201
  general of Tennessee militia 47, 48–
    49, 54–55, 58–66
  governor of Florida Territory 92–94,
    97–98, 118–19, 155–56
  and "hard money" 181
  health and physical condition 63,
    64–65, 68, 70–71, 83, 91, 94, 97–98,
    111, 158–59, 185, 194–95, 203–4
  and honor 9–11, 22–23, 44–46,
    189, 205
  inauguration as president 117–18
  and Indian Removal 133, 138–39,
    141–49, 180–81, 186–87, 193–94
  and John Sevier 46–49
  and "Kitchen Cabinet" 174–75
  legal education and law practice 20–
    21, 24, 27–28, 31–32, 43, 44
  marriage 29–32, 44, 109–10
  martial law controversy 70–71, 77–
    78, 197–98
  and Masonry 37–38, 46, 53–54, 110,
    122–23, 129
  as a military commander 58–
    60, 134–35
  in Natchez Expedition 63–64
  and Native Americans 32–33,
    69–70, 83–84, 91, 99, 110–11, 133–
    38, 147–48
  nose pulled 194
  in Nullification Crisis 162–68, 180–
    81, 182–83, 188, 193–94, 204–5
  as parent and/or guardian 57–58, 79,
    195–96, 197

  and political parties 184–86, 189
  political principles of 33–34, 81,
    98–99, 103, 161–62, 166–67,
    173–74, 175–77, 178, 179–80, 184–
    85, 205–6
  presidential candidate 1824 97–
    99, 103–8
  presidential candidate 1828 108–11,
    115, 185
  presidential candidate 1832 146–
    47, 180–81
  presidential messages to
    Congress 118, 174, 175–76, 188
  and Rachel Jackson 28–31, 115–17,
    118, 123, 129
  racial views 70–71, 134, 136, 154–55,
    156–57, 160–61, 168–69
  religious beliefs x, 6–7, 19–20, 33–34,
    36–37, 60, 68, 69, 74, 81, 82–83,
    100–2, 103, 116–17, 118–20, 157,
    168–69, 189, 194–95, 198
  and religious freedom 33–34, 102–3,
    110, 118–20, 187, 205
  removals of officeholders 173–
    74, 175–76
  representative in Congress 41–43,
    47, 48–49
  in retirement 193, 194–206
  and slavery 21, 27, 28, 31–32, 153–
    63, 166–69
  as Superior Court judge 43–44
  in Tennessee politics 31–32, 33,
    178, 185–86
  and Texas 201–3
  and Unionism 164–65, 166–69
  U.S. Senator 42–43, 44, 103–5,
    107, 108
  and U.S. Supreme Court 146, 179–
    80, 193–94
  vetoes 176–77, 179–81, 188
Jackson, Andrew (father) 1, 7–
  8, 147–48
Jackson, Andrew Jr. 57–58, 78–79,
  92–93, 161, 183, 195–97, 198–99,
  203, 204–5

Index

221

Jackson, Elizabeth 1–2, 6, 7–8, 9, 10, 13–14, 17, 18, 28–29, 80, 82–83, 102, 109–10, 133–34, 147–48, 198
Jackson, Hugh 2, 7–8, 13–14, 28–29
Jackson, Rachel Donelson Robards 28–29, 31–32, 35–36, 41, 43, 44–45, 50, 51, 53, 54–55, 63, 66, 69, 78–80, 87–88, 92–93, 94, 97–98, 100–1, 102, 104, 107, 108, 115, 118, 122, 123, 129, 133, 153–54, 155–56, 157, 158–59, 195–96, 197–98, 203, 204, 205
  death of 101–2, 115–17
  marriage to Jackson 30–31, 109–10, 115–16
  marriage to Lewis Robards 29–30
  religious beliefs 37, 68
Jackson, Robert 2, 7–8, 14–17, 28–29
Jackson, Sarah Yorke 195–97, 198–99
Jefferson, Thomas 48–49, 53–54, 61–63, 83, 138–39, 140, 154, 164–65, 173–74, 177–78, 184–85
Johnson, Richard M. 118–19

Kendall, Amos 168, 174–76, 179–80, 181–82, 197–98, 200–1, 202–3
"Kitchen Cabinet" 174–75

Lambert, John 72, 73
Lee, Henry 79–80
Lewis, William B. 103–4, 108, 124–26, 174–75, 181–82, 183, 195–96, 201–4
Louailler, Louis 77–78
Lumpkin, Wilson 141
Lutheran Church 110–11
Lyncoya 135–36

Macay, Spruce 21, 23–24
McCamie, George 2, 15
McCamie, Margaret ("Peggy") 2, 15
McCoy, Isaac 143
McKenney, Thomas L. 143, 145–46
McLane, Louis 166, 178–79, 181–82

McNairy, John 21–22, 24–25, 27–28, 46, 101–2
Madison, James 57, 62–63, 64–65, 69, 78, 79–80, 83–84
Marshall, John 146, 193–94
Masons, Masonry 37–38, 46, 53–54, 101–2, 122–23, 129
Maysville Turnpike Veto 176
Methodists, Methodist Church 35–37, 45, 73–74, 82–83, 90, 100, 103, 110–11, 120–21, 122–23, 143, 161–62
Mississippi Territory 53–54, 62–63, 65, 140
Monroe, James 69–72, 84–85, 89–90, 91, 93–94, 97–98, 103–4, 106, 120, 136–38, 139–40, 146
  in Florida controversy 86–87, 88–89, 126
  relationship with Jackson 85–86, 93–94

Nancy 27, 153
"Nashville Junto" 103, 106, 108
Natchez, Mississippi 28, 29–31, 47–48
  Natchez Expedition 63, 64–66, 68
National Republicans 176–77, 178–79, 180, 182–83
Native Americans 27, 32–33, 41–42, 58, 59, 61, 63–64, 70, 86, 89–90, 99, 110–11, 133–38
  and Indian Removal 133, 138–49, 176, 180–81, 193–94
New Orleans, battle of 59–60, 71–74, 77, 80, 81–82, 94, 97–98, 154–55, 197–98
Niles' Weekly Register 73–74
Nullification Crisis 162–68, 180–81, 182–83, 193–94, 204–5

O'Neal, William 120–21, 122–23
Onís, Luis de 86–87, 88–89, 91
Oregon Territory 201–2
Overton, John 27–28, 29–31, 42, 44, 98, 103, 108, 127, 194–95

222 *Index*

Pakenham, Edward 72
Parton, James ix, 22–23, 51, 58–59, 74, 97, 116–17, 154, 203–4
Pinckney, Thomas 64–65, 66–68, 69
Plauché, Jean B. 197–98
Polk, James K. 201–5
Poplar Grove 31–32
Poor Poll 204
Presbyterianism, Presbyterian Church 3–6, 9–11, 14, 15, 16, 18–19, 33–36, 37, 102, 103, 110–11, 115, 118, 119–20, 139–40, 142–43, 157, 186–87, 197–99

Red Sticks, *see* Creeks
Reid, John 83
Remini, Robert V. ix, 87–88
Republican Party 41–42, 48–49, 54, 100, 110–11, 157, 186–87
revivals, revivalism 4–6, 35–37, 100, 110–11, 157, 186–87
Rhea, John 86–87, 126
Richardson, Agnes Craighead 4, 6
Richardson, William 4–6, 10, 13–14, 35
Roane, Archibald 47–48
Robards, Lewis 29–32, 44
Roberts, Isaac 66–67
Robertson, James 45

Sabbatarianism 118–19
Sampson 156–57
Scots Irish 1, 2–4, 5, 7–8, 13
Scott, Winfield 84–85, 105
Seminoles 86–88, 92, 93, 133, 136, 146–47
Sevier, John 32, 46–49, 50, 54, 63
Shakers 100, 101
slavery 3, 21, 92–93, 99, 153–64, 166–69, 185–86, 201
Smith, Daniel 52–53
Smith, James 198–99
Snow Riot 167–68
Southwest Territory 31–33, 41–42
"Specie Circular" 185–86
"Spoils System" 173–74

Stokes, John 23–24
Sumter, Thomas 14–15, 16
Supreme Court, U.S. 146, 177–78, 179–80, 193–94
Swann, Thomas 49–51, 61–62
Swedenborgians 101

Talladega 65
Tallushatchee 65, 135–36
Taney, Roger B. 181–82, 193–94
tariffs 92–93, 106–7, 162–67
Tarleton, Banastre 14, 15
Tecumseh 62–63
Texas 49, 52–53, 88–89
  annexation issue 201–3
Timberlake, John 120–24
Tocqueville, Alexis de 100, 144–45
Trist, Nicholas P. 117, 158–59
Tyler, John 200–2

United States Telegraph 122, 125, 164–65, 174–75

Van Buren, Martin 108–9, 120, 125–26, 127–29, 142, 164–65, 173–76, 180–82, 183–84, 185–86, 193, 194, 200–3

Washington, George 32–33, 41–42, 61, 73, 103
Washington *Globe* 145–46, 164–65, 174–75, 180, 201–3
Watts, Isaac 5–6, 80, 123
Waxhaws 1–6, 7–11, 13–16, 17, 19–20, 23–25, 35, 133–34
Weatherford, William 134–35
Whig Party 182–83, 186–87, 189, 200–1, 204–5
White, Hugh Lawson 128–29, 144, 185
Wilkinson, James 53–54, 63–64, 74
Williams, John 45, 103–4
Wirt, William 146, 180
Wise, Henry A. 101
Woodmason, Charles 4–6
Wood, John 66–68, 109–10

Titles in the *Spiritual Lives* series:

George Eliot
Whole Soul
Ilana M. Blumberg

Ebenezer Howard
Inventor of the Garden City
Frances Knight

Walter Lippmann
American Skeptic, American Pastor
Mark Thomas Edwards

Mark Twain
Preacher, Prophet, and Social Philosopher
Gary Scott Smith

Benjamin Franklin
Cultural Protestant
D. G. Hart

Arthur Sullivan
A Life of Divine Emollient
Ian Bradley

Queen Victoria
This Thorny Crown
Michael Ledger-Lomas

Theodore Roosevelt
Preaching from the Bully Pulpit
Benjamin J. Wetzel

Margaret Mead
*A Twentieth-Century
Faith*
Elesha J. Coffman

W. T. Stead
Nonconformist and Newspaper Prophet
Stewart J. Brown

Leonard Woolf
Bloomsbury Socialist
Fred Leventhal and Peter Stansky

John Stuart Mill
A Secular Life
Timothy Larsen

Christina Rossetti
Poetry, Ecology, Faith
Emma Mason

Woodrow Wilson
Ruling Elder, Spiritual President
Barry Hankins